GOD'S PEOPLE
AND GOD'S PLAN

GOD'S PEOPLE
AND GOD'S PLAN

Trevor H Shannon

ATHENA PRESS
LONDON

ISBN 1 84401 760 5

First Published 2006 by
ATHENA PRESS
Queen's House, 2 Holly Road
Twickenham TW1 4EG
United Kingdom

Printed for Athena Press

Contents

Introduction

The aim of this book is to make the Old Testament more accessible and comprehensible to the man or woman in the pew – the pew of any Christian denomination. I am uncomfortably aware that sermons based on the Old Testament are increasingly rare, and that the Old Testament reading is sometimes omitted in acts of worship. Christians, however, ignore or undervalue the Old Testament at their peril. It is the sacred Scripture of the Jewish faith and it is the record of every Christian's spiritual ancestry. It is the Scripture on which Jesus was nourished and which he quoted constantly. He died uttering a verse from the Book of Psalms. It is a vast reservoir of inspiration, instruction and guidance to all who seek the eternal God who lives in every page.

Many of the stories in this book were written to be read aloud at Evening Prayer in the churches of St Margaret and St Clement, Ilford in the late 1990s. The congregation at those services was generally small and almost without exception those present had already worshipped at the Parish Eucharist and had heard a sermon based on readings for the day. They were a group of loyal and often lifelong worshippers with a broad, if patchy, knowledge of the Old Testament. They readily admitted that though they knew many Old Testament stories – the call of Abraham, Jacob's dream, the Joseph story, David and Goliath, Isaiah's vision – they were less sure of their context or significance. The history of the people of Israel, especially the period of the divided kingdoms, the Babylonian exile and the post-exilic period were areas where they walked with uncertainty.

The Old Testament readings at Evening Prayer provided a starting point from which to try to help people forward. Stories that combine multiple sources in their Scriptural version might be simplified. Sometimes meditative techniques were introduced, imagining what people present at a given scene might have seen or thought. This approach was often suitable when the biblical passage itself was already in narrative form. With the prophets narrative had to be 'invented', using and expanding whatever biographical material was available in the text.

It is hoped that:

1. Familiar stories may be given freshness by suggesting thoughts, motives and consequences that do not necessarily appear in the text. This is not an unfamiliar outcome of meditation on Scriptural passages.

2. The general outline of the history of Israel may become clearer. The grouping together of the historical books and the prophetic books in their separate collections in the Bible can be confusing. For example, the historical situation lying behind, say, the Book of Amos, predates the events recorded in the Books of Ezra and Nehemiah by several centuries, yet in the printed Bible Amos comes much later. The stories in this book try to put prophets and their words clearly in their historical setting.

3. Central themes – Israel as God's chosen nation, the hope for God's ultimate intervention on Israel's behalf, the political and social importance of the prophets – emerge without explicitly being mentioned.

The stories start with Abraham because he is the first reasonably 'historical' character in the Old Testament. The 'prehistory' stories such as Adam and Eve, the Tower of Babel and Noah and the flood are omitted, not because they are of no value, but simply because I wanted to concentrate on the history of the people of Israel and their importance in the Christian heritage, and that begins most obviously with Abraham.

Before each story there is an introduction. With the patriarchs, Moses and Joshua it seemed necessary to indicate little more than where the stories could be found. With Gideon, the chosen example of a Judge of Israel, I thought it would be helpful to explain something of the motives behind the story. The prophets are placed in their historical setting, with approximate dates if possible. The composite nature of the Book of Isaiah is explained as well as the nature of the Book of Job.

The stories actually run off the page at the end of the Old Testament, and the story of Judas Maccabeus, from the Old Testament Apocrypha, is told in order to build a bridge between the Old Testament and the time of Jesus.

The stories were originally designed to be read aloud, and they therefore contain colloquialisms and contractions found in normal speech. Longer stories have been divided into sections which might be of acceptable length for reading in public worship.

It is hoped that the stories which follow will illuminate what readers already know, introduce them to some things of which they may be unaware, and that enjoyment and enlightenment can mingle and help the reader to grasp more of the riches of the Old Testament.

Some Notes to Help Readers

References. In the earlier stories I have rarely given chapter and verse to justify what I have written. This is to allow the story to flow. I have quoted verbatim very rarely in these stories. In the stories of the prophets, however, I have quoted much more frequently and have generally included references. This is because I have had to construct narrative from the usually sparse biographical or autobiographical material that is included in the prophetic books. Also, material in the prophetic books is often not in date order, and it is therefore necessary to jump around the text to produce a consecutive narrative.

Themes. There are two great themes running through all the stories. One is God's choosing of Abraham and his descendants to bring blessing to all people. The other is the impossibility of separating religion from everyday life – social, political and economic. This comes out clearly as we read of the works of the prophets, both in their own writings and in earlier narratives in the books of Samuel and Kings.

The Lord God. In the Old Testament the word 'God' or 'god' or 'gods' is a translation of the Hebrew word *Elohim*. That is the word used when speaking of the deity as in the first verse of the

Bible: 'In the beginning God [*Elohim*] created the heavens and the earth.'

In Old Testament times it was a common belief that there were many gods, some local and some connected with a particular tribe or nation, others on a grander scale. These gods had names, and in the Bible we read of Moloch, the god of the people of Tyre, Dagon the god of the Philistines and many others, often collectively referred to as *baals*.

The God who revealed himself to Abraham and the other patriarchs and later to Moses also had a name. It was revealed to Moses at the Burning Bush (Exodus 3) and consists of four Hebrew letters. So sacred is the name of God that Jews do not say it. Whenever they come to the name in reading their Scriptures (the Christian Old Testament) they say either *HaShem* (which means 'The Name') or *Adonai* (which means 'My Lord'). Because the name of God has not been pronounced for centuries it makes it difficult to know exactly how we should say those four sacred letters. Perhaps the nearest we can come to it is to say 'Yahweh'. At the Burning Bush God told Moses that his name was 'I Am', so naturally when humans use the name we say 'He Is', and 'Yahweh' is not too far from that.

In our Bible the divine name is usually translated as 'Lord', though the Jerusalem Bible boldly opts for 'Yahweh'. To use the name 'Yahweh' seems to emphasise the uniqueness of the God of Israel and to remind us of the gradual discovery that there is only one God.

Source. All direct quotations from Scripture in the stories have been taken from the Revised Standard Version published by Wm Collins Sons and Co. Ltd in 1952. I have chosen this version because it seems to me to combine literary elegance with scholarly accuracy.

The Patriarchs

Abraham is the dominating figure in the Book of Genesis. He is revered as their founding father by both Jews and Arabs. Jews trace their descent through Isaac and Arabs through Ishmael. After shadowy and probably mythological figures such as Adam, Noah and Methuselah in the early chapters of Genesis, we meet Abraham in Chapter 12 and at once feel on much firmer historical ground. Some of the stories may reflect the later fortunes of his descendants but as we read the stories we seem to be meeting a real person.

Jacob, Abraham's grandson, is also a towering figure. His name was changed to Israel, and it was his twelve sons who were known as the children of Israel and the founding fathers of the twelve tribes which formed the nation of ancient Israel. Isaac, though certainly a patriarch, appears chiefly as the son of Abraham and the father of Jacob.

God's promise to Abraham that he would found a nation through which God's blessing would come to all people is in danger of foundering in each patriarch's generation. Wives are barren, children's lives are at risk. This is seen clearly in the stories of the 'Binding of Isaac' and the story of Joseph's being sold into slavery in Egypt. Also in the Joseph story, we can see how both the misfortunes and the successes of an individual are used by God to ensure the survival of the children of Israel and the continuance of the promise of blessing. The Joseph story also begins to set the scene for the great deliverance of the Exodus.

The stories about Abraham are in the Book of Genesis, Chapters 12–25.

The stories about Jacob are in Genesis, Chapters 25–36.

The stories about Joseph are in Genesis, Chapters 37–50.

Abraham's Story

God's Call

It was the name that was the problem. When we first meet him his name is Abram, which means something like 'exalted father'. And we might wonder how many times in his life Abram had squirmed with embarrassment that that was his name: exalted father.

He was the eldest son of Terah and his brothers were Nahor and Haran. Abraham grew up and, at the appropriate time, married Sarai, whom Jewish legend says was the most beautiful woman in the world. Sadly their marriage was childless. The Bible blames Sarai and her barrenness, but we might wonder how much was due to unreasonable expectations placed on Abram by his name. Whatever the reason for their childlessness, Abram must have been painfully aware of how odd his name sounded: exalted father...

Terah and his family lived in Ur of the Chaldees, one of the great cities of the ancient world, a centre of political power, of trade and culture. It was in Mesopotamia, 'the land between the rivers'. The rivers were and are the Tigris and the Euphrates, and Ur stood on the east bank of the Euphrates in what is present-day Iraq.

For a reason not disclosed Terah decided to move away from Ur. Not all the family went. Abram's brother, Nahor, and his family stayed in Ur. One of Terah's sons, Haran, had died and Nahor had assumed responsibility for Haran's dependants by marrying one of his daughters. So Terah took Abram and Sarai and his grandson Lot, one of Haran's sons, and travelled west toward the land of Canaan.

It wasn't a simple journey; no long journey was in those days. To reach Canaan from Ur wasn't a matter of going as the crow flies. They would first go north, then west, then south, travelling round the Fertile Crescent, with its safe, well-travelled trade routes, its towns and cities. All this was necessary to avoid the desert and its dangers.

After travelling over five hundred miles they reached one of the cities of the Fertile Crescent called Haran. They settled down and prospered and there, after a time, Terah died. This meant that Abram, though still childless, was now the head of an extended and growing family. They did well. The Bible speaks of 'their possessions' and 'the people who had joined them in Haran' and we get a picture of an increasingly wealthy family group, their women well dressed and bejewelled, and with property counted in servants and sheep and cattle.

Life was good for Abram. Terah's dream of going to Canaan had died with him and was now no more than a memory, and Abram's only regret, the only cloud on the horizon, was that he was getting older and he was still childless.

Suddenly the settled peace of life in Haran was shattered. God spoke to Abram: 'Go from your country and your kindred and your father's house to the land that I will show you. And I will make of you a great nation, and I will bless you, and make your name great, so that you will be a blessing. I will bless those who bless you, and him who curses you I will curse, and by you all the families of the earth shall bless themselves.'

The next words in the Bible are, 'So Abram went, as the Lord had told him.' It doesn't say whether he went after much thought. It doesn't say whether he talked to Sarai or consulted Lot. He just went, and we are left to assume that such was Abram's faith in God that to question or delay was simply unthinkable.

What God had said sounded very fine, but undoubtedly it demanded a great deal of Abram. First it meant a break with a very satisfactory way of life. It meant uprooting the family, giving up the security and prosperity he'd worked for, and facing the uncertainties and possible dangers of a new life in a new place. On top of that, God didn't tell him where he was to move to. It wasn't like Terah's dream of getting to Canaan. It was simply an order to move to 'the land that I will show you'. Then thirdly, God promises that Abram will be the founder of a great nation. That must have been the really difficult bit, the part that hurt

Abram. He was seventy-five years old and despite his name, he was still childless. Abram could be forgiven if he had thought that God was mocking him, as no doubt many people had mocked him throughout his life. Abram, the exalted father! More like Abram, the childless one.

Whatever hurt or hope Abram felt, he obeyed God. He left Haran and, in the absence of any specific instruction from God, he continued his father's journey, travelling toward Canaan. We don't know how long it took, how difficult the journey was, nor what Sarai and the others thought or said about it. They travelled on in obedience to God's call, and in time they came to Shechem, deep in the land of Canaan, about thirty miles north of Jerusalem.

Abram immediately went to the local sacred place, the oak of Moreh, and there God spoke to him again, confirming that this was indeed the land of which he had spoken when he first called Abram. And God said, 'To your descendants I will give this land.' What did Abram think and feel as he listened to God? Was he filled with hope? Or did he perhaps think, To my descendants! What descendants? I'm the famous 'exalted father' who has no children. But Abram didn't question God. Instead he worshipped him, building an altar and no doubt, on that altar, offering the best of his flocks and herds, tokens of his total commitment to God.

The journey wasn't over. In a sense it never would be because it was not only a journey across God's earth, it was also Abram's journey to God, a journey that could never end. So Abram moved on. First he camped near Bethel and built another altar there. He then moved further south to the Negeb, the barren hill country around Hebron. In that harsh land famine was not uncommon, and on one occasion, in order to survive, Abram had to take his vast family and his possessions of flocks and herds to Egypt. Making this journey he foreshadowed a journey that his grandson, Jacob, would make with momentous consequences. Abram didn't stay long in Egypt, and a rather confused story, which imagines Sarai as a young woman rather than a childless sixty-five-year-old, suggests that what Abram did or said in Egypt to ensure his survival was not entirely honest. Whatever happened, they did survive and moved back, first to the Negeb and then to the vicinity of Bethel, where Abram had earlier set up an altar.

Lot was still with Abram, and both men were wealthy. The Bible says that there was strife between Abram's herdsmen and Lot's. It wasn't surprising. The vast company of people over whom Abram was the head, was getting too big and was beginning to fragment. Loyalty to the whole group or clan was too difficult for most people, and easier, lesser loyalties were becoming more important. So there was strife.

Abram realised that the only way to deal with the problem was for him and Lot to go their separate ways, each taking his family, his servants, flocks, herds and all other belongings with him. Graciously Abram allowed Lot the first choice of territory. Lot chose the Jordan valley with its established cities of Sodom and Gomorrah. Abram was left with the rest of the land of Canaan which, conveniently enough, was the land that had been promised to him by God – promised by God and reached by Abram, but we should remember that it wasn't an empty land. It was somebody's home. As the Bible says, 'The Canaanites and Perizzites were then in the land.' Was this the beginning of the problems and disputes about land which still tear and scar the Middle East?

Lot had gone and Abram was on his own. God spoke to him again, confirming the earlier promises in even stronger terms. He is told to look north and south and east and west. Everything he can see will be his, given to him by God. His descendants will be so many that they cannot be counted; they will be 'as the dust of the earth'. Abram moved his camp close to another sacred tree at Mamre near Hebron, and again built an altar to the Lord. And we might wonder if he still said to himself, Descendants, what descendants? One would be nice, never mind the dust of the earth.

God's Promise

Abram wasn't the only person distressed about childlessness. The Bible assumes that the problem was really Sarai's, that she simply couldn't have children. In her desperation, and knowing how important it was to her husband and how unhappy he was, Sarai suggested that he take her Egyptian servant, Hagar, and try to have a child by her. He did, and Hagar became pregnant. But it was not a happy solution. Hagar the servant now despised her childless mistress and Sarai became jealous of Hagar. She began to treat her badly – so badly that Hagar ran away and only returned after an encounter with an angel who promised that she would have a son. She was told that the boy was to be called Ishmael and that through him she would have many descendants. The angel also predicted that Ishmael's life would be full of conflict. So at last Abram had a son, but Ishmael is not the son through whom God's promises will be fulfilled.

When he was ninety-nine years old Abram was told by God that his name would be changed. This would be very significant because it was believed that a name revealed the character of its bearer. Abram must have been relieved to hear that he was going to lose the millstone of his 'exalted father' name. But relief must have turned to disbelief when he was told that it was going to get worse. Not Abram but *Abraham*: not 'exalted father' but 'father of multitudes'! God promises to be with Abraham's descendants as he had been with Abraham. He will give them for ever the land that he has promised. That is God's side of the covenant, the agreement between God and Abraham. Abraham's part will be to worship, trust and obey God and, as a sign of his obedience, to mark himself and every male descendant with the mark of circumcision. It will normally be done when a male child is eight days old. Abraham accepted all this and the covenant between God and his descendants was confirmed.

God then tells Abraham that the first crucial step to the fulfilment of the promises will now be taken. Sarai will also have a new name reflecting her new role. She will be called Sarah – 'princess' – and, said God, she will have a son. When Abraham heard all this he laughed. He could have been forgiven if he'd wept. But he laughed; he fell on the ground and laughed. He couldn't forget that he was one hundred and Sarah was ninety. And he asked God why he wouldn't accept Ishmael as the son through whom the promises could be fulfilled. But no, he was told, it cannot be Ishmael; it must be, and it will be, the son of Abraham and Sarah.

Another story of God's promise of a son for the elderly couple tells of Sarah laughing. Abraham was sitting at the door of his tent when he saw three men approaching. He assumed they were men. With normal Middle Eastern hospitality, he hurried out to meet them and invited them to come into his tent to wash, rest and eat. They accepted the invitation. Abraham's words were, 'Rest yourselves under the tree while I fetch a morsel of bread.' It was rather an understatement. He rushed to find Sarah, told her to start baking, then dashed off to his herds, selected a suitable calf, slaughtered it and had it cooked while he entertained his guests with a cooling drink of curds and milk.

The men, or whoever they were – angels, perhaps – told Abraham that in the following spring Sarah would have a son. Sarah, doing the baking, overheard and, just like Abraham, could not stop herself laughing. She too might have wept.

The months passed and, as the Bible says, 'The Lord did to Sarah as he had promised.' She gave birth to a son and she rejoiced. The unhappiness she had lived with for so long was over and, typical of Sarah, she saw the funny side of it. Abraham had laughed and she had laughed when God's promise was made. Now that it was fulfilled she said, 'God has made laughter for me.' And not only that, God had made laughter for many others because, Sarah said, all who heard her story would laugh with surprise and happiness.

For Abraham there was joy, but above all there was relief. At last his name was no longer a reproach and a burden. He was the father of a healthy son, and could indeed now become the father of a mighty nation. In accordance with God's command, eight days after birth he circumcised his son, keeping his part of the covenant. And he named his son Isaac – meaning 'one who laughs.'

A Matter of Justice

Abraham enjoyed an intimacy with God that any believer might envy. It was rather like Adam's closeness when God used to walk and chat with him in the Garden in the cool of the evening. Abraham trusted God completely and was not afraid to ask questions and even to challenge God.

It had come to God's notice, perhaps through his three angels or agents who had called on Abraham and Sarah, that the cities of Sodom and Gomorrah were very wicked. What their precise wickedness was, if it was precise, we are not told. The origin of the word 'sodomy' has given a traditional clue. But more likely it was the sin of self-centred wickedness, greed and hard-heartedness, which could qualify every city, town and village for destruction. Whatever it was, God was considering drastic action.

In a sort of limited repeat of what he had done with the flood in the days of Noah, God was contemplating wiping out the two cities as they nestled comfortably and unaware near the southern end of the Dead Sea. Sodom and Gomorrah had been unwisely built, or their site had been unwisely chosen. The Dead Sea was and is on a fault in the earth's surface and lies well below sea level. Earthquake and flooding have been constant dangers in the area. In Abraham's day people didn't have our scientific knowledge. All they had were folk tales of ancient disasters. And how easy it is for those who have not experienced a disaster to believe that reports have been greatly exaggerated or possibly invented, and if it happened, it's not likely to happen again – lightning doesn't strike in the same place twice. So the people of Sodom and Gomorrah lived in blissful ignorance of their peril.

The destruction of the cities obviously weighed heavily on God because he decided he must speak to Abraham about it. As the man chosen by God to be the one through whom all the nations of the world would receive blessing, he was a person of importance in God's scheme of things. This story tells us how important morality is to God. Abraham, too, as God's chosen agent knows that good and evil must not be confused, nor the difference between them undervalued.

God told Abraham that he intended to wipe out the cities. Abraham's experience of God was that he was just and merciful. So he asked God if he intended to destroy the good people of Sodom and Gomorrah along with the evil. 'What if there are, say, fifty good people? Surely you wouldn't be so unjust as to kill them along with the evil?'

Abraham appealed to God's justice and even reminded God that he is the judge of everyone – the good as well as the bad. 'Shall not the judge of all the earth do right?'

God conceded that Abraham had a point and said that if he was able to find fifty righteous people he would not destroy the cities.

Encouraged by his success Abraham tried again, pushing a little harder. 'What if there are forty-five good people? Surely you won't destroy the city if there are a mere five less than the fifty?'

God conceded, and was asked, 'What if there are forty?' 'All right.' 'Thirty?' asked Abraham.

'Yes,' said God. 'Twenty?' said Abraham.

God said, 'If there are twenty good people I will not destroy the city.'

Abraham staked everything on his closeness to God and on God's merciful nature, and asked if he could make a final request. 'What if there are ten good people?'

God agreed. 'For the sake of ten, I will not destroy it.'

What a strange story, and what confidence in God Abraham shows! At a time in human history when there were many religions and many gods, fear was the most common attitude in worshippers. Yet Abraham fearlessly threw himself on God's merciful nature. In most people's minds an action would be considered right because their god did it or ordered it to be done. But not for Abraham. He knew God better than that, and his words, 'Shall not the judge of all the earth do right?' express exactly his confidence in the righteousness of God, in God's fairness and moral perfection. An action was not right because God did it, rather God did it because it was right, and it is God's nature to do right.

The Binding of Isaac

We are told nothing of Isaac as a child and young boy. All we know is that the jealousy between Hagar and Sarah burst out again and Sarah asked Abraham to send the servant and her son, Ishmael, away. Naturally Abraham hesitated. He was proud and fond of his elder son. But God told him to do as Sarah had asked, and Hagar and her son were sent away. Life was not easy for them, but they survived, and Ishmael became a skilled hunter and warrior, an expert with the bow. Eventually he married an Egyptian girl and was said to be the father of twelve princes, each of whom became the head of a tribe. So despite the harsh treatment, Ishmael prospered and through him, like it or not, Abraham was the father of many nations.

The Bible explains all that in order to clear the stage for the real stars of God's plan, Abraham and his son Isaac. No doubt the loss of Ishmael hurt Abraham, and because he did not know whether Hagar and her son lived or died, Isaac would have become all the more precious to him as the one precarious life through whom God's promise could be fulfilled. How he must have watched over him and worried when the child was ill or if he fell or went missing, as children do. Abraham's worries, like those of most parents, were largely unnecessary, but nonetheless real. But Isaac was strong and healthy and survived all the usual hazards of childhood. Soon he would be old enough to marry and have children – sons – of his own. Then Abraham would be able to relax. Then his work would be done, his job would be over. God's plan to make a nation dedicated and loyal to himself, who would bring blessings on all other nations, would be on the way to fulfilment.

But when we seem to have weathered the worst storms and life appears simpler and easier, then we are very vulnerable. And so was Abraham. God hadn't finished with him; he hadn't pensioned him off into a pleasant and pointless retirement. God spoke again.

It began very innocently. 'Abraham,' said God

'Here I am,' said Abraham, perhaps wondering what pleasant task God might have for him.

God said, 'Take your son, your only son, Isaac, whom you love, and go to the land of Moriah.'

No problem so far. Being sent somewhere by God was no hardship to the nomadic Abraham, and hadn't God, in the very words he used, recognised the very special love which existed between Abraham and his only son? But pleasant anticipation changed to horror as God went on, 'Go to the land of Moriah and there offer Isaac as a burnt offering upon one of the mountains of which I shall tell you.'

His love for his son, his pride in him, the hopes he'd built on Isaac, this child of joy and laughter, all were now to be destroyed. And besides all that, this young man was the only hope of God's promise ever being fulfilled.

And then God says, 'Kill him!'

Abraham was used to sacrificing the best of his flocks and herds, giving them as gifts to God as tokens of his own love and commitment. He was pleased to give God what he thought was the best, but it had never entered his head that God would ask for what was really the best – Isaac.

Just as with God's first call to Abraham, when he was told to leave Haran for an undisclosed destination, so now we are told that Abraham neither hesitated nor questioned nor argued. He didn't talk to Sarah about it, or mention it to Isaac. The story goes straight on: 'So Abraham rose early in the morning, saddled his ass, and took two of his young men with him, and his son Isaac.'

They travelled for three days and there is no record of their conversation. Perhaps Abraham could not find words for his thoughts. Perhaps silently and urgently he prayed that God would withdraw his terrible demand. On they went in silence and on the third day came in sight of the place. Calm and stern, Abraham made the arrangements. The two young servants were to remain in camp; he and Isaac would go on alone to make a sacrifice to God. Isaac carried the wood and Abraham carried the knife and the fire.

Perhaps in view of Abraham's terrible silence and the absence of any animal for sacrifice, Isaac already had a good idea of what was going to happen. He spoke to his father: 'We have everything for the sacrifice except the lamb.' Abraham still couldn't tell his son the truth and was evasive, replying, 'God himself will provide a lamb for a burnt offering.' And Isaac had to be satisfied with that. And on they went together.

When they reached the mountain top, Abraham built an altar and laid the wood in place. He took the uncomplaining and by now fully aware Isaac and bound him on the altar as the sacrificial gift. He took the knife and raised it. We are not told if there were attempted explanations or words of farewell. We are not told if Abraham and Isaac could look into each other's eyes. We are not told if tears poured down Abraham's face. Isaac lay still, silent, his eyes shut against his own fear and the appalling act that his father was to perform. The knife was raised.

And then, in the sound of the wind on the mountain top came

the voice of God, or of God's angel: 'Abraham, Abraham.' There is urgency in the voice. It wouldn't do to be late; the timing was critical. But Abraham was ready for any excuse to pause. He said, 'Here I am.' And the voice said, 'Do not lay your hand on the boy or do anything to him.'

The crisis was over. Abraham lowered the knife and it must have seemed as if he were waking from a nightmare. The voice went on, 'Now I know that you fear God.'

Slumped over the altar, his son still bound, Abraham could scarcely breathe, so relieved was he.

Could Isaac hear the voice? Or was he still rigid with fear, eyes clamped shut, waiting for the pain of the knife stroke? Perhaps he sensed something, some pause, and opened his eyes to see his father, limp with exhaustion, gazing over his inert body. Then the knife was used. Abraham cut the ropes binding Isaac and told him to climb down. And now Isaac could turn and see what Abraham was looking at so intently. It was a ram with its horns entangled in a thicket. His father had been right. God did provide the animal for sacrifice – and not a moment too soon.

The ram was sacrificed. In one sense this sacrifice cost Abraham nothing, but in a far more real sense it had cost him more than could be counted. God spoke again and commended Abraham for his absolute trust. So strong was his faith that God would fulfil his promises, that he was willing to risk losing – risk killing – the one person through whom the promises could be fulfilled. And so the promise was renewed, in even stronger terms. Without doubt he would be the father of people innumerable as the stars of heaven and the sand on the seashore.

And so the testing of Abraham was over. God was sure of Abraham and Abraham was sure of God, sure that unlike many of the gods worshipped by neighbouring peoples, Yahweh, Abraham's God, did not demand human sacrifice. His did not want parents to kill their children in an effort to win his favour or avert his anger. And so the custom grew and still exists that Jewish firstborn sons are offered to God and 'bought back', in the knowledge that what God wants is a life of obedience, not the death of a child.

Jacob's Story

The Cheat

Jacob is not an easy man to like. We meet him as he is born the younger of a pair of twins, and almost before we've started we find him cheating his brother. Later he does it again, making it worse the second time by also deceiving his aged and blind father. Because of his dishonesty and greed he has to run for his life. He's not a very attractive character but, despite that, or perhaps because of that, he is of immense importance in the story of the people who bear his name, the people of Israel, because Jacob becomes Israel.

How do we move from the deceitful young man with an eye to the main chance to the person of whom Jesus speaks with respect when he says, 'People will come from east and west and will take their places in the kingdom of heaven with Abraham and Isaac and Jacob?'

Jacob's story falls into that section of the Book of Genesis that contains the patriarchal history. Running beneath and behind the stories of the three great men, Abraham, Isaac and Jacob, is the theme that God has chosen to establish a family which will become a nation through which the glory and the love of God will be made known to all people. The Bible's words are, 'Through you shall all the nations of the earth be blessed.'

God's plan is beset by problems. Abraham is old. His wife Sarah is old, childless and barren. But against all odds and because of the grace of God a son is born and is named Isaac. Then Abraham is told to sacrifice Isaac who is the sole hope of the family continuing and of God's plan being fulfilled. At the last moment he is saved and once again God's plan can go forward.

Isaac lives and marries Rebekah. She, too, is barren and again it looks as if the line will die out. But once again God's grace carries forward God's plan, and against all odds Rebekah becomes pregnant. She has twins, Esau and Jacob. Esau is the firstborn and therefore the important one, bearing the honour and the responsibility of carrying on the line and fulfilling God's promise.

Perhaps this is where we can begin to understand Jacob and his deceitfulness. Born a second or two after his brother – for the story says that he was clinging with his hand to his brother's heel as they were born – that tiny period of time divided them, and it meant that Esau was of immense importance to the family while Jacob counted for little. As they grew up, however, it became clear that Esau was in no way capable of carrying the responsibilities which his position as firstborn placed on him. He was an outdoor man, living for the moment, thoughtless, careless of the future. And who knows, he might also have used his position to bully the gentler and perhaps physically weaker Jacob.

It was a typical day. Esau was out in the fields hunting and trapping. Jacob was at home cooking. He had made a wonderful hot, lentil stew. In came Esau, exhausted and very hungry. What happened next gives us a very clear picture of the capacities of the two brothers. As soon as he smelt the stew Esau said, 'Give me some of that, I'm starving.'

Maybe as a joke, maybe not, Jacob said, 'I'll sell it to you for your birthright.'

Not seeing the joke or the trap, and not for a moment considering the implications, Esau said, 'What good will it do me being the eldest son if I die now of starvation? You can have the birthright. You'll have it anyway if I starve to death.'

And so the rights of the elder son passed to Jacob, and we have been given a glimpse of the very different characters of these twins: Jacob, quick-thinking and not averse to gaining an advantage: Esau, rather shallow, thoughtless, with little interest in the past and the future.

Some time later there was a similar and more serious incident. It seems as if it had become clear to Rebekah that her sons had been born the wrong way round. Esau had his strengths. He was an excellent hunter, protector and provider; he didn't take other matters too seriously and he didn't bear grudges. As long as the hunting was good, nothing much mattered to Esau. Jacob on the other hand was the clever one, the one fitted for responsibility.

He, not Esau, was the one who could carry the burden of being the head of the family when Isaac was dead – and Isaac was already old, his powers failing.

And so Rebekah – the archetypal Jewish mother, fixing things, actually ruling the family although the father was nominally in control – Rebekah helped Jacob deceive Isaac and cheat Esau of his father's blessing. A father's blessing just before death was rather like the stating of a will. It meant that if Esau knelt before the blind and aged Isaac and received the elder son's blessing, it would have undone and overridden his weak and foolish surrender of the birthright years before. So Rebekah, with the very best of intentions for the future of the family, planned to deceive her husband. She told Jacob to put some goatskin on his shoulders and arms so that he would both feel and smell like Esau, the man of the fields.

Isaac was blind but he was not stupid and immediately suspected something. But Jacob blatantly lied, and in the end the deception worked and he received the blessing of the firstborn son. His status as the elder son was now confirmed. Esau's even temper had been pushed too far. The Bible says, with some understatement, 'Esau bore a grudge against Jacob because of the blessing.' That is putting it mildly, for the anger of the hunter was aroused and the man who didn't normally bear grudges erupted in fury against his brother.

In this story we can hear echoes of another famous pair of brothers, the elder jealous of the younger. The grudge that Cain bore against Abel led to murder. But Jacob was nothing if not clever, and skilled at nothing if it were not self-preservation. So he ran away and denied Esau the chance of becoming a Cain.

The Dream

Reversing the journey taken by his grandfather Abraham, Jacob left Beersheba and fled toward Haran. When night came, exhausted by his flight, he lay down to sleep and was tired enough to use a rock as a pillow. As he slept something happened to this frightened, self-seeking man. Something made him aware of the presence of God, drawing from him the words, 'Truly, the Lord is in this place and I did not know it.'

Perhaps it wasn't really a surprise that God should be in such a godforsaken place as that barren desert where Jacob happened to be resting for the night. Perhaps the real surprise was that God should be concerned about such a godforsaken cheat and liar as Jacob, who seemed to give very little thought to God.

Jacob dreamt of a ladder reaching from earth to heaven with angels moving up and down it. Clearly this was a place where heaven and earth met. Jacob learned through his dream that there is no place beyond the reach of God and no person beyond God's forgiveness. Jacob learnt that whatever he had done, he could never be so bad that God didn't care about him.

After this profound experience of God we don't suddenly find Jacob changed. There was no overnight change of character and way of life, because Jacob was Jacob, as you are you and I am I. And we know that change of character and habit is a long, slow and difficult process, no matter how uplifting a spiritual experience we may go through.

So Jacob remained Jacob, and when he took refuge with his cousin Laban, the cheating and the seeking for advantage went on. Laban, however, was no Esau. Jacob found himself in the novel position of pitting his wits against a very crafty and worthy opponent. And so at first it was Jacob who was cheated. He thought he'd worked seven years to win the lovely Rachel as his bride, but found, on his wedding night, when the veil was removed, that he was married to Leah, the no doubt admirable but less attractive of Laban's daughters. Jacob liked to get what he wanted, and he wanted Rachel. To his great credit he was willing to work a further seven years to count her as his wife. We learn a lot in this part of the story about the strength and patience of Jacob's character. He was in the business of outwitting people, and he didn't seem to bear a grudge when he was himself outwitted. He stored it away and put it down as experience.

In the end he came out on top, as we would expect. By clever farming and selective breeding Jacob became the owner of a large flock of sheep, and those lovely speckled and blotched sheep we today call 'Jacob Sheep' are witness to Jacob's bouncing back and getting the upper hand. So, having arrived at Laban's camp a poor vagrant, a refugee fleeing for his life, Jacob left a wealthy family man. What is more, he now felt strong enough, confident enough, to meet his brother Esau again. Perhaps he thought the years that had passed would have calmed Esau's temper.

The Fight

It's interesting that Jacob's first encounter with God had been when he was running away from Esau. A second and more transforming experience of God happened when he was on his way back to meet his brother. We might ponder the closeness and importance of human, and in particular family, relationships. In this case it was as if the thread joining these twins was unbroken, despite the strains they had both put on it throughout their lives. Their antagonism was perhaps the result of their closeness and their basic likeness. This reminds us that God is in the middle of even the most turbulent relationships among family and friends.

Meeting Esau after so many years was not something Jacob could do lightly. He was still afraid, afraid of what his wronged elder brother might do, afraid that Esau's grudge would still be alive. So, practical as ever, Jacob sent messengers ahead to meet Esau. They were to say, 'Your servant Jacob is returning; he is now a rich man and hopes to meet you on good terms.'

The messengers returned and their news was not encouraging. They said, 'We met your brother Esau. He was already on the way to meet you with four hundred men!'

Jacob prayed. He reminded God of how prosperous he had become through God's grace, and how this was in accordance with God's plan and how he now needed God's help quite desperately. But he didn't only pray; he planned as well. He divided up his possessions into groups, so that if Esau met one group and destroyed it, he might have had his fill of killing and destroying when the second group of flocks and herds came along. Jacob also sent lavish presents ahead to try to take the steam out of Esau's expected anger: 200 she-goats, twenty he-goats, 200 ewes and twenty rams, thirty milchcamels with their young, forty cows and ten young bulls, twenty she-asses and ten he-asses. Quite a sweetener.

He had reached a river. He could have kept it between himself and his brother, giving opportunity for retreat and escape, but he didn't. He committed himself by organising the crossing of the Jabbok ford for his wives, slave girls and his eleven sons. Then he returned to be alone, to wrestle with his fear of Esau, and with the fact that God had seemed to be with him and to favour him. Surely he wouldn't turn his back on him now.

Jacob's second close experience of God again came in the night. Perhaps it was real or perhaps it was a dream so real that in the morning it was impossible to believe that it was a dream. Jacob wrestled with God, or with a man, or with an angel. The story is unclear, or perhaps just dream-like, about who Jacob's opponent was. They wrestled all night and there was no clear winner. As day broke, Jacob's opponent was anxious to get away. He partly disabled Jacob by injuring his leg. But still Jacob hung on. He refused to give in or to let his adversary go before he received a blessing from him.

The blessing was given in the form of a new name. In the struggle a change had taken place or perhaps simply been completed, a change in Jacob's character. Perhaps it was something Jacob had been striving for all his life. We know how far short we fall of what we could be and should be; how far short of what God intends us to be. It is a lifelong struggle. So it was for Jacob, and for him that struggle somehow came to a head on the night before he met his brother Esau again. The night-long battle was the climax of a lifelong battle and Jacob emerged from it a different man. His name was changed too to make the change permanent. His opponent – man, angel or God – said, 'You shall no longer be called Jacob, you shall be called Israel, because you have wrestled with God and with men and have prevailed.'

So Jacob and Esau met and they were reconciled. But life's problems were not over for Jacob. No one can have children and be free from anxiety, pain and tragedy, and Jacob had his full share. His twelve sons, whom we can now accurately call 'the children of Israel', were the founders of the twelve tribes of Israel. God's plan and promise were being amply fulfilled. And Jacob's place in the memory of Jews and Christians was assured. To us he is an example of how God searches for his prodigal sons and daughters, how we can never be out of the reach of God's mercy, how God never gives up, however unpromising or downright bad we might be. If there was hope for Jacob, and there was, there is hope for you and for me.

Joseph's Story

Joseph and His Dreams

Joseph as a youngster was clever, good-looking, spoilt and totally lacking in tact. Why didn't he keep his mouth shut about his dreams? No wonder his brothers didn't like him.

God's promise to Abraham that his descendants would be as the stars of heaven, as the sand on the seashore, as the dust of the earth, was moving very nicely toward fulfilment, and Jacob was largely responsible for that. Married to Leah by accident, and by choice and effort to his beloved Rachel, he also had children, as the custom was, by their maidservants, Bilhah and Zilpah. The full team of his sons was: by Leah – Reuben, Simeon, Levi, Judah, Issachar and Zebulun; by Rachel – Joseph and Benjamin; by Bilhah – Dan and Naphtali; by Zilpah – Gad and Asher. There are rivalries and jealousies in almost all families, and in Jacob's large family there was the additional factor of them being the children of four different mothers. It was a family group which needed all the tact and sensitivity that could be found.

Everyone worked. The flocks had increased, and finding pasture for them in the arid land around Hebron took all the manpower they had. Jacob was proud of all his sons, but he had his favourites. He knew from his own experience what it was to be a younger son and he had fought successfully to change that. Perhaps that left him with a particular inclination to favour his younger sons. Perhaps he knew that the older brothers gave them a hard time. Also Rachel, now dead, had been his great love, and her children, Joseph and Benjamin, his youngest sons, reminded him of her, and he loved them in a very special way. This probably didn't help relationships between the brothers.

Benjamin was still young, still about the house or, we should say, about the camp. He was the youngest child and spent time among the older adults and the servants. He would be spoilt and he probably enjoyed it. Joseph was older, about seventeen, and he worked partly at home and partly with his brothers, looking after the sheep. Theirs would be a hard life, constantly on the move seeking fresh pastures, sleeping out, charged with the responsibility of protecting the sheep from predators. Joseph would be unsure of himself among his elder brothers. Their maturity, their language and their jokes would surprise and probably hurt him – as they were intended to. He would be the butt of coarse humour, some good-natured, some not. Life would not be easy for Joseph.

Unfortunately Jacob, in his blind old man's love for his son, gave him a new coat. In the east in those days the gift of clothing was an accepted way of honouring someone. The coat Jacob gave to Joseph was long; it reached to the ground and had long sleeves. It wasn't a coat for working in. A working garment would be cut off at the knees and have short sleeves, for freedom of movement and safety. The gift of a special coat – the Bible's 'coat of many colours' – would not make Joseph any more popular with his brothers. So perhaps it wasn't tactlessness, perhaps it was embarrassment about the coat that made Joseph feel the need to assert himself. Perhaps he felt he had to attack in order to survive the taunts of his brothers. Whatever it was, something led Joseph to act very unwisely about his dreams.

He had had two dreams. The first was rooted in the stuff of everyday life. It was harvest time and all the brothers were working in the same field, binding sheaves of corn. 'And,' said Joseph, 'your sheaves all bowed down to my sheaf.' He must have dreamt it; he wouldn't have made it up. Perhaps he felt so little, so useless and weak compared to his elder brothers that in his dreams he compensated and imagined himself better and more powerful than them all. That wouldn't be surprising. But he lacked the guile of his father, and he spoke out when it would have been wiser to keep silent. And his brothers hated him all the more.

So he told them his second dream, and that was worse. Now he imagined himself a cosmic hero. The sun and the moon and the eleven stars of heaven bowed down to him. The brothers didn't need a skilled interpreter. They knew what it meant, or at least, what Joseph meant. His parents as well as his brothers would kneel before him. It seemed as if he couldn't stop himself saying stupid things and taking matters from bad to worse. This time he told his father of the dream. Jacob rebuked him and showed commendable restraint. But secretly Jacob stored the dream safely in his memory. He seemed to know instinctively that there was something in it.

The Brothers' Revenge

Sometimes, because Joseph was still quite young, Jacob used him as a messenger between camp and flock so that he could know where his sons were moving as they looked for suitable pasture. It also meant that he could hang on to his favourite son a bit longer.

One day he sent Joseph off to Shechem. That was where the flocks had been the last time they had heard from the brothers. He was to find out if they needed anything, if all was well, and then return and report to Jacob. It was a journey of some forty miles. When he reached Shechem there was no sign of his brothers and the sheep. He wandered a long time in that vast area, not knowing in which direction his brothers had gone. Then, by chance, he met someone who had seen them and heard them say that they would be moving on to Dothan. So Joseph set off for Dothan, a further twenty miles.

As he spotted the flocks and then his brothers, they spotted him, a solitary figure in that wide landscape. They knew it was Joseph because of his long, flapping coat – not really practical for the long journey he had made. His brothers were weary. Finding pasture was an endless and exhausting task and they were not feeling patient or charitable. 'Here comes the dreamer,' said one of them. 'The last thing I need is him telling me how to do my job and how wonderful he is.' Another said, 'Well, this is our opportunity. We are miles from anywhere. We could kill him and pretend that a lion or a bear has done it. No one would suspect anything.'

Reuben, the eldest, didn't like what he heard. He had no great love for Joseph, but to talk of killing him was beyond reason. But the murmurs of the brothers showed that he was in a minority, perhaps a minority of one. He thought quickly and, trying to convince his brothers that he was as tired of Joseph as they were, he suggested that they put him in a pit – a water cistern dug in the ground. It would be a nasty and effective prison because it would be bottle-shaped with a narrow opening to minimise evaporation, and it would be impossible to climb out. Reuben hoped his suggestion would appeal to his brothers because he hoped to save him. He knew that if Joseph were left in such a pit, with the intense heat of the day and the intense cold of the night, he wouldn't last very long. So the brothers might agree. Joseph would be dead, but they wouldn't exactly have killed him. But Reuben hoped his brothers would agree to his plan because, secretly, he intended to lift Joseph from the pit as soon as he could.

Joseph arrived and, though he was very tired, greeted his brothers cheerfully. He was quickly aware that something was wrong; there was something in the atmosphere, something strange in the way they wouldn't look at him properly. No one offered him water or tried to explain why they'd moved from Shechem. Then one of them said, 'Let's have that flashy coat,' and got up and began to tear it off Joseph.

Joseph fought back and others joined in and he began to realise that this was not horseplay, this was serious. The coat was torn off and he was punched and kicked and forced into the dry cistern. So far, Reuben's plan was working.

But then the unexpected happened. The brothers had settled to their meal – lamb, of course. The conversation was strained and muted because they were all thinking about Joseph and what they were doing to him. They heard the noise of camels and men; snorting animals, clinking harnesses and deep voices. A caravan of traders were on their way to Egypt. They might have been Ishmaelites or Midianites – the Bible uses both terms – but naturally they would stop and make camp for the night. The accepted customs of hospitality would ensure that the brothers would invite them to share their meal. Another lamb or two would be killed and cooked and there would be much talk and exchange of news – very welcome to both groups of men, whose way of life involved much loneliness and little company.

The story makes you think of mob psychology. It was as if, as individuals, each of the brothers disliked Joseph and was jealous of him. But that was all. The violence and the death threats seem to have arisen as one egged on another and as they said and did things that would impress the others. None of them wanted to look weak or soft in their treatment of Joseph. But already Reuben had misgivings and secret plans to save Joseph, and now it was Judah's turn.

Judah was the fourth eldest of the brothers and, like Reuben, he was not happy with what was going on. He saw the traders as an opportunity to save Joseph. He said to his brothers, 'We gain nothing by killing him, and we shouldn't do it; after all he is our brother. Let's sell him. These fellows will take him off our hands and we'll make a little profit.'

It seemed a good idea, perhaps getting all the brothers out of a situation that had got out of hand. After the usual and expected haggling, the traders handed over twenty shekels of silver, and the next morning Joseph was taken away to be sold as a slave in Egypt.

Back in the brothers' camp things were not happy. Reuben, for some reason, was not aware of Judah's intervention, and he went to the cistern to release Joseph only to discover that he wasn't there. There was a lot of talk and arguing. None of them wanted to take responsibility for what had happened, and by now they all regretted it. They had begun to realise for the first time what this would mean to their father. What could they tell him? They had to be practical. They still had Joseph's coat, so they killed another of the flock and soaked the coat in the blood.

When they returned to Hebron they showed their father the tattered, bloodstained coat. 'We found this,' they said. And Jacob saved them the trouble of lying further. Like most worried parents, he imagined the worst. He said, 'It is Joseph's coat. No doubt a wild animal has attacked him, and my son is dead.'

The brothers didn't dare tell him that things were not that bad, and that the last time they had seen Joseph he was alive and reasonably healthy. They had to act out the part of distressed brothers, supporting their bereaved father. Jacob refused their sympathy. He knew they had never liked Joseph and perhaps he sensed something false in their sorrow and their words of comfort to him. He said, 'No, don't comfort me. I shall never cease to mourn for my son, until I too go to the grave and join him in death.'

A Prisoner in Egypt

The traders reached Egypt and did a good deal over Joseph, selling him to a high-ranking officer in the Egyptian army whose name was Potiphar. They got far more than the twenty shekels they had paid for him. Potiphar was a good judge of men, if not of women, and his experienced eye realised that Joseph would be very useful to him. He employed him in his luxurious home and it quickly became clear to everyone that Joseph was exceptionally able. Soon he was in charge of all the other servants and slaves and of the total running of the household. Joseph had landed on his feet and all was going well. As the Bible says, 'The Lord was with Joseph.'

God's plan was complex and was going to land Joseph in greater trouble than anything he'd faced from his brothers. Probably he didn't think of it at all as God's plan; he probably thought it was just his bad luck. Mrs Potiphar was an attractive woman, rich and totally spoilt by her successful and very busy husband. She was bored. She had become increasingly aware that the new slave, who was such a help to her husband, was not only intelligent and hard-working but also very good-looking. After making sure that he was in her presence more and more and could hardly be unaware of her undoubted charms, she finally ordered him to her bed. Joseph refused out of loyalty to his master and to his God. The first time he refused, Mrs Potiphar accepted it. But she tried again – and again. Joseph's behaviour was impeccable. The Bible says, 'Although she spoke to Joseph day after day, he would not listen to her, to lie with her or be with her.' There was always a strength and an innocence about Joseph, as when he naively told his brothers his dreams and when he cheerfully went looking for them. It is all part of Joseph's character that he would not even consider doing the wrong his master's wife proposed.

One day, when there were no other servants about who might be witnesses, Mrs Potiphar made her final bid. Again Joseph refused and left the room. She tried to stop him and as he went out she grabbed his tunic. Again his clothes were going to get him into trouble. Like the brothers with the bloodstained coat, Mrs Potiphar made up a story. She told her husband that Joseph had tried to force himself upon her. She said she had cried out for help and Joseph had fled leaving his tunic behind: 'Here it is – the evidence.'

Perhaps Potiphar knew his wife better than she thought. If he really believed that Joseph had done what his wife said, surely he would have had him put to death immediately. But in fact Joseph was put into prison in the Round House, and perhaps Potiphar therefore joins Reuben and Judah as one of those who worked secretly, even unconsciously, to ensure Joseph's survival – unwitting agents of God.

Even in prison Joseph prospered. Again the Bible tells us that 'the Lord was with him.' Before long he had gained the confidence of the prison governor, who sensibly used Joseph's administrative talents to help run the prison. It occupied Joseph, developed his gifts and made the prison governor's life a great deal easier. Joseph was in prison a long time and, patient though he was, he could hardly be expected to think that his life was following a plan laid down by God.

The prison then gained two celebrity inmates, the former Chief Butler and Chief Baker to Pharaoh, ruler of Egypt. Both men had held positions of great importance and influence in the court. The Superintendent of Bakeries supervised all the catering and was therefore responsible for the diet and health of Pharaoh and his court. The Chief Butler was the man who 'placed the cup in Pharaoh's hand'. He was physically close to Pharaoh, always at his shoulder to receive confidential messages, and day by day he had to ensure that no dangerous drink passed Pharaoh's lips. Perhaps Pharaoh felt ill and looked immediately to those responsible for his food and drink. For safety's sake he had them held in prison while the incident was investigated. While they were in prison, Joseph was instructed by the prison governor to look after them. After all, they were as yet uncondemned and Joseph was an experienced personal servant. Very quickly his intelligence and good nature led them to depend on him and trust him.

These two men, used to life in court, would feel deep shame that they were in prison. They would feel fear and anxiety about when they would be released, or if they would be released. Behind all their hopes and fears would be the great fear that it all might end in execution. One night they both had memorable and worrying dreams. When Joseph waited on them in the morning he could tell that something was worrying them, so he asked them what it was. They told him that they had both had vivid dreams and they were worried because they could not understand them.

Joseph said, 'The skill to interpret comes from God,' and he let them know that he had that skill. It was a very reasonable claim to make in view of his own experiences. After all his brothers had nicknamed him 'The Dreamer'. He was an expert.

They told him their dreams, the butler first. Not surprisingly he had dreamt of wine and drinking. In his dream he saw a vine with three branches which budded, sprouted and produced grapes with astonishing speed. He picked the grapes, pressed the juice into Pharaoh's cup and gave the cup to Pharaoh. That was the dream. What did it mean?

Joseph explained that the three branches denoted three days, and that within three days the butler would be released from prison and restored to his former position at Pharaoh's table. 'Please,' said Joseph, 'when you are back in favour, don't forget me. Like you I am in prison though I have committed no crime.'

Encouraged by this favourable interpretation, the baker told his dream. He, too, had dreamt about his job. He was carrying three baskets piled up on his head. In the top one, open for all to see, were all sorts of good things he had baked for Pharaoh. But they didn't reach Pharaoh, for as he walked along birds came and ate them out of the basket.

Joseph interpreted. 'The three baskets mean three days. In three days you will be executed by hanging and the birds will come and eat your flesh.'

Events took place exactly as Joseph had predicted. The baker was executed and the butler restored to his position. But, either because he was too busy re-establishing himself, or because he was a selfish man, the butler forgot Joseph and Joseph continued to serve his long, undeserved prison sentence.

Pharaoh's Dreams and Joseph's Promotion

Two years passed, and dreams, which had caused Joseph so much trouble, eventually came to his rescue. This time it was Pharaoh who dreamt, and, in keeping with his status, he had two dreams. They were both rather complicated. In the first, seven healthy, well-fleshed cattle were grazing in the rich pastures on the banks of the Nile. Then seven more cattle, gaunt and thin, appeared. They did not feed on the lush vegetation, but devoured the seven fat cattle. Then the dream changed. He saw, on one stalk, seven ears of grain, plump and full. But immediately seven thin, blighted ears appeared and they swallowed the fat grain.

Egypt was famous for its wise men, sorcerers, magicians, diviners and soothsayers, and Pharaoh had plenty of them. Usually they could answer his questions and satisfy his enquiries, but not this time. Not one of them could tell Pharaoh what his dreams meant – or perhaps they were afraid to be the bearers of bad news. It was all the gossip at court, Pharaoh being tormented by his dreams and no one able to interpret them. And, of course, the butler heard the gossip. Eventually he remembered Joseph. He spoke to Pharaoh and told him about how, when he was in prison, a young Hebrew prisoner had interpreted both his and the baker's dreams and done so correctly.

Joseph was sent for. He was told to shave and given decent clothes and rushed along into the presence of Pharaoh. Pharaoh explained the situation and the failure of the wise men. 'I believe you can interpret the dreams for me,' he said.

'It's not me, 'said Joseph, 'It is God who will give an interpretation.'

So Pharaoh told his dreams. Joseph didn't hesitate. He spoke calmly and confidently; he knew about dreams. 'The two dreams are really the same. They are the way God has chosen to reveal the future to Your Majesty. The seven fat, healthy cattle are seven years of plenty. The seven gaunt and thin cattle are years of famine. It is the same with the fat and thin ears of grain. God is warning Pharaoh that after seven years of plenty, famine will eat up the land and make it seem as if the good years had never happened.'

Joseph knew he was making a good impression and he wasn't going to let the opportunity pass. He continued, 'What is needed, therefore, is a man, discreet and wise, who can be put in charge of things so that enough is collected and saved during the good years to see the nation through the bad years. All must be done, of course, to keep everything under the authority and control of Pharaoh.'

Pharaoh liked what he heard; Joseph had talked himself into a job. Pharaoh and the court agreed that they could think of no one wiser or more discreet than this man, who seemed to add divine guidance to his own considerable gifts. So Joseph was appointed, and prison became only a memory. From imprisoned slave he became second only to Pharaoh, and was given a signet ring as the sign of his authority. Naturally his new position brought wealth and status. He dressed magnificently and wore a gold chain round his neck. He rode in the second state chariot and as he passed through the streets his bodyguards shouted to the people, 'Bend the knee!' On top of all that, Pharaoh arranged a very advantageous marriage for Joseph with the daughter of a high-ranking priest. So Joseph, who entered Egypt as a slave, had become, at the age of thirty, a member of the Egyptian aristocracy.

Joseph Meets His Brothers

As in the case of the butler and the baker, Joseph's interpretation of Pharaoh's dreams proved accurate. He carried out the policies he had outlined, and during the seven years of plenty stored up an enormous reserve of grain. Then the famine came and, as Joseph had predicted and planned, the position of the monarchy was strengthened because, through Joseph, Pharaoh controlled all the supply of food. People came and bought from the state storehouses established by Joseph. He drove hard bargains, and when the people had spent their money he took their livestock and even their land in exchange for the grain they needed to eat and to sow for the coming year. The monarchy became richer and stronger, and Joseph's own position was very powerful indeed.

The famine was not confined to Egypt; the whole of the Middle East suffered. Soon merchants were carrying the news that there was grain in Egypt, and back in Shechem Jacob heard about it. He spoke sharply to his sons. 'Don't stand there looking at each other and doing nothing. You've heard there's grain in Egypt. Go and buy some before we all starve to death.' He wouldn't let his youngest son Benjamin go, but the other ten set off.

Once in Egypt, they found their way to the supply point and, as foreigners, were taken to be interviewed before being allowed to buy the precious grain. Imagine Joseph's surprise when the next travel-stained, weary and humble group was ushered into his presence, begging for his help and bowing to him in unconscious fulfilment of his childhood dream. He recognised them at once. They were not much changed. There was Reuben, dignified despite being worn out, and the others uncomfortable and embarrassed, shifting from foot to foot in the presence of this Egyptian overlord. They didn't recognise him, of course. It was ten or eleven years since they'd seen him and he had since grown from a youth to a man. What's more, everything about him was Egyptian – his clothes, his manners, even his language, for he used an interpreter.

Who can blame Joseph for taking the opportunity to get his own back, for twisting the knife a little? He was aggressive in his questions. 'Where are you from?'

'Canaan,' they replied.

'Ah, so you're spies.' This wasn't an entirely unreasonable accusation. Egypt was always at risk from the intrigues of the other nations of the Middle East. They all posed threats to Egypt's security and prosperity; all would have like to have laid their hands on the prosperous land with its fertile Nile valley. Joseph said, 'Yes, you are spies. You have come to see if the famine has made Egypt weak enough to be attacked.'

'Oh, no, not at all. We are all the sons of one man. There were twelve of us in all. The youngest has stayed behind and one is no longer with us.' That ambiguous statement was quite accurate from the brothers' point of view, because they didn't actually know whether Joseph were dead or alive. They'd sold him, and his father had assumed that he was dead, but they didn't really know. Joseph must have been bitterly amused when they said,

'One is no longer with us.' It was the exact opposite of the truth. He was with them, in the very same room.

He decided to let them stew. Speaking to them only through the interpreter, he said that they would have to prove their story by bringing their youngest brother. Meanwhile they could recover from their journey by spending three days in prison. Perhaps Joseph thought, 'What's three days, after all, compared to the years I spent in prison because of them?'

When the three days were over he interviewed them again and announced his decision. 'I have decided to let you go home with the grain you want. However, one of you will remain here as a hostage. He will be released when you all return, bringing your youngest brother with you. You had better discuss it among yourselves.'

They all started to talk at once, totally unaware that Joseph understood every word. They knew what their father would say if they returned without one of them and how difficult – impossible – it would be to persuade him to let Benjamin go back with them. In their uncertainty their consciences began to speak and they started to connect their present problems with their cruel treatment of Joseph long ago. Even Reuben, rather peevishly, said, 'Didn't I tell you not to harm him? But you wouldn't listen to me.'

What a scene it must have been, and how Joseph must have enjoyed it! They were talking quite freely about him, totally unaware that the elegant Egyptian overlord who had their lives in his hands could understand everything that they said. In fact Joseph understood so well that he was overcome with emotion and had to go out of the room and, once outside and alone, he wept.

When he had recovered himself he went back in and briskly made arrangements that Simeon should stay as hostage and the others take the grain and return to Canaan. The brothers were glad to go, despite having to leave Simeon behind. They travelled all day putting as many miles between themselves and Egypt as they could. At night they stopped and made camp. One of them opened his sack to give some grain to his ass and there, in the mouth of the sack, was his money. We can imagine his feeling of despair as he saw it. Everything was going wrong.

They reached Shechem, and Jacob could immediately see that something was wrong. First, where was Simeon? What had been going on? They tried to explain. They told him how the 'lord of the land' had treated them; how he had suspected that they were spies; how he had demanded a hostage; and how Simeon would only be released if they took Benjamin back with them. When they had told their tale they emptied their sacks and found that the money had been put back into every one of them. It had been planted. They were being set up. That was the only possible explanation.

Jacob was bewildered and distraught, an unhappy and confused old man. 'What are you doing to me?' he said. 'You have taken two of my sons away, and now you want to take Benjamin as well.'

It wasn't quite fair, but we can sympathise with Jacob. Reuben, characteristically, tried to heal things. He must have been a very strong man, and perhaps confident that everything would eventually work out, because he said that he would stand surety for Benjamin's safety, and if he did not bring him back, then his own two sons could be killed. It seems grossly unfair on his sons, but things were seen differently in those days, and perhaps Reuben knew quite well that Jacob would never kill his own grandsons. Jacob had no option. In the end he had to agree and after further discussion and bickering, the brothers set off once again for Egypt, this time taking Benjamin with them.

Jacob was very low. He really had no choice but to accept the situation, but he felt as if his children were being torn from him one by one and being destroyed. His words of resignation are desperately sad: 'If I am bereaved of my children, I am bereaved.'

The brothers had work to do. They had to be practical. They took double the money they needed so that they could not be accused of stealing their money back on their first visit, and they made their way to Egypt and once again into the presence of Joseph. When Joseph saw that Benjamin was with them, he ordered his servants to prepare a special meal at which all the brothers would be his guests. When they were told this, they could only imagine that it was a plot by which the powerful Egyptian lord was going to further humiliate and accuse them.

They felt, in some uneasy way, that it was all connected with the return of their money. They fully expected to be accused, condemned and made slaves.

They tried to explain about the money – that they had paid, and how surprised they all were to find it in their sacks. But something seemed to have changed. The man didn't seem too concerned about the money. He even suggested that God might have done it. (They wondered which god he might have meant.) Then Simeon was brought out and reunited with them. Things seemed almost too good to be true, and it worried them. But the kindness and the hospitality continued. Arrangements were made for them to clean themselves up after their journey and to get ready for the meal with the Egyptian lord.

Joseph arrived and joined them. They gave him the present they had diplomatically brought with them and were surprised that his first words were, 'How is your father, the old man of whom you spoke?'

They replied that he was still alive and well. And then he looked at Benjamin and innocently asked if this was the youngest brother whom they had mentioned. This charade was a great strain on Joseph, and at this point he had to go out of the room to hide his emotions and his tears.

When he had controlled himself and washed his face he went back and instructed his servants to serve the meal. The brothers were all together at one table and Joseph alone at another, still keeping up the pretence that he was an Egyptian who could not eat with foreigners because of Egyptian religious and social customs. The meal was a great success. Benjamin was treated with special consideration, but they all ate and drank well and it was a happy occasion.

But Joseph hadn't finished with his brothers yet. He was being drawn back to them, his affection returning almost in spite of himself. But he still had a few ounces of revenge to take. He ordered the sacks to be filled for their return journey the next day. The money was to be replaced as before, but this time his servants were to put his own silver cup into Benjamin's sack.

In the morning the farewells were loud and cheerful. They were all going home, and their father Jacob would be reunited with them all, including Simeon and Benjamin. He would be thrilled and content, and they would all have sufficient food to see them through the rest of the famine. Things were beginning to look good.

When they had been travelling only a short time Joseph sent a servant after them. He was to accuse them of ingratitude and theft. Why, when they had been treated so well did they steal the Egyptian lord's silver cup? Did they think no one would notice? They respond that there must be some mistake. So confident were they of their innocence that they proposed that a search be made. If the cup was found, whoever's sack it was in should be put to death, and the rest of them would be slaves to the Egyptian lord. Joseph's servant, who must have been in on the trick, was rather more moderate and suggested that it would be sufficient, if the cup were found, that the man who had stolen it should become a slave and the rest should go free. A search was made and, of course, the cup was found where it had been planted – in Benjamin's sack.

Their confidence, the energy with which they were travelling home, the shared happiness of all being together again and safe – all drained away. Despondently, they packed their baggage, loaded the asses and trudged wearily back to Egypt.

Confronted by Joseph yet again, Judah tried to explain. He spoke of their guilt – and was thinking mainly of their cruel treatment of Joseph and the way they were now being punished for it. He desperately tried to deflect the death penalty that hung over Benjamin and offered himself and his brothers as slaves. Joseph was totally in control. He had made his brothers suffer terribly, but he hadn't finished yet. He had one last piece of malice to get out of his system. He said he would not dream of enslaving them all, just the one who was found to have the cup. He knew quite well what the prospect of returning to their father without Benjamin would do to his brothers. It was the thing they feared most. Judah explained just how difficult it had been to persuade their father to let Benjamin go with them, and what his failure to return would do to the old man. 'When he sees that the lad is not with us, he will die.' Unwittingly, in this emotional plea, Judah spelt out that he and his brothers understood the full enormity of their treatment of Joseph, and what it had done to their father. They hadn't fully understood before, but they understood now with the prospect of Benjamin being torn from the family.

Judah explained that he had stood surety for Benjamin's safe return and so it is he that should now become Joseph's slave. 'How can I go back to my father if the lad is not with me? I fear to see the evil that would come upon my father.'

Judah spoke well, and the atmosphere was charged with emotion. Joseph had done enough; he'd had his revenge and was beginning to think he'd overdone it. He sent out his servants and bodyguards, leaving himself alone with his brothers. They were baffled and worried to see this powerful Egyptian break down before them and weep. Was it another trick? But it wasn't, and Joseph, in their own language, told them who he was. Beneath the Egyptian clothes and manners and language he was Joseph, their brother. This explained many things of course, but it didn't remove the brothers' worries. They knew now why they had been pushed around, tricked and made to suffer – but there was no guarantee that it was over. It could get worse. Now that he had revealed himself, Joseph could take the ultimate revenge.

So fearful were the brothers that Joseph had a hard time convincing them that it was all over. He had to tell them not to feel guilty about their treatment of him years before. They were God's instrument, he said. If they had not sold him he would not have been where he is now, with the means of providing food for the whole family, saving them and ensuring that God's plan to bring blessing on the world could move forward. He said, 'So it was not you who sent me here, but God.' One can only admire this generous reinterpretation of his brothers' malice.

Joseph had been thinking and planning during the time he had been taking his revenge. He was very much in control and knew exactly what he intended to happen. He had the power, the influence, the wealth and, more important, the high moral ground. The brothers were all shocked and unsure of themselves, and Joseph had the initiative. He ordered them to return to their father with the news that he was still alive and 'lord of all Egypt'. What's more, they were to make arrangements to bring Jacob and the whole clan to Egypt, where they could settle and receive preferential treatment.

While all this was happening, news had been travelling. The Egyptian court now knew that Joseph's brothers were with him. Pharaoh confirmed that the suggested move of all Joseph's relations to Egypt was agreeable to him. Perhaps he thought that a few more like Joseph could only do good to the tottering Egyptian economy. So he confirmed the invitation and suggested that the brothers take wagons from Egypt to assist the moving of their women and children when the journey eventually took place. The wagons were provided, and Joseph showered his brothers with gifts for themselves and for all at home. They must have accepted the gifts, especially the silver and the gold, with mixed feelings. But the bitterness was over. These were real gifts and, weighed down with them, the brothers left for Canaan. Joseph's final words to them show what an astute judge of men he was, what common sense he had. 'Do not quarrel on the way,' he said.

How well he knew his brothers!'

Jacob Goes to Egypt

The brothers arrived back in Shechem and told their father that Joseph was still alive. It was too much for Jacob; he couldn't believe it. But when they showed him the wagons and presents that they'd brought from Egypt, gradually he was able to accept the staggering news. Plans and preparations were made, and eventually Jacob and all his family set off for Egypt. It was a long time since Jacob had made such a journey. When they rested for the night near Beersheba, Jacob offered sacrifices to God. There had been several occasions in Jacob's life when he had been acutely aware of the presence of God, and twice, on momentous journeys, God had spoken to him in the night. It happened again.

Encouraging the old man, God said, 'Do not be afraid to go down to Egypt, for I will there make of you a great nation.'

Years ago, in his first night-time encounter with God at Bethel, the promise had been made that his descendants would be like the dust of the earth. This latest experience, near the end of his life, reassured Jacob that God and God's purposes had not changed.

There were about seventy people in Jacob's extended family and they all moved to Egypt. As they came toward the end of their journey Judah, who several times had proved himself trustworthy, was sent ahead to let Joseph know that they were close. With great courtesy and the proper respect of a son for his father, Joseph went out to meet Jacob. He did it in style, travelling in his state chariot. He knew that his father would like that, that it would make him proud to see his son so successful. Their reunion, not surprisingly, was very emotional. Joseph wept and Jacob wept, and Jacob declared that now he was ready to die, happy and at peace.

Immigration formalities had to be gone through, including the brothers being interviewed by Pharaoh about how they would support themselves and their dependants in Egypt. They had been coached for this by Joseph and they said that they were shepherds. As had been arranged they were allotted some good pasture land in the district of Goshen. Then, more as a courtesy than a necessity, Pharaoh spoke with Jacob. He was very gracious with the father of his senior civil servant, and gently asked Jacob's age.

'I am 130,' said Jacob, 'nothing compared to my ancestors.'

The interview ended with Jacob blessing Pharaoh. He then joined his family as they settled into their new homes in a strange land.

Time passed. They prospered, and the family and its wealth grew. Jacob lived another seventeen years before he made preparations for his death by handing things over to his sons. He spoke to Joseph and made him promise that he would not be buried in Egypt, but with his father and grandfather in Canaan. Joseph brought his sons, Manasseh and Ephraim, for their grandfather's blessing. As they knelt before him, Jacob crossed his hands so that his right hand was placed on Ephraim, though Joseph had intended it should rest on the firstborn, Manasseh.

It was as if Jacob was remembering his own deceitful stealing of his brother's blessing long ago. Was he expecting his own son to try to deceive him? Joseph pointed out that the boys were receiving the wrong blessings, but Jacob insisted. He knew what he was doing, and the boys were getting the blessings he thought right for them, and that was the end of the matter. Jacob later called all his sons to him and gave them each a personal blessing.

Jacob died and Joseph called on the expert embalmers of Egypt to care for his father's body so that his wishes about being buried in Canaan could be carried out. Also, because he was the father of Joseph, Jacob was honoured by a period of national mourning of seventy days. When that was over, Joseph asked permission to go to bury his father in accordance with his final wishes. Permission was granted. The whole thing was done with great style and solemnity. Neither time nor expense was spared, and Jacob was buried, as he wanted to be, in the field of Machpelah, with his father Isaac and his grandfather Abraham.

When they had all returned to Egypt it became clear that the brothers were still not quite sure about Joseph and what he might do. They feared that with their father dead, Joseph might take terrible revenge on them. They tried to pre-empt any such thing by going to Joseph and formally apologising for the way they had treated him. For Joseph, it was all in the past and their fear of him reduced him to tears; it was so unnecessary. He told them again that it was part of God's plan, and so they should have no regrets and they must not fear. He, Joseph, would care for them and their families.

So all Jacob's descendants were in Egypt, prosperous and secure. Joseph lived to see his own great-grandchildren and died at the age of 110. Several of his brothers outlived him and before his death he called them to him. He spoke to them solemnly, and they heard this man, who was both their brother and a powerful Egyptian ruler, tell them that Egypt was not their home. In time, God would take them back to Canaan, the land promised to their ancestors, Abraham, Isaac and Jacob. He told them that when they left Egypt they must take his bones with them so that he too could be buried in Canaan. So Joseph died. Few men in history have had Joseph's gifts or his experience of the ups and downs of life, failure and success, misery and fulfilment. In the working out of God's plan for the human race, Joseph was, as he recognised, a link in the chain, a means whereby God would bring blessing to all people.

The Exodus and Wilderness Years

Moses is the dominant figure in the Old Testament. His story is contained in the Books of Exodus, Numbers and Deuteronomy. Most people know about his birth and his being hidden in the rushes by the Nile. They know of the plagues which beset Egypt, of the Burning Bush and the crossing of the Red Sea. But how do these stories carry forward God's plan to bring blessing to all people? We read of a man who could have chosen a comfortable life as a member of the Egyptian ruling class, but who chose instead the uncomfortable role of leader of the downtrodden Hebrews. The stories reveal a man who, in the space of forty years, transformed a rabble of fleeing slaves into a nation with religious and social laws, a nation with the military capability of invading a foreign land, which they believed had been promised to them by God.

As we read the story of Moses we find a man so close to God that they speak to each other 'as friends'. We also begin to appreciate what his love for God and his obedience to God cost Moses. We read the Passion Story of Moses.

The first five books of the Old Testament – Genesis, Exodus, Leviticus, Numbers and Deuteronomy – have traditionally been called the books of Moses. They are also known as the Pentateuch, which simply means 'five tools' (or books). Together they form the first scroll, the Torah Scroll, of the Jewish Scriptures. We can accept that they are the Books of Moses, not in the sense that he actually wrote them, but in the sense that, with the exception of Genesis, he dominates them. Moses does not appear at all in Genesis.

The 'Books of Moses' came into their present form by editors linking together older material which they had collected. Scholars usually identify four main sources used by the editors and which together make up the Pentateuch. One strand of narrative uses the name Yahweh or Jahweh when speaking of God, so this is called the J source. Another strand uses the Hebrew word *Elohim* when it mentions God, so this is called the E source. The book of Deuteronomy stands more or less on its own and is called the D source. Material which is concerned with religious ceremonies and ritual laws is thought to be the work of priestly writers and is known as the P source. Woven together, with some repetition and overlapping, these four sources make up the bulk of the first five books of the Bible.

The main narratives about Moses are in the Books of Exodus and Numbers. The Book of Deuteronomy, as its name suggests, is a second and fuller version of the Law. It contains in the last chapter a moving account of the death of Moses.

Moses' Story

The Birth and Early Life of Moses

Among the giants of the Old Testament, Moses stands supreme. He towers like a great oak over lesser trees.

He should never have lived, of course. He was born into a family of Hebrew slaves at a time when people and policies in Egypt had changed. The Pharaoh who had promoted Joseph was dead. The Hebrews no longer had influence at court and had sunk into slavery. Also Egypt had become worried about its immigration policy. It was regretting having let in too many foreigners. It had been all right at first. The economy benefited, and the Hebrews had been moved from their agricultural work to the service and construction industries. They were virtually slaves. They were a strange people. They wouldn't give up their traditional ways, which were often not at all what civilised Egyptians were used to. And they bred; how they bred! They had taken over some areas almost completely, and people were beginning to say that the immigrants would soon outnumber the native population.

And so steps were taken. Midwives were ordered to kill at birth all male children born to Hebrew women. The midwives, compassionate women and professionally upright, made excuses and said that in most cases the birth was over before they got there. So a further order was given that all newborn Hebrew boys were to be thrown into the Nile and drowned.

We know the story of Moses in the bulrushes; how he was put into the Nile as Pharaoh had commanded, but put in not to drown but to survive in a waterproof basket. We know how he was hidden in the rushes, discovered by Pharaoh's daughter and, through a combination of good luck and good management, not only survived but was brought up as the princess' son, with his own mother as the hired nursemaid. It must have been his mother who saw to it that the young Moses never forgot who he really was. The education and privileges of being brought up in Pharaoh's court were grasped, but he was never allowed to forget who his people were, and that they were being held in cruel slavery.

As he grew up, it may be that the young Moses was not quite sure what he was – Hebrew slave or Egyptians prince, not sure whose side he was on. But it all became clear when he saw an Egyptian strike a Hebrew slave. Moses intervened, and he intervened so strongly that the Egyptian was killed.

Such things cannot be hidden. The truth will always come out, and not long afterwards when he tried to act as peace maker between two quarrelling Hebrews, he was asked, very bitterly, if he was going to kill one of them as he had killed the Egyptian.

Moses had declared himself. By his actions he had placed himself alongside the Hebrew slaves, and in the eyes of his Egyptian patrons and protectors he was a traitor, a murderer, a man without an ounce of gratitude or decency in him. His very life was at risk. And so he ran away, just as his ancestor Jacob had done many years before.

Moses in the Desert

He escaped to the safety of the vast spaces of the wilderness, that desert area where vegetation was sparse and where herdsmen could only find pasture for their flocks by being constantly on the move. It was with one of the most distinguished of these nomadic peoples that Moses found a livelihood. Reuel, or Jethro as he is more commonly known, was the priest of Midian, and within a short time had become not only Moses' employer but his father-in-law as well. It was while he was looking after Jethro's flocks near Mount Horeb, deep in the Sinai Desert, that Moses experienced something that changed his life. He was called by God.

Something caught his eye. A bush was burning. That in itself, in the heat and dryness of the desert, was not unusual. What was unusual was that though the fire raged, instead of the bush disappearing in a crackle and roar of flame, it remained whole. Moses was no coward and he moved in to have a closer look. He was stopped in his tracks by a voice that ordered him to approach no further. He was told to remove his sandals in reverence, because the ground on which he was standing was holy. Then God, for it was God who was speaking, told Moses that he was the God of Abraham, Isaac and Jacob, Moses' ancestors, and that he knew of the plight of the Hebrew people in Egypt and had decided to rescue them. And he would do it by the hand of Moses.

Impressed though he was, Moses was not enthusiastic. He was safe in the desert. He had married and had a young son. He liked his new life, and the prospect of giving it all up and returning to the country where he was a wanted man didn't appeal at all. So he began to argue. 'Who am I,' said Moses, 'that I should go to Pharaoh and that I should be another Jacob and lead our people from one place to another?' Then he thought of a good excuse. 'When I speak to the Hebrews and they say, "Who has sent you?" what am I to say? I can't say I talked to a bush in the desert.'

Moses' excuses were cut short when God revealed his name, a name so holy, so awesome, so sacred, that for centuries Jews have never uttered it. In the Bible every name reveals the character of the person who bears the name, and God's name reveals that God is simply God. In the end it is not enough to say that he is Creator, Almighty, Father, Eternal and so on. He is so far beyond human comprehension that all that can be said of God is that he is God.

'I am who I am. Tell them that "I am" has sent you to them.' That is what God said. Yahweh is probably the nearest we shall get to pronouncing the name correctly, but even that is a guess. Jehovah is quite wrong. We know how to write the name – just four letters in Hebrew – but we are not sure how to pronounce it because there are no vowels in the Hebrew text of the Bible, and because of the prohibition against uttering the sacred name. Moses knew the name of God because God chose to reveal it, and in revealing his name, God revealed his character to Moses.

Despite this overwhelming experience, Moses' mind went back to his wife and child and the dangers, real or imagined, that awaited him in Egypt. And so more excuses. 'They still won't believe me, even if I tell them your name.' But God was not to be thwarted, and he provided Moses with a staff that could become a serpent, and the ability to make his own flesh leprous at will and, equally at will, to restore it to full health. But it was still not enough for Moses. 'It's no good,' he said, 'I've never had any ability at speaking or arguing. I shall never convince the Hebrews to follow me, and I shall never convince Pharaoh to let us go.'

By this time God was getting impatient. 'Who gives man his tongue? I will help you to speak.' Still Moses argued and God said, 'You have a brother, Aaron. He is an accomplished speaker. He will be with you and help you. So now go.'

Moses went back to his father-in-law, Jethro, and told him that it was time he went back to Egypt to see how things were with his enslaved fellow Hebrews. Very graciously, Jethro accepted the situation and said goodbye to Moses, and, surely more painfully, to his own daughter and to his own grandson. So Moses returned to Egypt.

He met his brother Aaron, whom God had forewarned and sent out to meet him. We might want to ask how Aaron survived the slaughter of the male Hebrew children, but the Bible doesn't offer an answer. It tells us that this talented pair of brothers gathered the Hebrews together, and Moses told them what God had said. He backed up his words with demonstrations of the supernatural powers which God had given him. What he suggested to the Hebrews was escape from Egypt and from slavery. And at this point the suggestion was warmly welcomed.

Moses and Pharaoh

The next step was always going to be more difficult; Pharaoh had to be persuaded. Moses had more sense than to say that he proposed to remove from Egypt the whole workforce of Hebrew slaves. Such an act would cause economic and social chaos. So the request was that they should be allowed to leave the country and go to Mount Horeb, a mountain sacred to their God. It was in the desert, and there they were to keep a pilgrim festival.

Pharaoh was not impressed and refused to cooperate. Whose fault that was is hard to decide from the biblical narrative. On the one hand Pharaoh was hard-hearted and inflexible, and on the other it says that God hardened Pharaoh's heart. Whichever it was – perhaps it was both – the result was the same. Moses said, 'Let my people go,' and Pharaoh said, 'Never!' Pharaoh also ordered the overseers and the foremen to make the Hebrew slaves work even harder. Previously, straw to bind the clay used in brick making had been supplied. The new legislation required the Hebrews to provide their own straw without reducing the number of bricks manufactured each day.

Moses wasn't popular. Not only was he getting nowhere with Pharaoh, but his own people were suffering. They were told, 'You are lazy, you are lazy,' and the number of bricks to be made daily was increased, and they groaned under ever increasing burdens. And they complained, usually about Moses, and wished that they had never heard of his hare-brained scheme for freedom and escape.

God seemed to have put Moses into an impossible situation, and Moses complained. After all, he hadn't wanted the job in the first place. 'Why, O Lord, has you brought misfortune on this people, and why did you ever send me?' Precisely the questions the Hebrew slaves themselves were asking.

God solemnly assured Moses that all would be well. 'With mighty acts of judgement I will bring my people, the Israelites, out of Egypt.'

But the problem of persuading Pharaoh still remained. Moses first threatened and then inflicted a series of disasters on the people and land of Egypt – the nine plagues. There was a certain natural logic about them. The river turned to blood; that was the first. Those who like to rationalise biblical miracles talk of unusually heavy rains washing red soil down from the hills into the river and making it dense and, in appearance, blood-like. If that were the case it is not surprising that there was next a plague of frogs, as they left the polluted waters of the Nile in search of purer streams. And so it went on. The frogs died in the heat and they were piled, it says, into countless heaps, and the land stank. Not surprising then that there were gnats, another plague; and flies, another; and cattle suffering from some disease and people being plagued by boils. And each time disaster struck Pharaoh said that the Israelites could go. And as soon as the danger had passed, he changed his mind, he hardened his heart and refused the exit visas.

So then it was hail, and then locusts, and then darkness. And each time Moses pressed, 'Let my people go.' Each time Pharaoh wavered; first 'Yes,' and then, as it says, 'The Lord made Pharaoh obstinate and he refused to let them go.'

Then God said to Moses, 'One last plague I will bring upon Egypt. After that he will let you go.'

The tenth and last plague was the angel of death. Precisely what happened is hard to say. There seems to be one strand of the story which suggests that the term 'the firstborn of Egypt' referred to Pharaoh's eldest son, the heir to the throne. His death would be a terrible blow to the whole land, but especially to Pharaoh himself. He had already suffered a great deal with his people. To add to that a personal grief of the most terrible kind, the death of his child, might well be sufficient to make the distraught man say, 'What does politics or economics or anything else matter now? My son is dead. You can take your people into the desert or any-where else you like.'

That might be the truth behind the story of the death of the firstborn of Egypt, or it may have been the death of a vast number; in the words of the book of Exodus, 'from the firstborn of Pharaoh on his throne to the firstborn of the captive in the dungeon, and the firstborn of cattle.'

The Hebrews – or the people of Israel, as they came to be called – were exempted. God told Moses and Aaron that each family, or perhaps two small families joining together, should take a lamb, kill it and eat it with cakes of unleavened bread. Some of the blood of the lamb was to be smeared on the doorposts and lintels of the houses of the Hebrews. That mark would be a sign to the angel of death, and he would pass over that house. And so the feast of the Passover and Unleavened bread was born, to be for ever a festival when the people of Israel would remember and rejoice that God saved them and brought them out of slavery.

The Exodus

Moses and Aaron had their victory. The Book of Exodus tells us that seventy people had travelled with Jacob to join Joseph in Egypt. Four hundred and thirty years had passed and now, not counting dependants, we are told that 600,000 left Egypt, led by Moses. You can imagine the euphoria, the feelings of triumph among this vast concourse of people. They were free! They had been born into slavery but they had thrown off its bonds. And they didn't leave empty-handed. They had been told to borrow gold or silver or jewels from their Egyptian neighbours. And their neighbours gave. Possibly they were generous, trying to help these people who were making themselves refugees. Or, most likely, the Egyptians were ready to pay a price to get rid of this troublesome race who were in some way responsible for the terrible plagues Egypt had suffered. Whatever the reasons, the Israelites carried wealth away with them and left in high spirits and with triumph in their hearts.

Moses was in charge. He could be sure of two things: first, that he was doing what God had told him to do; and second, that every time anything went wrong, he would be the one who would be blamed.

He was the leader, but where was he to lead them? Their destination was the holy mountain, Horeb or Sinai (it is given both names), where Moses had met God at the Burning Bush. And God would guide them. A pillar of cloud by day and a pillar of fire by night would lead them on. We might wonder whether Mount Sinai was a volcano, its smoke visible during the day, and the flames, disappearing in the bright sunlight, becoming visible against the blackness of the night sky. Perhaps it was a volcano, but volcanoes are hard to find in that area and anyway, in the Old Testament, both fire and cloud are symbols for the presence of God. Whatever we might speculate, it means that God was leading them on, toward himself and toward their Promised Land.

It was no straightforward route; there were obstacles every step of the way. We remember that every time a plague persuaded Pharaoh to let the Hebrews go, just as quickly, when the plague ended, Pharaoh changed his mind. He did the same even after the devastating tenth plague in which he lost his own son. Perhaps, after his immediate collapse in grief, he determined that Moses, the man responsible for his son's death, and all the people with him, would pay for it. The army was mobilised. It wasn't a difficult assignment for the Egyptian guards. They had mounted soldiers and chariots, so they could travel at speed, and they were pursuing a vast number of people, among whom were the elderly and infirm, pregnant women, nursing mothers, children and babes in arms – a very slow-moving company of people. What is more, they had set out in the wrong direction if they were to get clear away from Egypt. Between them and the Sinai peninsula, in which even their great numbers might be hard to find, stood the Red Sea. The Hebrews were trapped and it didn't take the Egyptian army long to close the gap. Soon the advancing troops were clearly visible to the people of Israel, who by this time were weary and footsore.

Jubilation had drained away and terror took its place as they watched the cloud of dust churned up by the ever closer horses and chariots. The Egyptian army was narrowing the gap. Naturally they blamed Moses. 'Were there no graves in Egypt, that you have brought us here to die in the wilderness? Didn't we tell you to leave us alone? We'd rather be slaves and live, than come out here and die.'

We feel sorry for Moses; he was only doing what God had told him to do, and he hadn't wanted to do it in the first place.

But Moses trusted God and he told the Israelites to stand firm and to have faith that God would do what he had promised. Moses stretched out his rod over the sea and the sea parted – driven aside, it says, by a strong east wind. Meanwhile the Egyptian army was delayed because the pillar of cloud, the sign of God's presence, had moved to stand between them and their pursuers. It says the cloud brought darkness and early nightfall, and the Egyptians could not see which way to go.

The Israelites passed over what had been the sea as if on dry land. Late on the scene came the Egyptian army and very unwisely, it seems to us, drove their chariots on to the barely dry soft sand and mud. They were caught; they were trapped. The wind changed, the sea returned and they were drowned. And Chapter 14 of Exodus ends: 'When Israel saw the great power which the Lord had put forth against Egypt, all the people feared the Lord and they put their faith in him and in Moses his servant.' If only that had remained true!

We might want to ask if it really was God's doing and God's will that the Egyptian army should perish in that way, or indeed whether the death of the firstborn has anything at all to do with the God and father of Jesus. But we are reading a story, and the people who wrote it believed that God fought on their side. If we reflect for a moment we realise that people have believed very similar things in two world wars, and in many conflicts since – that God is on *our* side.

Israel in the Wilderness

First it was water, which is not surprising as they were in the desert. Exodus says, 'They came to Marah, but could not drink the water because it was bitter. The people complained to Moses.' Moses was resourceful and, on God's instructions, threw a log into the water and the water became drinkable.

But the people weren't satisfied for long. Soon they were complaining again. 'If only we had died in Egypt where we had meat dishes and plenty of bread, but you have brought us into this wilderness to starve to death.'

There was no jubilation now, no mention of freedom. The Red Sea had been forgotten and Moses was universally unpopular. And again, an object lesson to all believers and particularly to all leaders, Moses poured out his troubles to God. It never entered his head that he could deal with the situation because of his own strength or cleverness or abilities; there's no suggestion that he could solve the problems. Only God could do that.

God again proved to the people that it was his plan and his will that the Israelites should escape from slavery in Egypt to become his people, to enter their Promised Land and bring the whole world to know and worship the one true God. Neither Pharaoh nor drought nor hunger would stand in God's way. And so meat flew in the shape of quails, and bread was given in the form of manna – God's gift, bread from heaven or, as the Psalmist puts it, 'So man did eat angels' food, for he sent them meat enough.'

There were other difficulties, but eventually Moses, guided by the pillar of cloud and fire, led the Israelites to the holy mountain. That was their first objective. Moses was taking them to the holy place where he had encountered God. There they were to meet their God, the God of Abraham, Isaac and Jacob, and there they would make a covenant with him. God, for his part, would make them his people and he would care for them and take them to the Promised Land. On their side, they would observe the laws which God would give them.

It was a very dramatic business. God told Moses that he would speak to him in the hearing of the people, though they would not see him. 'I am coming to you in a thick cloud,' he said.

Precautions had to be taken. God's holiness is not something to be trifled with. It is a searing, terrifying holiness. If a man thinks be can be chummy with God, he is wrong. As the writer of the Letter to the Hebrews put it, 'It is a terrible thing to fall into the hands of the living God.' And because that has always been so, care had to be taken. God told Moses, 'You must put barriers around the mountain and tell the people, "Take care not to go up the mountain or even to touch the edge of it."' The rules were to be strictly enforced. 'Any man who touches the mountain must be put to death. No hand shall touch him; he shall be stoned or shot.' It was as if the holiness of God were contagious, as though holiness were a force too great for an ordinary person to experience and live.

The people had to prepare themselves by bathing and washing their clothes so that they were as pure and prepared as possible when God came among them. They had three days to do it; then, it says, 'On the third day when morning came, there were peals of thunder, and flashes of lightning, dense cloud on the mountain and a loud trumpet blast. The people in the camp were all terrified.'

So the Lord came down upon the top of Mount Sinai and summoned Moses to the mountain top.

With all that going on, Moses had to be a brave man to go up the mountain alone. But he went and there he received the Law that would govern Israel's relationship with God, with each other and with other nations. The core of the Law was, and is, the Ten Commandments.

The first four tell us how we should regard this wonderful and terrifying God who revealed himself through Moses. First, we must accept that there is not and there cannot be any god other than Yahweh. God is One. Second, God is so far above and beyond the comprehension of man, so wholly other, that we must not reduce or belittle God by imagining that he can be depicted or portrayed in wood or stone or metal. No idolatry. Third, God's holy name must not be used as if it were a magic charm. How well the Israelites kept this; so well that God's name is never uttered by a devout Jew to this day. Fourth, God's Sabbath is a day when God comes before everything else, before work or pleasure; that day must be observed. These four rules are there to ensure that God is given his rightful place at the centre of life, not pushed out to the edges, to be used when we are worried or ill or when we need a favour. There is great wisdom in the first four commandments, and we are the poorer if we do not observe them properly.

The fifth commandment demands respect for parents, 'Honour thy father and thy mother.' The sixth requires respect for all life, 'Thou shalt not murder.' The seventh demands respect for the institution of marriage, 'Thou shalt not commit adultery.' The eighth requires respect for the persons and property of others, 'Thou shalt not steal.' The ninth demands respect for the truth, 'Thou shalt not bear false witness.' And the tenth is a command to be satisfied with what is your own, and not to be envious or jealous of what someone else has. It is a command-ment to make advertising agencies weep!

We are a long way from keeping the commandments and, as we shall see, so were the people of Israel. Oh, they deceived themselves, they even tried to deceive Moses, and they thought they were deceiving God when in response to Moses' reading of the Commandments they roared out as one man, 'All that the Lord has said, we will do.'

At the time, no doubt, they meant it and it was a great day for Moses. But his problems and their complaints, and what we might call the passion of Moses, were by no means over.

Toward the Promised Land – The Passion of Moses (1)

We have followed the career of Moses from his birth, on to his exile in the wilderness, his meeting there with God and his return to Egypt to lead a campaign to liberate his people from slavery. We saw his triumph as he led them out, no longer slaves but proud to be free. We saw how quickly people's gratitude turned to criticism when they thought they were trapped between the sea and Pharaoh's army. We saw their gratitude quickly fade when they were hungry or thirsty. They blamed Moses, and time and again in the Book of Exodus, we read that the people complained to Moses. Usually they didn't complain openly and honestly, rather they 'murmured' – that's the word the Bible uses. It conjures up sly, underhand criticism by those who didn't have the courage to speak directly to Moses. It was the voice of the moaner, the sower of seeds of discontent, the person who starts rumours and hides behind whispers and hints and insinuations.

I wonder how many times Moses wanted to give up. 'Why me, Lord?' he must have asked. He was only in a position of leadership because God had insisted, but his reluctance did not in any way lessen the worry and unhappiness that Moses experienced.

Accompanied by an awesome display of thunder, lightning, dense cloud, trumpet calls and a shaking of the earth, God's Law had been given and Moses had read it to the people. And the people had said, 'All that the Lord has spoken we will do, and we will be obedient.'

Fine words, but like a New Year's resolution, soon forgotten. Would any party leader or local candidate ever put themselves forward for election if they had thought deeply about the story of Moses? The burdens of leadership are immense, and no one who has not carried them can really understand what is involved. After an election, the voters get on with their lives. For those elected, the problems begin. So it was for Moses. The Law had been read and the people had said that they would obey. In a sense it was all over for them. The decision had been made and they could get back to the their tents, to their families, to their petty squabbles and jealousies, keeping an eye on the people in the next tent, keeping up with the Cohens.

But for Moses it was the beginning of new responsibilities and new problems. He went back up the mountain to be with God for forty days and forty nights. He carried with him two burdens, his responsibility to God and his responsibility to his people. It was a crucial moment in Moses' life, and he went away to think about the future, to be with God and to pray for God's guidance in the enormous task ahead – the task of leading his truculent and hard-to-satisfy people to their Promised Land.

Worried about the future, with social, political and military decisions to make, Moses decided on his priorities. The Book of Exodus tells us that in those forty days God gave Moses instructions about the making and furnishing of the Tabernacle, the special tent set apart as God's dwelling, a place for the worship of God. It was as if Moses, beset by multiple problems, decided that a right relationship with God was of first importance; get that right and all the rest will fall into place.

So Moses was on the mountain top, agonising about his people. What were they doing? They were getting very impatient and, of course, complaining. They knew that Aaron was a weaker character than his brother, and Exodus says that they went to Aaron and said, 'Come, make gods for us.' And then, very callously, they said, 'As for this Moses, we do not know what has become of him.' Moses was out of sight and therefore out of mind.

Aaron was weak. He told the people to bring all their jewels and trinkets, many of them looted from the Egyptians. With the precious metal Aaron made a golden calf – an image, he said, of God. No one was denying that God existed, or rather that gods existed. No one was denying that Yahweh, the God of Abraham, Isaac and Jacob, had freed the Israelites from slavery in Egypt. They were simply making it easier for everyone to worship God by giving him a shape. That is what the Egyptians did; they had gods in the shapes of birds, animals and humans. It was what all the surrounding nations did. They depicted their gods in some recognisable form. But Moses had realised that the one, true God cannot be depicted, and the second commandment had told them, 'Thou shalt not make for thyself any graven image.' But the people didn't have Moses' insight about God, nor did Aaron though he had the title, 'the priest of the Lord.'

By this time the forty days had passed and Moses came down the mountain carrying in his hands the two tablets of stone on which were engraved the Ten Commandments including, of course, the one which said, 'No graven images.' As he made his way down the mountain side he could hear sounds from the camp below. Was there a battle? Were they sounds of victory or defeat? As he got nearer he realised that the noise was revelry and drunken shouting and singing. And at the centre of all the disgusting behaviour stood the golden calf – their god. By belittling their God they belittled themselves and, as they reduced the divinity of God, so they behaved in less than human ways.

Moses was appalled, and in anger and astonishment he threw down the tablets of stone and smashed them. We can wonder if the Israelites realised that his angry reaction was a symbol of their moral failure. They had broken God's Law, which should have been written on their hearts. Moses merely broke the stone tablets on which the commandments were written.

Most people would have given up in despair, but that wasn't Moses' way. He had a job to do, given to him by God, and he was going to do it, however unpleasant it was for him or for the Israelites. He didn't feel like being pleasant at this point. He had the offensive golden calf ground into dust. The dust was mixed with water, and he forced his rebellious people to drink it. But that wasn't the end of it. He asked Aaron what on earth he had been up to, letting them, encouraging them, to do such a thing. And weak Aaron could only lie in his defence. And it was such a poor excuse. He said the people came, asking him to make an image of God. 'I took their gold,' he said, 'and threw it into the fire and the golden calf came out.' Moses didn't even bother to reply.

He turned his back on his brother and ignored him, but he hadn't finished with the people. He stood where he could be seen and heard by all and said, 'Who is on the Lord's side?'

Most of the men of the tribe of Levi went and stood by Moses. They were told to arm themselves and go about the camp and kill the offenders, even if they were their own brothers, companions or neighbours. Three thousand men died by the sword that day, a terrible price to pay for their own impatience and stupidity, and for Aaron's weakness.

When the people had been punished and reminded of their covenant responsibilities, Moses went back up the mountain for a further forty days and nights. When they were ended he returned, coming down the mountain with two more tablets of stone inscribed with God's Law. This time they were not smashed, and tradition says that they were kept in the Ark of the Covenant, the wooden box symbolising God's presence, which was kept in the Tabernacle while they were in camp, and carried by the Israelites whenever they moved on.

Continuing Opposition – The Passion of Moses (2)

Despite all the problems that beset him, Moses faithfully led the people forward toward their Promised Land, the 'land flowing with milk and honey', which had been promised to them by God. What a vision that must have been for the people as they trudged wearily through the wilderness, often hungry and always thirsty! How that vision must have kept them going – a vision of rivers and fresh streams, well-watered pastures, vines, olives and fig trees. The picture drew them on but it didn't stop them complaining, nor did it stop people challenging Moses.

First it was his own brother and sister. You would have thought that they would have understood. After all they had seen at close quarters the greatness of their brother, the way he put up with unjust criticisms, the way he laboured for the people and sought the best for them. But perhaps we never see the greatness in those closest to us. A greater man even than Moses quoted a well-known proverb when he said, 'A prophet will be held in honour except in his own house and in his own country.' And Moses' own house certainly didn't give him the honour and support he deserved.

Moses had married another wife. It was not unusual and certainly not against the law. His new wife was a foreigner, a Cushite, probably an Ethiopian. The new sister-in-law was clearly not welcomed by Aaron and Miriam, but they didn't say so directly. (How true to life this story is!) They didn't dare tell Moses that they disapproved of his wife so they found another way to attack him. They questioned his authority: 'Has the Lord indeed spoken only through Moses? Has he not spoken through us also?'

The next verse must be one of the most surprising in the Bible. It says, 'Now the man Moses was very meek, more than all men that were on the face of the earth.'

This is the man who faced Pharaoh and steadily wore him

down – and Pharaoh was a mighty ruler. This meek Moses was the acknowledged leader of hundreds of thousands of men, women and children. He had organised their social, religious, political and military life. He raged at their unfaithfulness and made them drink the dust of the idol they had made. Was he meek?

Yes, he was meek, because he did nothing in his own strength. He let himself be the instrument of God. He was not power-mad, on an ego trip of leadership. And so when Miriam and Aaron say, 'Has the Lord indeed spoken only through Moses?' he does not rush to his own defence. He claims nothing for himself. He says and does nothing. A meek man.

But God did something and said something. God vindicated Moses. He said, 'Hear my words. If there is a prophet among you, I, the Lord, make myself known to him in a vision: I speak to him in a dream. Not so with my servant Moses. With him I speak face to face; clearly, and not in dark speech.'

Miriam and Aaron were put in their places by God, and perhaps they came to realise that Moses was in the position he was, not because he sought it, but because God put him there. Certainly Miriam seems to have been so ashamed of her part in all this that she was ill for a week. It looked as if she had leprosy and she was excluded from the camp, in accordance with the Law. Again this incident serves to show the greatness and the compassion of Moses. When he discovered that Miriam was ill he didn't say, 'It serves her right.' He cried to the Lord, 'Hear her, O God, I beseech thee.' Moses seems to have been a better brother to Miriam than she was sister to him.

Then there was a rebellion among the Levites. They, of course, had special tasks and responsibilities in the worship of the people. But they were not as important, it seemed, as Moses, who spoke to God face to face, and Aaron who was the priest of Yahweh. It was another case of jealousy. One of the Levites, a man called Korah, sowed discontent. He had two henchmen, Dathan and Abiram, and together they raised a force of two hundred and fifty men, all quite prominent in the community. They went to Moses and Aaron with the sort of argument that is often heard from people who want power for themselves but are too ashamed or too clever to say so. They didn't want to admit their own ambition. It was power for the people they wanted, justice, human rights for everyone. They said to Moses and Aaron, 'All the people are holy and the Lord is among them. Why then do you exalt yourselves above them?'

Of course, they judged Moses by their own standards. They wanted position and power and they assumed that a similar ambition drove Moses. They failed totally to realise that meek Moses was only doing the will of God.

A competition was arranged – Moses and Aaron on one side, Korah, Dathan and Abiram and their families and supporters on the other. It is not very clear what the competition was; it was something to do with censers and incense. But though the actual competition might be a little obscure, the outcome was crystal clear. As Moses finished his prayer, the ground under Korah, Dathan and Abiram split. It says in the Book of Numbers, 'The earth opened its mouth and swallowed them up with their households and all the men that belonged to Korah and all their goods.' Again God vindicated Moses.

But we wonder how much more of criticism, murmuring, jealousy and rebellion this meek man can take. We remember that he didn't want the job of leading Israel in the first place. We know that on one occasion he had said to God, 'I am not able to carry all this people alone. The burden is too heavy for me.' Everything he did as leader of his people was a matter of duty, a response to the call of God, a labour of love. But we would misunderstand Moses completely if we thought he enjoyed it and revelled in the power and influence it gave him.

His final task was to get his people to the Promised Land, that land which would flow with milk and honey. But, of course, it wasn't an empty land; people lived there, and they wouldn't welcome invaders. The Israelites couldn't just walk in. The land would have to be fought for in some places, infiltrated gradually in others. So Moses sent out spies, men who could slip, unnoticed, into the country and carefully weigh things up. How strong were the cities? How big were the armies? How well were they armed? Was the land as fruitful and prosperous as God had promised?

The spies went off and did their job. They came back and

reported, 'The land flows with milk and honey. Yet the people who dwell in the land are strong, and the cities are fortified and very large.' The report soon became common knowledge and by now we know what reaction to expect. The people murmured against Moses and Aaron. They went back to the old complaints and said, 'Would that we had died in the land of Egypt, or that we had died in the wilderness. Why has the Lord brought us to this place to die by the sword?'

This lack of trust, which was not just lack of trust in Moses, but lack of trust in God, so angered God that he swore than none of the people who left Egypt would enter the Promised Land, only their children and grandchildren. There was one exception, the man Caleb – but that is another story. Moses was a true leader. He shared the fortunes and fate of his people. It seems most dreadfully unfair, but Moses himself was not to enter the Promised Land. Like every good leader he had groomed a successor to take over his job, and it would be Joshua who would have the honour of leading God's people into their Promised Land.

Despite his heroism, despite his total trust in God, despite his patience, his loyalty, his courage, his meekness, Moses would not enter the Promised Land. God had passed that sentence on him when, momentarily, he lost faith in God's ability to provide water in the desert. When the end was near it was as if God had relented and would dearly have loved to take Moses into the Promised Land. But it was not to be. Moses was old and tired. He'd had enough and it didn't bother him that he would not tread the soil of the land flowing with milk and honey.

On the borders of the Promised Land was Mount Nebo and, as so often in the past, Moses climbed the mountain and was with God. And it says, at the end of the Book of Deuteronomy, 'The Lord showed him the whole land, and the Lord said, "I have let you see it with your eyes but you shall not cross over there." Then Moses, the servant of the Lord, died there. Moses was one hundred and twenty years old when he died; his sight was unimpaired and his vigour had not abated.'

The Book of Joshua

After a long apprenticeship under Moses, Joshua had the task of planning and leading the invasion of Canaan. Sadly, all that is remembered of his career by most people is the collapse of the walls of Jericho. But there was much more to Joshua than that. He was a man of the highest integrity and courage, prepared to do his duty under all circumstances. Neither unpleasantness nor unpopularity was allowed to deflect him from the course of duty. He was of that rare breed of admirable men, the godly soldier.

His story is found in the Old Testament book that bears his name, though there are important details in the Books of Numbers and Deuteronomy. The Book of Joshua gives one view of the entry into the Promised Land. It sees it as a rather one-sided conquest in which, despite one or two setbacks, the Israelites, with God on their side, drove out all before them and occupied their promised territory. This view has to be tempered by the situation which lies behind the narratives in the Book of Judges, where we read of a more gradual and piecemeal settlement.

Joshua's Story

The New Leader

Moses was a hard act to follow – impossible, you might say. But the times had changed. The days of leading out, out of Egypt, were over. Now it was the time for leading in, into the Promised Land. And with the new times came the new man, Joshua, the son of Nun.

His task would not be easy. The land of promise was not empty, and the people of the land would not take kindly to a large influx of immigrants, who had strange customs and an even stranger God. These 'people of the land', the Amorites, Perizzites, Jebusites, Hittites, Philistines, and the rest of those names we hear in the Old Testament, didn't want foreign refugees on their ancestral lands, and they were ready to keep them out by force of arms. Years earlier, when Moses had sent spies into the land, they had come back and reported that the cities were strong and well fortified, and that their men were well armed.

But as they say, 'Cometh the hour, cometh the man.' This was the hour of war, the hour for fearless leadership and for brilliant military strategy. Perhaps it happens in the history of all nations, a time when they need a Napoleon, a Churchill, a Joshua.

Joshua, the son of Nun, had been Moses' right-hand man. He knew what a thankless task it was to be the leader of the Israelites. And as Moses handed over the reigns of leadership he stressed the qualities that Joshua would need. He said to Joshua, 'Be strong and resolute, for it is you who are to lead this people into the land. The Lord himself goes at your head; he will be with you; he will not fail you or forsake you. Do not be discouraged or afraid.' There was more than a hint in Moses' words that the job was no sinecure.

Then Joshua was commissioned by God. The Book of Deuteronomy says, 'The Lord gave Joshua the son of Nun his commission in these words, "Be strong, be resolute, for you shall bring the Israelites into the land ... And I will be with you.'"

In each of these statements there is warning and encouragement. The repetition of 'be strong, be resolute' must have been a warning to Joshua that problems lay ahead, that leadership brings heavy burdens, and that he would need strength and determination to face not just the enemies of his people – the Amorites, Perizzites and the rest – he would need courage to face the critics and the backbiters and the moaners among his own people. 'Be strong, be resolute...' Joshua knew there were problems ahead.

But there was encouragement too. He didn't have to carry the burdens alone. God said, 'I will be with you,' and Moses, speaking from his own vast experience of the problems of leadership, said of God, 'He will not fail you or forsake you.' If only Joshua could keep that in mind when the going got tough, he would be reassured and know that though his responsibilities were enormous, it didn't all depend on him.

Like every other character in history, especially those who have to make decisions in times of national crisis, when the very survival of the nation is at stake, Joshua must be judged in context. Some of the things he did, some of the things he allowed, may seem to us excessive, even immoral. But we certainly do not need to defend or justify Joshua. We need only to understand him and his place in the story of God's dealing with his people, Israel.

We can begin with the story of the character who has since appeared in a thousand books and almost as many films – the prostitute with the heart of gold, or at least with a firm grasp on reality. In this case her name was Rahab.

Joshua knew his job. He had to invade and conquer a settled and well-defended country. There were walled cities to be besieged and overthrown, and the first of those, and perhaps the greatest, was Jericho, gateway to the Promised Land. Joshua knew how vital up-to-date, accurate information was, so he sent spies into Jericho. It was an ancient, busy, bustling city, and two strangers would not readily be noticed until they started asking questions. It was a stroke of genius to go to a house which all sorts of men regularly entered and left – the house of Rahab the prostitute. We don't know whether the spies used their own initiative or whether they were acting on Joshua's orders, but whichever it was, it was an inspired move. For whatever reasons, Rahab was convinced that the army of Israel would overcome Jericho with terrible consequences for the people of the city. So she hid the spies when a search was made for them, and bargained to ensure her own safety and the safety of her relations when Jericho was defeated.

The bargain was struck and in order that all the Israelite soldiers would know which was the house where the occupants had to be left unmolested, she was told to put a red cord in her window. It was the beginning of a long tradition.

That was by way of preparation and information gathering. But before Jericho could be besieged and destroyed, the River Jordan had to be crossed. The Israelites numbered hundreds of thousands, and not all were able-bodied. There were the old and the sick; there were pregnant women, nursing mothers and children; there were priests and Levites as well as soldiers. The Jordan is a great river, and in Joshua's day, crossing it was a major undertaking.

See how history repeats itself. The problem which had confronted Moses at the Red Sea now faced Joshua at the Jordan. And again the solution was not in Joshua's hands, but in God's. God had said, 'I will not fail you or forsake you,' and now God told Joshua what he must do.

Orders were given for the sacred Ark of the Covenant to be carried by the priests until they were standing in the water. The Book of Joshua says, 'When the priests reached the Jordan and dipped their feet into the water, the water coming down from upstream was brought to a standstill.' The priests stood there, bearing the Ark, and all the people passed over on dry ground. It was like the crossing of the Red Sea all over again, but it was for a different generation of Israelites under their new commander. Joshua's reputation grew. 'That day,' it says, 'the Lord made Joshua stand very high in the eyes of all Israel, and the people revered him, as they had revered Moses all his life.'

Jericho was Joshua's obsession. It filled his mind. That great city, the oldest inhabited city in the world it is said, protected by great walls and a strong army, was the gateway to the Promised

Land. Unless Jericho were conquered there could be no further advance into the land. It must have looked an impossible task and perhaps, in his heart of hearts, Joshua was not sure that he could do it. We are told a strange story in Chapter 5 of the Book of Joshua. It tells how Joshua went out alone, away from the Israelite camp, and came nearer to that great city that was his objective and his obsession. Perhaps he looked at its great walls and towers and wondered if it could ever be taken. Then, the story says, as he looked he saw a man standing in front of him with a drawn sword in his hand. Joshua asked him who he was and in whose cause the sword was drawn. He received the startling answer, 'I am here as captain of the army of the Lord.' It was startling because that was precisely what Joshua thought *he* was: captain of the army of the Lord.

It was a sign to Joshua that it was not he who would lead Israel against Jericho, but God. And this strange encounter is the equivalent of Moses' experience at the Burning Bush. The man, or the angel, or the Lord himself, whoever it was, used the very words that God spoke to Moses: 'Take off your sandals; the place where you are standing is holy.'

Reassured, Joshua began the campaign against Jericho. And this is the part of the story that everybody knows: 'Joshua fought the battle of Jericho, and the walls came tumbling down.'

It was a war of nerves. The people of Jericho knew of the reputation of the Israelites, how they had already fought and defeated several strong tribes. And no doubt there were fear-fed rumours that made these fanatical invaders seem even more frightening. Joshua played on this. There were no sudden attacks; no premature advances. Those defending the city were on the lookout for surprise tactics, but nothing happened.

Day after day, for six days, it looked as if something might happen. The army of Israel formed up, rank on rank, and silently marched behind the priests who carried the Ark of the Covenant. The priests carried their ritual trumpets, the rams' horns. But the priests did not blow the horns, nor did the soldiers attack. In eerie silence they circled the city, just out of bowshot, and fear and uncertainty grew within the walls of Jericho.

On the seventh day, just as the people of Jericho were getting used to the daily, silent routine, things changed. Instead of returning to the camp after the circuit of the city, this day they went round a second time. Then a third, and in all seven times. You can imagine the tension and the terror in the hearts of the people of Jericho. Suddenly as the seventh circuit was completed there was a tremendous blast of trumpets and a colossal shout raised by every man in the Israelite army.

The war of nerves was over. The people of Jericho were helpless. Their nerve and their resistance had been eroded and broken... 'And the walls came tumbling down.' Whether it was by human strength or the power of God doesn't really matter. The fact is that the city lay open to Joshua and the people of Israel.

And then we read things that disappoint us and make us say, 'Surely, God didn't want that.' The Book of Joshua says, 'The city shall be under solemn ban; everything in it belongs to the Lord. No one is to be spared, except the prostitute Rahab. So they destroyed everything in the city; they put everyone to the sword, men and women, young and old, also cattle, sheep and asses.'

We read that and we say, 'Was it really necessary? Did God really want it and order it?'

After Jericho

Jericho fell and its people, its men, women and children were killed, and all its animals, in accordance with God's command. We cannot condemn Joshua, nor should we even criticise him. Who are we, successors of the generation of Belsen and Auschwitz, of Stalags and Gulags, of Coventry and Dresden, of Hiroshima and Nagasaki, to condemn mass killing? At least in Joshua's eyes the people of Jericho were an offering, a sacrifice to God, not simply the victims of total war. So let's suspend our criticism and follow Joshua's story a little further.

After Jericho the next objective was Ai. Compared with Jericho it was going to be easy; a small town with modest fortifications. Joshua's practised military eye summed it up and he decided that it was not necessary to deploy the whole army. He sent a force of three thousand men. And then came the humiliation. The Book of Joshua says, 'They fled before the men of Ai and the men of Ai killed about thirty-six of them and chased them before the gate as far as Shechem.'

What had gone wrong? Joshua took the problem to God in prayer, and God's answer came in a form that a disciplined, life-long soldier like Joshua would certainly understand. God said, 'Stand up on your feet, man. Stop grovelling.' It's there, Chapter 7, verse 10. And it was revealed that the defeat at Ai was the result of God's orders regarding Jericho not being properly observed. Someone, instead of sacrificing everything to God, had stolen some of the booty. Someone had looted Jericho, stolen things that had been declared holy and given to God.

The process of justice began. The guilt was narrowed down to one of the tribes, then to one of the clans of that tribe, then to one of the families in that clan, then to the guilty person in that family. It was Achan. To be fair to Achan, he didn't deny the charge, he didn't try to excuse himself, he didn't try to wriggle out of it in any way. He said, 'I confess. I have sinned against the Lord, the God of Israel. This is what I did. Among the booty I caught sight of a fine mantle from Shinar, two hundred shekels of silver, and a bar of gold weighing fifty shekels. I coveted them and I took them. You will find them hidden in the ground in my tent.'

It was a brave confession, complete and frank. Achan didn't expect to get away with it. He knew the seriousness of his crime and he knew the consequences, not just for himself but for others. He had stolen things which were holy, devoted to God. And the belief was that holiness was contagious. If you touched a holy thing you became holy, and anything you touched also became holy and therefore dedicated to God. Achan was stoned to death so that no one had to touch him, and so were his sons and daughters, his oxen, his asses and his sheep, his tent and every-thing he had touched. The sin, the stain, had to be purged from Israel. It is a sad and frightening story.

Cleansed once more, and reconciled to God, Israel, under Joshua, again became invincible and feared. The Gibeonites, one of the tribes whose ancestral lands were part of what Israel was claiming as its Promised Land, decided that if they were to avoid the fate of the people of Jericho and Ai, they would have to resort to trickery.

A number of them deliberately dressed in old garments,

tattered and travel-stained. They carried stale bread and little water and limped into the camp of Israel. There they made themselves out to be travellers from far away and suggested that they and the Israelites, who were themselves travellers, should make a treaty never to attack or molest each other. They were such good actors, such good liars, that they totally deceived Joshua and the Israelites, and the treaty was made.

It wasn't very long after this that Israel's advance into the Promised Land brought them to the territory of the Gibeonites. Israel prepared to attack, but the Gibeonites said, 'Oh, no. You have promised never to attack us. We made a treaty only a few weeks ago.' It might have been expected that Joshua would be furious at the trickery, and perhaps he was. But he was a man of honour, and he stood by the promise he had made. He didn't attack and wipe out the Gibeonites, but made them slaves and servants, condemned to perform menial tasks for the Israelites, their masters. In the words of the Bible, they were to be 'hewers of wood and drawers of water for ever'.

There is nothing like common adversity to draw people together; the friendliness of Londoners in the Underground air raid shelters is legendary. People who in peacetime had little time for each other, who would walk past each other without a word, were drawn together by a common predicament and a common fear. That happened to the small tribes of Canaan. The kings of Jerusalem, Hebron, Jarmuth, Lachish and Eglon were drawn into an alliance in an attempt to be strong enough to defeat Joshua. The armies were drawn up for battle, and God assured Joshua that he would gain the victory. The five kings were defeated. It seemed as if nature itself fought on Israel's side. As the armies of the five kings fled in disarray, a storm burst and the Bible says, 'More died from the hailstones than the Israelites slew by the sword.'

That same day, as the sun went down and it looked as though the Israelite army was being denied total victory by the onset of darkness, Joshua prayed, 'Stand still, O sun, in Gibeon; stand, moon, in the valley of Aijalon.' And so it was, or so it appeared, that the sun and the moon stood still and time was granted to Israel to complete the rout of the five kings. The kings themselves were captured and executed.

The Book of Joshua continues its tale of bloodshed and violence. It is full of the names of the clans, the kings and the heroes defeated and sometimes exterminated by Joshua and his army. In Israel's terms it is a story of wonderful success, as they advanced steadily, surely to take possession of their Promised Land. Chapter after chapter records in detail Joshua's brilliant conquest of Canaan.

He was by now an old man. He had done his duty. A born soldier, he had served in the army of the Lord, doing his duty whether it were pleasant or unpleasant, whether he personally agreed with it or not. Now his day had passed, and it was time for other men – in the main lesser men – to help Israel settle and survive in the territories Joshua had won for them.

He called the people to him and gave them his final orders. They were not orders about weapons, battles and treaties, they were orders about worshipping God. He said, 'Hold the Lord in awe; and worship him in loyalty and truth.' And the people said, 'The Lord our God we will worship and his voice we will obey.'

They didn't, of course, but at the time they meant it. And Joshua, simple, brilliant soldier that he was, took them at their word. He had always kept his word and done his duty and he imagined others would do the same. He was too generous in his judgement, but at least it allowed him to die a happy man. And the Book says, 'Joshua, the son of Nun, the servant of the Lord died; he was one hundred and ten years old.' He was faithful to the end; a loyal, honest, incorruptible man, the soldier and servant of the Lord.

The Book of Judges

The Book of Joshua gives a picture of rapid advance into the Promised Land with opposition swiftly swept away. The Book of Judges depicts a much more gradual occupation with failures almost as frequent as successes.

We see the different clans and tribes of Israel as they settle into different parts of Canaan. Naturally they meet with opposition from the people of the land who object to foreigners invading and stealing their ancestral lands. Nothing changes. In recent history, the founding of the state of Israel, though legal and probably absolutely necessary, was not welcomed by the Palestinians, today's people of the land, and the conflict goes on with no likely end in sight.

The writer or editor of the Book of Judges describes the process of settlement and interprets what happens by religious standards. He sees God's hand and God's judgement in everything that happens. A pattern is repeated, an ever-turning cycle of events. The Israelites settle in, cease to be nomads and begin to farm. Sensibly, they copy the farming methods of the people of the land, but are tempted too to copy some of their religious practices and to worship their nature and fertility gods. So they neglect Yahweh, the God of Israel. God punishes them by letting the people of the land get the upper hand and oppress the Israelites. When they repent God raises up a leader, a Judge, and he, or she in the case of Deborah, fights against the people of the land and defeats them. And again Israel prospers until they fall away again and the pattern is repeated.

Different Judges are raised up in different areas of Canaan. Samson fights against the Philistines, Deborah against the Hazorites, Jephthah against the Ammonites, left-handed Ehud struggles with the Moabites, and Gideon fights the Midianites.

It is Gideon's story that we shall look at to get the flavour of the Book of Judges and a picture of the difficult and troubled process of settlement in the Promised Land.

Gideon's Story

God Chooses a Judge

Gideon was one of the Judges. We would probably not use the word 'judge' to describe him and his work. It is more likely we would call him a leader or a hero. We meet him in rather strange circumstances. The story says, 'Gideon was beating out wheat in the wine press.' That sounds rather strange: wheat in the wine press! It's rather like having your car serviced at the hairdressers, which would certainly confuse people. And that was exactly what Gideon wanted to do – to confuse and mislead – and in particular, to confuse and mislead the Midianites.

The Midianites were a nomadic people just as the Israelites once had been. By this time Israel was becoming settled, a nation of farmers on land which they had invaded, conquered and stolen from the people of the land. But now the tables were turned. The Israelites were the settled landowners and the Midianites were the raiders, coming and going as they chose, harrying, destroying property and frightening the Israelite farmers, who only wanted to be left to get on with their lives in peace.

Things don't change much in that land we still choose to call 'holy'. Still there is conflict. What we hear, what we are told of today's conflict, of Israeli settlers driving Arabs from their ancestral soil, of Palestinian suicide bombers and of casualties on both sides, is supposed to be unbiased reporting. The Book of Judges makes no such claim. It is written from the point of view of Israel, and any heroes are going to be Israelite heroes. And Gideon was one of them, a hero, a Judge.

The story tells how the Israelites had become too settled, too comfortable in their farming lives. They had forgotten that it was God who had given them the land and continued to give sun and rain to grow their crops. They had started to behave like the people they had conquered, following their customs, worshipping their gods. When that happened, God punished them. He let their enemies regain strength and attack and harass the Israelites. Then, if they repented, he would raise up a Judge to lead them and to win back their freedom. This pattern of sin, punishment, repentance, a leader and victory was repeated again and again. So we read that after forty years of peace, 'The people of Israel did what was evil in the sight of the Lord, and the Lord gave them into the hand of Midian seven years.'

The Midianite raiders, mounted on swift camels, drove the Israelites from their homes. They were forced to live in caves and shelters in the hills. They had tried to be good farmers and had worked the land well. But the Midianite raiders trampled the sown fields, they destroyed the crops and stole anything that was left. And that was why Gideon was threshing wheat in the wine press. It was not the time for grape harvest and so the Midianites would not bother to check the wine press sheds. There Gideon could hide both himself and the precious grain he had saved.

The Midianites didn't find Gideon in the wine press, but, the story says, the angel of the Lord did. 'The Lord is with you, you mighty man of valour,' said the angel.

Gideon, with the down-to-earth good sense of a countryman, was not impressed by the angel's courtly and extravagant greeting. He brought the angel down to earth by asking why, if the Lord was with him, was he hiding here in the wine press for fear of the Midianites? If the Lord was on Israel's side, why didn't he do something for us? It was a fair question.

There is always a danger that if we ask God to do something he will say, 'Yes, I will do it; and you are the person I will use to do it.' We ought to remember that when we ask God to feed the hungry and shelter the homeless and care for the sick. He is quite likely to say, 'I'm glad you asked; I'll come with you and help you.' That is how it was with Gideon. God said that he would save Israel and that Gideon was the man through whom he would do it.

Gideon was quickly on the defensive. 'How can I do it? My family is obscure and I'm the youngest in the family. No one will take any notice. I think you've got the wrong man.' But God said, 'I will be with you, and you will smite the Midianites.'

The first thing Gideon had to do was to issue a rallying call to unite the Israelites and fill them with enthusiasm and devotion for Yahweh, their God. He had to bring them back to faith in Yahweh alone. Their sacrifices and devotion to the local gods, the *baals*, had to stop. Many had let themselves slip in this regard, thinking they were in some way making themselves better farmers. Even Gideon's father had deserted the true faith and built an altar to the local gods and goddesses on his land.

Gideon knew that he had to act, but he still wasn't confident. He was afraid. He gathered together some friends he could trust and at night, under cover of darkness, they destroyed the altar of Baal and the wooden pole that was the symbol of the local goddess.

In the morning the vandalism was discovered and the culprit was soon known. Someone had seen them, or one of the group had talked. It's always like that. This was a crossroads for Gideon. He could say, 'Sorry, we'd had too much to drink. It doesn't mean anything,' and he could have let the Israelites continue to worship the false gods and suffer as a consequence. Or he could say, 'Yes, I did it, and now come and join me and make a stand for Yahweh, the one true God.' He pressed them further. He said, 'What good has Baal done for you? You worship him and you are driven off the land. You live in caves and shacks. That's what Baal has done for you. Disown Baal. Fight for Yahweh.' And because Gideon was convinced, and because he was brave, he carried the day, and the despondent Israelites found that they had a leader, a Judge.

Such things can never happen in secret, and the Midianites soon knew that the situation had changed. No longer were there easy pickings. No longer were they able to raid and destroy without fear of opposition. No longer was it a light duty, a soft option for Midianite soldiers to be sent on a raid against Israel. Now there was real opposition, and the Midianites decided they would have to deal with it once and for all.

We are told, 'All the Midianites and the Amalekites and the people of the East came together, and crossing the Jordan they encamped in the valley of Jezreel.'

Gideon, now under the inspiration of God, responded. He

sounded the trumpet, and Israelites from many clans and families rallied to his call. There were Abiezrites, men of Manasseh, of Asher, of Zebulun, of Naphtali – a great army. Gideon was on the crest of a wave of popularity and power. His people trusted him; they believed that God was with him and that he would lead them to victory and freedom.

That was what it looked like on the outside. Inside Gideon was full of fear and self-doubt. Perhaps it's like that for all leaders. Perhaps only fools have complete confidence in themselves. Gideon needed reassurance. Secretly he asked God for a sign, for proof that he was with him. He said he would place a bundle of sheep's wool on the ground overnight. If, in the morning, the wool was wet with dew but the ground all around it dry, then he would believe that God was on his side. Dawn came, and sure enough, the wool was wet and the ground was dry. But still Gideon wasn't satisfied; his doubts were still greater than his faith. So he asked again. 'This time,' he said to God, 'let the wool be dry and the ground all around it wet.' The next day dawned and the wool was dry while all around it the ground was soaked with dew.

So Gideon was convinced that God was with him and he took his Israelite army to face the might of Midian and its allies.

Gideon's Victory

Gideon's army was large – 32,000 strong. One might have thought, the more the merrier, or at least, the more the safer. There's strength in numbers, and a great army under a good leader seemed the best hope for an Israelite victory over Midian. We can assume that is what Gideon and his men thought. But it was not what God thought. No sooner had Gideon organised his vast army than God spoke to him. 'The people with you are too many,' he said.

It would probably have made more sense to Gideon if God had said they were too few. But no, it was too many. God wanted the people of Israel to know that it was by his will and his power alone that they were to triumph and to continue to live in the Promised Land. There must be no opportunity for them to think that victory was due to their own skill or courage, or to the sheer weight of numbers. So Gideon was told to announce that if anyone was in any way afraid of the battle and would prefer to go home, he should do so. Twenty thousand men were honest enough, and indeed brave enough, to admit that they were afraid and would prefer to be at home with their wife and family. And so they left and the army now numbered 10,000 men; a much reduced and fearless elite.

God spoke to Gideon again; 'There are still too many.'

This time there was a more elaborate weeding-out process. Gideon was told to take his 10,000 men down to a stream for a drink. He was to watch how they drank. The vast majority knelt down, scooped up water in their hands and brought it to their mouth. Perhaps they were the cautious ones. They never relaxed completely; they stayed mainly upright, alert and ready to move into action. The others, a mere 300, threw themselves flat on the ground at the river's edge, thrust their faces into the water and lapped like dogs. They would have been helpless if attacked.

'Now,' said God, 'it's that 300 that I want as the army of Israel.'

Gideon must have been appalled, or thought it was a joke, but he said nothing and did as he was told. By now Gideon had realised that it was not the size of the army, nor the courage of his soldiers, nor his own inspired leadership that would win the battle. It would be God himself; he would bring victory.

So Gideon and his 300 men waited for the battle. Night is the time when worries grow like mushrooms in the dark. Problems which disappear with the coming of day, at night seem insoluble. We all know that, and so we understand Gideon's not sleeping and worrying about what might happen; imagining the worst, as we all do at night. God decides that as Gideon is not sleeping he might as well do something useful. He suggests that Gideon take a companion with him and creep stealthily into the Midianite camp.

Perhaps Gideon had tracked wild animals from the time he was a boy. Whether he had or not, he was able to creep, unseen and unheard, into the camp of Midian. First impressions were not reassuring. He could see the camp fires around which the

Midianites were sitting, talking, dozing, waiting for the battle. So many fires, so many soldiers. The Book of Judges says, 'They lay along the valley like locusts for multitude.'

He crept nearer to one of the groups, and heard one soldier telling another that as he was dozing he had a terrifying dream. He had dreamt that a great loaf of bread had rolled into the Midianite camp, crashed into a tent and upended it. In those days it was believed that dreams were one of the ways God communicated with men. We might remember the story of Joseph. Joseph himself had dreams; there were Pharaoh's dreams and the dreams of Pharaoh's butler and baker. So perhaps this soldier's dream contained a message from God. The dream was full of symbols and meanings. A loaf of bread could be a symbol for a settled farming community, one that grew grain and made bread – like Israel. A tent, on the other hand, was the home of a nomad, which is what the Midianites were. And the loaf knocked down the tent. There could only be one meaning: Israel would defeat Midian.

Gideon had heard enough. He slipped silently away and returned to his men, a battle plan already formed in his mind. He divided his men into three companies, one hundred in each. They would strike before dawn. They were armed, of course, with swords and shields, spears, bows and arrows. But these conventional weapons were to be of minor importance in Gideon's strategy. Some probably had to be discarded. The rest would be tucked into belts or slung on backs, because they needed their hands free.

Each man was given a trumpet. Not a brass trumpet, but the Jewish ritual trumpet, the shofar, the ram's horn, which makes such an eerie sound and which had played so important a part in the battle for Jericho. Each man was also given a torch, which was placed in an empty jar to hide its light. 'Watch me,' said Gideon, 'and do as I do.'

Armed in this unusual fashion the three bands of men advanced silently to surround the Midianite camp. It was night still, very dark and very quiet.

At Gideon's silent command the trumpets screeched, the jars were smashed with a great noise, the torches blazed, the men shouted and the sleeping, unprepared Midianites found themselves surrounded by noise and fire. There was panic. The Midianites weren't reluctant to fight, but where was the enemy? They were half blinded by those torches and each man grabbed his sword or spear and prepared to kill anyone who came near him. Some just ran about aimlessly, hacking indiscriminately to left and right. The men of Israel, Gideon's 300, needed only to stand by and shout and wave their torches and watch the chaos as Midian defeated Midian.

For the writer of the Book of Judges, it was all God's doing. 'The Lord set every man's sword against his fellow and against all the army; and the army fled.'

Israel had triumphed. Gideon the hero, the Judge, had been used by God to protect and preserve his people. Then, the book says, 'The land had rest for forty years in the days of Gideon.'

The Book of Ruth

The little Book of Ruth is a literary gem. It is a beautiful, self-contained short story. It can be read simply as a story of tragedy and happiness, of death and the hope of life. It can be linked with other biblical stories of women whose role in the fulfilment of God's plan of blessing for mankind was at risk because of the inability to have children. We saw it in the stories of Sarah, Rebekah and Rachel; and we shall see again in the story of Hannah. In this story it is widowhood that threatens the carrying out of God's plan.

In the Bible, the Book of Ruth stands between the Book of Judges and the Books of Samuel, which will tell the story of the founding of the monarchy in Israel. The Book of Judges ends with the words, 'In those days Israel had no king; everyone did as he saw fit.' (Judges 21:25) Immediately following those words the Book of Ruth looks forward to the end of such anarchy and the founding of the monarchy, and, in particular, the reign of David.

It is possible that the book was written to praise and promote the house of David, perhaps at a time when there was strong opposition such as that lead by the prophet Ahijah, who told Jeroboam that God had chosen him to be king in place of Rehoboam, David's grandson.

The fact that Ruth was a foreigner, a Moabitess, suggests further motives for the story. As we shall see later, when the people of Judah returned from exile in Babylon in the sixth century BCE, leaders like Ezra and Nehemiah struggled to re-establish the nation. They had to rebuild both the city and the community. One of the rules they insisted on, and enforced with great vigour, was the prohibition of foreign marriages. It was their attempt to create religious purity and social solidarity. Not everyone shared their view. It could be that the Book of Ruth was written to counter Ezra and Nehemiah's point of view by showing how God had chosen the foreigner, Ruth, just as surely as he had chosen Abraham, to carry forward his purpose of bringing blessing to all people.

The book is a delight to read. It tells a wonderful story and, as you will see, Ruth is not its only, nor indeed its main, heroine.

Ruth's Story

This story begins in Bethlehem – like another very famous story. But this isn't about a baby and its mother but, rather surprisingly, about a mother-in-law. This story turns on their head all those popular stories and jokes about mothers-in-law. In this story the mother-in-law is the heroine. She is not jealous or nasty or funny. She is loving, faithful and has a great deal of common sense. Her name is Naomi, and it means 'pleasant'. Her story is placed in the Bible between the Book of Judges, with its tales of heroes like Gideon and Samson, and the First Book of Samuel, which tells the story of Samuel, a great leader who gave Israel its first king, Saul, and more important, its second and greatest king, David.

So between Judges and Samuel, pointing forward to David, stands this little book about Naomi – and it doesn't even bear her name. It bears the name of her daughter-in-law, Ruth.

The story starts in Bethlehem and times are hard. Naomi, the heroine, is married to a good man named Elimelech, and they have two sons, Mahlon and Chilion. Both young men are grown-up, but are unmarried and still living in the family home. Times are hard because there is a famine. A decision is made – a difficult decision, taken no doubt after much heart-searching and debate – and they decide to leave their home in famine-stricken Judah and try their luck in a foreign country – in Moab, a land on the other side of the Dead Sea; a land and a people who, on and off for many years, had been the enemies of the people of Israel.

They go to this foreign land to settle and find work and above all simply to eat and survive. It seemed a good move – at first. But then tragedy struck. Elimelech, the husband and father, died. We don't know what he died of; whether he was weakened by the famine, or crushed by the worry of the move and the responsibility he felt for his wife and his sons. We don't know what it was. But whatever the cause, the result was that Naomi became a widow.

But life went on. Despite their father's death, Naomi's sons, Mahlon and Chilion, clearly approved of the family's move to Moab, because before long they had both found Moabite girls and married them. One girl was called Orpah; she was Mahlon's wife. The younger son, Chilion, married Ruth.

There must have been much happiness in this family. They all lived together, and clearly Naomi was a mother-in-law in a million. She was loved not only by her sons but also by her daughters-in-law. Their life together in their new country began to settle down and prosper, and things looked good.

But no one can predict what might happen in life, and tragedy struck a second time for Naomi. This time her two sons died. Again we don't know why or how. Widowed ten years before, Naomi now went through that most terrible of trials that can face a parent, the death of her children. Yes, Mahlon and Chilion were grown men and married. But it doesn't matter how old they are. For the parent whose child dies before them, nothing can seem more unfair, nothing more unnatural. Almost every parent, I think, would gladly give their own life to save the life of their child.

But parents aren't usually given that option. They must go through the pain of loss and the feelings of guilt that they live while their child has died. Naomi must have felt all that; no husband, and now no sons.

But Naomi was not alone in the world. She had her two daughters-in-law, Orpah and Ruth. They too had been through the anguish of losing their husbands – both young men. And so there are three widows, one in vigorous middle age and the other two young, attractive women. All three are sensible and strong, and despite the fact that Naomi is a Judaean, and Orpah and Ruth are Moabites, they are friends, real friends, and they support each other through the dark days of their bereavement.

But bereavements cannot be dwelt on forever. Life must go on, and no one knew that better than Naomi. She became strictly practical and advised the young women to go back to their mothers' families, while she would return to her roots and relations in Judah. 'You are both young,' she said, 'Go back. Some young man will realise how lucky he might be, and you will marry again, and perhaps be blessed with a family.'

So generous in spirit was Naomi, she thought only of what was best for her daughters-in-law. No wonder they loved her. No wonder they both said, 'No, we will stay with you and go back to Judah with you.'

But she could see that that was not best for them. So she used humour – self-mockery – to persuade them. 'You want to stay with me?' she said. 'Do you think I might marry again? I'm not all that old. Do you think I might have two more sons? And will you wait for them to grow up so that you can marry them and be my daughters-in-law for a second time? Come on, be sensible. Go back home and built new lives for yourselves. That is best.'

Orpah thought about it and realised that what Naomi said was good sense. And so, not without tears and much sadness, she kissed her mother-in-law and said goodbye, and went back to her home to try to build a new life for herself.

But not Ruth. Her love for her remarkable mother-in-law was stronger even than the desire to return home and start life again. 'Don't ask me to leave you,' she said. In the lovely words of the King James Bible, 'Entreat me not to leave thee. Where thou goest I will go. Where thou lodgest I will lodge. Thy people shall be my people, and thy God my God.' Ruth's words: such loyalty, such gratitude, such love. Naomi didn't try to argue and so they both returned to Judah, to the little town of Bethlehem, where the story began.

Newly arrived back in Bethlehem, Naomi and Ruth walked through the streets, Ruth feeling lost in a foreign town. Naomi was wondering what sort of welcome she would get, noticing how things had changed since she had left, the shops that had closed, the new buildings, the new roads – all the sorts of things people notice when they return to a place after a long absence.

And people noticed her and wondered, Is that Naomi? She had changed, of course. When she left she had a husband and two fine sons. Now they were dead, and that experience must have marked and changed Naomi. And when they asked her, 'You are Naomi, aren't you?' she said, 'I was Naomi, but Naomi means "pleasant". Better now to call me Mara.'

Mara means 'bitter', and Naomi's experience of life had been very bitter.

Ruth knew that life was going to be hard for Naomi and herself. She was very like Naomi, loyal and loving and intensely practical. They were back in Naomi's country. They had a roof over their heads supplied by Naomi's kinsfolk – but how could they live? How would they eat?

They had arrived back in Bethlehem at the time of grain harvest. Practical Ruth said that she would go gleaning. She would join other poor people of the neighbourhood who were allowed to follow the reapers and gather up any stalks of grain that were dropped. A long day's work gleaning might just provide enough grain to make into bread for another day. It was a hard way to survive, but better than not surviving. So Ruth said, 'I'll go gleaning.' At once Naomi's quick intelligence and common sense saw how they could make the best of it.

She said, 'One of my husband's relations has a farm nearby. Go and glean there.' So she did. Elimelech's relation was Boaz, a fairly rich farmer. It was his practice to visit his fields to see how the harvest was progressing, and in the course of one of these visits he noticed Ruth among the gleaners who were following the main harvest workers. She must have been something special, not looking at all like of the normal run-of-the-mill gleaners. 'Who is that girl?' asked Boaz. And he was told. She was a foreign girl from Moab, and she'd come from there with Naomi. And she was a worker; she never stopped all day.

Boaz was smitten; it seems to have been love at first sight. He did two things. First he spoke to Ruth, and said how welcome she was as a gleaner on his farm – and indeed she didn't need to go to any other farm; she must always glean on his land. What's more, he said that she could join the regular harvest workers at break times and share the meal that was provided for them. Then he spoke to the harvest workers and told them to be a little careless in cutting the grain, and a little careless in trying up the sheaves, so that plenty was left for the gleaners. So Ruth gleaned until evening and took home to Naomi a quite remarkable amount of grain.

Naomi, as we know, was no fool. She could see that this was not the usual scrapings that came to a gleaner, and she asked Ruth about it. Ruth explained how kindly the rich farmer had treated her, inviting her back to glean again and providing a meal and making sure she was not harassed by any of the young men on the farm. She told Naomi that the farmer's name was Boaz.

'Boaz,' said Naomi, 'he's the relative I was talking about. Make sure you go back to him; he'll look after you.' And I think, into Naomi's mind, so saddened by her experiences over the years, came a new light. It was the light or delight at the possibility of a bit of matchmaking. She encouraged Ruth to see as much of Boaz as possible. And the story tells us that Boaz was not at all upset by that. And this story, which began as a triple tragedy, has turned into a love story.

But, naturally, the course of true love never does run smooth, and there was an obstacle in the way of Boaz and Ruth. And a mighty obstacle it was. It was the Law – the Law of Moses and the Law of God. And for Jews like Boaz it could not be ignored. The Law stated that if a man died, leaving a widow but no child, his closest relative should marry the widow and the first son born to the marriage should count as the child of the first, but now dead, husband. Boaz, as a relative of Chilion, Ruth's dead husband, would dearly have loved to fulfil the Law and marry Ruth. But he was not the closest relative. The first choice, the first claim on this lovely, loving and hard-working girl was not his.

Boaz was an honest man and so he called together an assembly of elders and, in their presence, he asked the man with the greater right if he wanted to claim his right – Chilion's property, including the widow Ruth. At first the man said, 'Yes.' But then he decided that to acquire another wife would complicate and confuse the arrangements he had already made for his own family. And so he changed his mind and said, 'No.'

Now the way was clear. It was all above board, all in accordance with the Law of Moses, and Boaz and Ruth were married. Eventually they had a son called Obed. Obed grew up, married and he had a son called Jesse. Jesse grew up and married and had eight sons, and the eighth son was called David – the David who killed Goliath, and who was the greatest king that Israel ever had. And he was the great-grandson of a foreign girl! What a lesson that was to the people of Israel, who thought that only Jews were God's chosen people. What a lesson to all religious people.

The Books of Samuel

The two Books of Samuel trace the history of Israel from the time of the settlement in Canaan until the last years of David's reign. Samuel himself might be thought of as the last of the Judges, though he was far more powerful and influential than any other Judge. Whereas they were local leaders and their influence was limited to a particular locality, Samuel's influence reached to all Israel. He thus provided a link between the local leaders at the time of the Judges and the centralised power of the monarchy. It is fitting that it was Samuel who was led by God to select and anoint the first two kings of Israel, Saul and David.

A little more about the make-up of the Books of Samuel will be found in the introduction to the story of Saul.

Samuel's Story

The Answer to a Prayer

Like so many of the early heroes of the Old Testament, Samuel should never have been born.

His mother, Hannah, was barren, as were some of the other great women of the Bible – Sarah, Rebekah and Rachel. Elkanah, Hannah's husband, was like those heroes of the faith, Abraham, Isaac and Jacob, a man who seemed to be cursed by God so that his wife could not bear him any children. There was a further resemblance to Abraham in that Elkanah had children by another wife, Peninnah. Not surprisingly, Hannah was unhappy and jealous.

It was Elkanah's custom to take the family each year on a pilgrimage to Shiloh, the great sanctuary where the Ark of the Covenant was kept. On the most important day of the festival they would make a feast. Elkanah was always mellow and generous on the festival day, and everyone ate and drank well. But it was obvious that he was more generous to Peninnah and her children than he was to the sad, childless Hannah. Peninnah took advantage of the situation and taunted Hannah, who wept and refused to eat.

Elkanah, who was a kind man, did not like to see Hannah upset and he tried to comfort her, saying that her childlessness didn't matter. 'Am I not more to you than ten sons?' he asked.

But it did matter, and Hannah refused to be comforted. She went off by herself into the sanctuary and wept and prayed. She was so desperate that she tried to bargain with God, promising that if God would give her a son, she would give him back to God, dedicating him as a Nazarite. That meant that her child's total commitment to God would be marked by never shaving or cutting his hair and by never drinking alcohol. To be a Nazarite was a symbolic return to the wilderness where, it was believed, Israel had been very close to God, when personal vanity counted for little and when there was no alcohol because nomadic people cannot cultivate vines. The promise or the bargain was a measure of Hannah's desperation.

She was distraught, and though her prayers were silent, in her emotional turmoil her lips moved and she seemed strangely uncontrolled. Eli, the priest in charge of the sanctuary, thought that she was drunk. He spoke sharply to Hannah and told her to stop drinking. Hannah explained that she was not drunk, just deeply unhappy. With great tact, Eli did not enquire further. He simply gave her his blessing and prayed that God would answer her prayer. Only Hannah knew what had happened between her and Eli and God.

The family returned home and life went on as usual. Then things began to happen. Hannah became pregnant, and in time gave birth to a son. She called him Samuel, saying he was God's gift, the answer to her prayer.

When the festival came round again, Elkanah told all the family to prepare for the journey. Hannah, much more confident now that she was a mother, said she would stay behind and look after the baby. When he was on solids next year she would join them on the pilgrimage again.

True to her word, when Samuel was old enough Hannah returned to Shiloh. We are not told whether she discussed it with Elkanah, nor are we told how difficult it was for her to give up this child she had so longed for. But she had made a bargain with God and he had kept his part, so Hannah would keep hers. She prepared gifts – a young bull, grain and wine – and went to Shiloh and found Eli. She reminded him of their previous meeting and of the promise she had made. And so Samuel was given, or as Hannah said, lent to God for the whole of his life. He was dressed in a linen *ephod*, the uniform of a young assistant in the sanctuary.

Time passed and Hannah had other children, three more sons and two daughters; she was clearly a fulfilled and contented woman. But she never forgot Samuel, God's answer to her prayer. Each year she made him a robe and took it with her when the family went on their annual pilgrimage. So Samuel began his lifelong dedication to the service of God. It was to lead him to a position of great power and influence.

God's call

The days when God spoke easily and openly to men and women seemed to have passed. He had spoken to Moses 'as a man speaks to his friend, face to face', but in Eli's day God did not speak at all – or perhaps no one listened carefully enough. Eli was old, he was going blind and he was tired. His sons, Hophni and Phineas, were not cut out for the priesthood. They went through the motions but had no sense of the presence of God and were more concerned with what material gain they could get out of their position. It must have been a strange apprenticeship for Samuel, seeing the dedicated, holy old man going gently about his work with reverence and a constant awareness of God in all that he did. And then the contrast: his sons, brash, greedy and quite oblivious of the inner meaning of the actions they performed and the words they spoke in the service of the sanctuary. Which example would win? Eli's or his sons'?

One night, the pilgrims and worshippers had left the sanctuary. All the lights had been extinguished except the lamp burning perpetually near the Ark of the Covenant. Eli had retired to his room to sleep, and Hophni and Phineas were nowhere to be seen. Samuel went to sleep, as he always did, in his place near the sacred Ark. He was its night-time guardian and was accustomed to sleeping there. He was almost asleep when he heard a voice calling, 'Samuel, Samuel.'

It must be the old man, needing some help. He jumped up and went into Eli's room and enquired what he wanted.

Eli said, 'I don't want anything; I didn't call you. You must be mistaken.'

Samuel went back and lay down. Again the voice came, 'Samuel, Samuel.' He was sure he heard it this time, so he went into Eli's room and asked what he wanted.

'Nothing,' said the old man, 'I didn't call you. Go back to bed.'

Samuel tried to sleep but again the voice called his name. He wasn't very pleased to hear it yet again, and quickly went to Eli and said, 'I am here. What do you want? You certainly called me.'

At last Eli realised what was going on. He gently told Samuel to go back to his bed and if the voice called again he was to say, 'Speak, Lord, for thy servant hears.'

Samuel returned and lay down, straining to hear the slightest sound. Again the voice came very clearly, 'Samuel, Samuel.' As Eli had advised Samuel said, 'Speak, for thy servant hears.' And God spoke to Samuel.

God's message was that he was going to do wonderful things for his people. The dead wood of the house of Eli would have to be cut out and Samuel himself would have to take on the role of the leader of the nation. It was not easy for the young man to relay this uncomfortable message to Eli, and he would gladly have kept it to himself. But in the morning Eli asked what God's message had been. He made it quite clear that he expected stern words from God and that he would not blame Samuel if the message were unwelcome. Samuel told him what God had said and the faithful old man said, 'It is the Lord; let him do what seems good to him.'

Samuel's experience of God as the voice in the night confirmed his position. No longer was he in God's service because his mother had placed him there. He was now in God's service because God had called him and would use him. As the years passed and Samuel grew to maturity, it became increasingly obvious to the people of Israel that he was God's prophet, God's spokesman whom they should obey.

Samuel's days of power came at the time when the tribes of Israel had successfully settled into many regions of Canaan, though conflicts with the Philistines, who occupied the coastal strip, were still frequent. The Philistines themselves were invaders, sea people from the Mediterranean. Sometimes the Israelites and Philistines lived in uneasy peace. But at other times skirmishes or even full-scale war broke out. Generally the Philistines had the better of the exchanges, and it was after a particularly humiliating defeat, with many deaths, that it was decided to boost Israelite morale by bringing the Ark of the Covenant, the sacred symbol of God's presence, to the field of battle. In everyone's minds this would be to bring God himself into the front line. Hophni and Phineas supervised the moving of the Ark, and it was received into the Israelite camp with a great deal of shouting and cheering.

From their front line, not very far away, the Philistines could hear the noise of jubilation in the enemy camp. Soon their spies told them what it was. The Ark had been brought into the camp of Israel. The Philistines were alarmed. They too believed that the presence of the Ark would mean that the God of Israel himself would fight against them, and they had heard what he had done in the past to the mighty army of Egypt and the city of Jericho. Fear strengthened their resolve, and pride gave them courage and in the battle which followed Israel was defeated. Thirty thousand Israelites were slaughtered. Others fled, not just back to camp; they deserted to their homes. The Ark was captured, and Hophni and Phineas gave their lives defending it. Perhaps by their courageous deaths they made up for the less satisfactory aspects of their lives.

The report of what had happened reached Shiloh. When Eli heard that the Ark had been captured and his sons killed, he collapsed, fell off his seat, broke his neck and died. It was a terrible time for the house of Eli. But it was not the end of the story.

The Philistines took the captured Ark in triumph to their great city, Ashdod, where the temple of Dagon, god of the Philistines, stood. They placed the Ark in the temple close to the image of Dagon. The next day when they went into the House of Dagon to pray, they found that the statue of Dagon had fallen. It was lying face down before the Ark of Yahweh. Quickly the image was lifted and put back in its place. The next day things were worse. Not only had the image of Dagon fallen again; this time the head and the hands of the statue had been broken off. The next thing was that illness began to spread through the city and the surrounding districts. To the Philistines it looked as if it could only be due to the malevolent presence of the Ark of the God of Israel.

So they moved the Ark to Gath, another of their great cities. The disasters followed. So it was taken to Ekron, but understandably the people of Ekron were not happy to receive the Ark that had caused so much trouble in Ashdod and Gath. A conference was held, and the Philistine leaders asked advice from the priests and wise men. Their advice was to send the Ark back to the Israelites, but not to send it empty-handed. Gifts should accompany it to buy off the anger of the God of Israel, whose honour had been soiled by the capture of the Ark. They directed that a new cart should be made to carry the Ark. Two cows, never before used as beasts of burden, should be used to pull the cart. In addition, as their people had suffered from tumours due to the presence of the Ark, golden models of tumours should be made, also golden mice, as an offering or a bribe to the God of Israel.

All this was done, and the cart with its sacred burden was sent off in the direction of the territory occupied by the Israelites. It eventually came to rest at Kiriath-jearim and it stayed there twenty years. Perhaps the ark's reputation for bringing trouble worried the Israelites also.

During those twenty years, Samuel found himself trying, as Moses had tried, to keep the people faithful to Yahweh. He struggled to stop them drifting into the worship of the gods of the people among whom they lived. On one notable occasion he called all the people together at Mizpah and publicly prayed for them. This had such an effect that the people confessed their sins and rededicated themselves to Yahweh. They asked Samuel to pray for them continually, and in response Samuel offered a lamb in sacrifice. The Philistines were aware that Israel was occupied in a great religious ceremony and callously chose that moment to attack. But they had miscalculated. The Israelites were so full of religious and national fervour, or God was so clearly on their side, that they routed the enemy in a memorable victory.

Samuel was leader, judge or prophet in Israel for many years. He kept in touch with his scattered people by travelling around the territory so that he knew their needs, their hopes and their fears. As he grew older he appointed his sons, Joel and Abijah, to share the responsibilities he had carried alone for so long. But they were not satisfactory. For Samuel it must have been a disappointment, but probably not a surprise. He had seen exactly the same thing happen in the case of Eli and his sons.

Though he was old, there was still one task for Samuel to carry out, and it would be the most important and far-reaching thing he ever did. He was to establish the monarchy of Israel.

Saul's Story

The story of Saul is found in the First Book of Samuel. The early part of the book is made up of at least two sources, which editors have woven together to make their narrative. One source is anti-monarchy (Ch. 8) and the other pro-monarchy (Ch. 9). The story which follows, like the Bible, tries to weave the two strands together.

The story of Saul is a tragedy. He was the victim of a political experiment in Israel. As the first king he had no role model to follow, he had no training for the job and no previous experience of leadership. He was big and strong and willing and looked the part – and if that sounds like a description of a not very successful heavyweight boxer, perhaps it's not too far off.

Saul was probably the best they could do when it came to finding a king, and we should remember how difficult born or trained leaders like Moses and Joshua had found the burden of authority in Israel. Saul simply could not fulfil the expectations placed on him.

A lovely incident seems to disclose the nature of Saul. After he had been told by Samuel that he was God's choice as king and had been anointed by the prophet, the public ceremony of coronation had to take place. Samuel called the nation together to Mizpah. Everyone was there, all Israel gathered in solemn assembly. But the man destined to be king couldn't be found. Shy and perhaps afraid, Saul had hidden himself among the piles of baggage. Perhaps he sensed even then that it would all be too much for him. He did his best.

In the Book of Chronicles, we find a harsh and probably untrue judgement of Saul – that he was unfaithful to the Lord. A far better epitaph is David's lament, the Lament of the Bow, in the first chapter of II Samuel. Saul died in battle like the brave and faithful soldier that he was. When he could see that there was no escape, rather than be taken by the Philistines, the enemy he had fought against for so long, he took his own life. David, who had been a constant thorn in Saul's flesh, saluted him graciously:

> Your glory, O Israel, lies slain on your heights,
>> How are the mighty fallen
>> O daughters of Israel,
>> Weep for Saul.

The Establishment of the Monarchy

Samuel's sons had neither the ability nor the integrity of their father. This was evident to all, and a number of prominent men in Israel got together, approached Samuel and put their proposition to him. 'Behold, you are old and your sons do not walk in your ways, now appoint for us a king to govern us like all the nations.'

Samuel didn't like it. He didn't like to be reminded of his own failing powers and the poor reputation of his sons. But there was more to it than that. One of the things he had constantly to watch was the tendency of the Israelites to copy and even to be absorbed by the people among whom they had settled. They copied their farming methods, which was sensible for people who had formerly been nomads. But too often what was considered good farming practice involved the worship of agricultural gods and goddesses. The stress on fertility – vegetable, animal and human – made for a morality which contradicted some of the laws of God, given through Moses.

Samuel could see that there was danger in having a king. It would be one more very large step toward becoming like the people around them, and Israel might drift steadily further from Yahweh, their God and covenant partner. He prayed about it, and as he prayed God told him that he should not take it personally. After all, in asking for a king to rule them, they were not rejecting Samuel, they were rejecting Yahweh himself. God told Samuel to accept their demand, but to warn them solemnly what having a king would mean.

He recalled the men who had approached him and gave them a very critical statement as to what a monarchy in Israel would involve. A king will lead the army as they want him to, but a king will also conscript some of their young men to the hazardous life of a professional soldier. He will set up a court and live in the style that befits a king. So other young men will be required to work the king's land, to run his farms and to harvest his crops. His court will be expected to live in style and luxury like the courts of neighbouring kings, so some of their daughters will be taken to work as servants at court, cooking, cleaning, being ladies' maids. A king will want to build up his wealth to be like other kings, and there will be favourites he will want to reward. So he will take some of their land and some of their cattle. And the days will come when the king will make slaves even of the free people of Israel. Freedom and equality before God will disappear. That is what a king will do.

However darkly Samuel painted the picture of life under a monarchy, the people could see no alternative, and they would not change their minds. Samuel had to find them a king. And God already knew who it would be.

There was a particularly striking young man who belonged to the small tribe of Benjamin, the descendants of Jacob's youngest son. His name was Saul. He was handsome and unusually tall and well built, head and shoulders above everyone else. He worked on the farm for his father, Kish. A problem had arisen. A number of valuable asses had strayed and no one knew where they were. Kish was aware he had an exceptionally energetic and able son, and he told Saul to take one of the servants with him and find the asses. He was confident that his son would soon find them and bring them back.

But it didn't work out like that. Saul and his companion travelled a long way and took a long time and eventually Saul, showing admirable common sense, said that by this time his father would be worrying about them, not about the asses, so they ought to return. The servant didn't dispute Saul's judgement, but made an alternative suggestion. He said that they were very near to a city where a man of God lived. This man was a seer – someone who, by God's guidance perceived things that other people could not understand. 'As we are so near, why not call on him? He might be able to help.'

Saul thought that this was a good suggestion and they made their way to the city. They enquired where they might find the seer and were told that he had just arrived back in the city and was about to offer a sacrifice because this day was a special day in their city. They were given directions, and as they walked along they met the holy man on his way to the sacred hill where he was to offer the sacrifice. Samuel was the seer, and God had already prepared him for this moment.

The previous day God had spoken to Samuel and told him that, using the loss of some asses as the pretext, he would guide to Samuel the young man whom he had chosen to be the first king of Israel. As soon as Samuel saw Saul, noticed his stature and the unmistakable light of intelligence in his face, he knew that God was saying, 'This is the man.'

When the two met, Saul politely enquired if he was going in the right direction for the house of the seer. Samuel replied, 'I am the seer,' and went on to invite Saul to join him at the sacred meal that would follow the sacrifice. He also said that he would like Saul to stay the night because he had something important to tell him in the morning. As for the asses, they were not to bother about them. They had been found and were safe and sound. He also made some hints about Saul and his family and their importance. Saul couldn't understand that, and modestly said that his family were not only members of the smallest tribe but were a rather unimportant family in it. Perhaps this modesty impressed Samuel as well.

Samuel took them to the meal and Saul was treated as an honoured guest. After the meal, Saul and his companion were shown where they could sleep and they retired for the night, no doubt baffled as to what was going on.

As day broke they were wakened by Samuel who took them down into the street to get ready to leave. Then Samuel said quietly to Saul, 'Tell the servant to go on ahead a little way; I have something to say to you in private, a message from God.'

When he and Saul were alone Samuel took a vial of oil and poured it on Saul's head, anointing him and declaring that God had made him king over the people of Israel. He also spoke in much more favourable terms about what Saul would do as king than he had used to the men who first asked him to make a king. He said that Saul would be the military saviour of his people.

And Samuel, speaking as a seer, a man of God, told Saul that the proof that what had just happened was in accordance with God's will would be demonstrated by three incidents. First, when he left Samuel he would meet two men who would tell him that the asses had been found and that his father was now worried about him. Secondly, a little later he would meet three men who would give him some loaves of bread, which he should accept. Thirdly he would meet a group of ecstatic prophets, dancing and playing musical instruments. When he met them, the Spirit of God, which was causing their ecstasy, would fall on him and he would join them in their fervour and be so changed that he would become like another person. All this would prove that God was placing his Spirit in Saul to guide and inspire him, so that in many ways he would be like a new man, a man fit to be the first king of Israel. Saul left, and all three signs took place and Saul became a man inspired by God.

What Samuel had done privately had to be declared publicly. He called an assembly of all Israel to meet at Mizpah. Samuel had everything worked out; he knew precisely how the choosing of Israel's first king had to be stage-managed. By the drawing of lots he chose one tribe out of all twelve – and it was the little tribe of Benjamin that was chosen. Out of that one tribe one clan was chosen by lot. Finally, by another drawing of lots, Saul was chosen. But where was he? Where was Saul when his first great public moment came? He couldn't be found. Shyness had overcome the country boy and he had hidden himself among the baggage. Eventually he was found, and by this time everyone was longing to get a glimpse of him. We wonder whether Samuel had stage-managed that too because when the people saw Saul they were greatly impressed. He was taller by a head than anyone else in the great assembly. Samuel called out, 'Do you see the man the Lord has chosen?' And all the assembly shouted, 'Long live the king!'

Saul's reign began in the best possible way. He went to the aid of the people of Jabesh Gilead who were being terrorised by Ammonite raiders. Saul mustered an army and routed the

Ammonites. The men of Jabesh Gilead never forgot their debt to Saul and when, many years later, he died in battle with the Philistines, they rescued his body from the indignities that the Philistines were inflicting on his corpse.

Saul's twelve-year reign was a sad story of decline and fall. The job of being king was new; there were no examples to copy, no role models to study, and Saul found he could not meet all the demands and expectations of the people, and especially of Samuel. As his power fragmented, so Saul sank into depression and mental illness. In the end Samuel despaired of Saul and decided that God must have rejected him in order to choose a new king. And so David came on the scene.

In one strand of the story, Saul and David came together because David was a skilled musician and his playing soothed Saul when he was in the grip of one of his depressions. In another strand they met because David, a young shepherd, took on and killed the Philistine champion Goliath – but that is another story.

So Saul's story and his life declined sadly to an end. Samuel had abandoned him. David was ruthlessly exploiting every opportunity to promote himself and claim the throne. Despite all that, something of the nobility of Saul's character showed through at the very end. With his warrior son, Jonathan, beside him, Saul died, as surely he would have wanted to, in battle against the old enemy, the Philistines.

David, who had caused Saul so many problems, knew the worth of this troubled man, and he composed a lament for Israel's first and tragic king and for the son who would never succeed him.

It is best to let David have the last, generous word:

> Saul and Jonathan – in life they were loved and gracious,
> and in death they were not parted.
> They were swifter than eagles,
> they were stronger than lions.
> O daughters of Israel,
> weep for Saul.

David's Story

David is second only to Moses as the dominant figure in the Old Testament. He was soldier and king, poet and musician. He was brave, he was generous. He was also lustful, ruthless, devious and ambitious.

The David story is told in the two Books of Samuel, with his death spilling over into the first two chapters of the First Book of Kings. There is also a parallel account, from the death of Saul to the death of David, in the First Book of Chronicles, Chapters 10–29.

Just as the first five books of the Old Testament have traditionally been ascribed to Moses, so the Psalms have been attributed to David, and in many editions the book bears the title, 'The Psalms of David'. It is unlikely that he was the author of all the Psalms, and indeed several of them bear other people's names. But we can be confident he wrote some of them. After all, he had a reputation as a musician. Also, after you have read the story of how the prophet Nathan made David aware of his sin in murdering Uriah and marrying Bathsheba, then read Psalm 51, which has the introduction: 'For the director of music. A Psalm of David. When the prophet Nathan came to him after David had committed adultery with Bathsheba.' There you will find the expression of David's profound shame and repentance.

In human terms, it was through ability, intrigue, courage and ruthless ambition that David made himself king of all twelve tribes of Israel. In biblical terms it was because God had chosen him and made a covenant with him, as he had before with Abraham, Isaac, Jacob and Moses.

Under David, the united kingdom of Israel was strong. He was perhaps fortunate that none of the neighbouring nations was particularly strong at that time and none posed a great threat to Israel. So the people lived in comparative peace and prosperity. David reigned for forty years and by the end of his reign the cracks were beginning to show in the fabric of state. After his death the cracks widened and within a generation the kingdom was divided.

David's reign shone as a bright jewel in the troubled history of Israel, and subsequent generations looked back to it as a golden age. Through the troubled centuries that followed – through the time of the divided kingdoms, through the destruction and disappearance of the northern kingdom, through the exile and return of Judah, and through the years under Persian, Greek and Roman rule – there was always the hope that God would save Israel again and make it great by sending another king like David.

David and Goliath

In the days when people had a better knowledge of the Bible than they do these days, one story you could guarantee they would know would be the story of David and Goliath. How it captured our imaginations! It was the biblical equivalent of the cowboy film with the hero, against all the odds, taking on the villains who outnumbered him six to one. In this story it is as if all six villains have been put together to make the one colossal figure – Goliath, the giant of Gath.

The story is set in the days when Israel was settling into its newly entered Promised Land. It hadn't all been as easy as the story of the collapse of the walls of Jericho might suggest. It wasn't a clear and clean conquest. Nor was it an empty land they walked into after forty years in the wilderness. Each of the twelve tribes of Israel had to drive out the original inhabitants or learn to live with them. They were not made welcome; foreign immigrants rarely are. Some of the people of Canaan put up very stiff resistance, and none more so than the Philistines. They had been invaders too, Mediterranean sea people who had settled on the coast, just south of what we now call the Gaza Strip. In fact, Gaza was one of their great cities, along with Ashdod, Ashkelon, Ekron and Gath. They were a civilised and prosperous people. They were merchants; trade was their main occupation and, like most trading nations, they were ready to go to war if their trade was attacked and their prosperity threatened.

When we pick up the story the armies of the two warring nations, Israel and Philistia are drawn up facing each other in the Valley of Elah. Each army is encamped on a steep hillside and between them is the valley. Being on a hillside, they can see each other very clearly, and all the emotions of men before battle are there. They are all afraid; few of them really want to fight. It is a patriotic duty and, in order to be able to carry out their distasteful duty, they encourage each other. There is boasting and bravado in both camps, saying what a poor lot the enemy are, how we'll wipe them out tomorrow. Anything to build up their courage; anything to convince themselves that they will be all right; that they'll win and return, unharmed, to their homes, their wives and children, their jobs.

It was amid this artificial pumping up of courage that Goliath stepped forward. What a sight he must have been. Ten feet tall, perhaps more, and built in proportion. We can tell from the weight of his armour that he must have had a mighty frame. And he was armed to the teeth. Goliath was probably the one man in both armies who really wanted a fight. Someone of his size had never lost a playground fight. Most people didn't fight him at all, they simply ran away when they saw him, which was the intelligent thing to do. Goliath, one suspects, was a rather stupid bully. He was used to frightening people and he liked doing it. And so, while the normal, brave but terrified men of Israel and Philistia pretended they were spoiling for a fight, Goliath strode out and roared out his challenge.

'We don't need armies!' he said. 'Send out your best man, and let us fight. If he kills me, we Philistines will be the slaves of Israel, and if I kill him, the Israelites will be our slaves.'

Of course, there was no 'if' in the mind of Goliath about who would win.

There was no 'if' in the mind of Saul, king of Israel and leader of the Israelite army. Saul was a big man, head and shoulders over his fellow countrymen. But Saul was just a big man, probably about six feet tall. He was strong and brave and a well-trained soldier – but he wasn't a ten foot giant and he knew he didn't stand a chance. And if he didn't, no one in his army did. What could he do? He could offer an incentive. So he made it known throughout the army of Israel that whoever would fight and kill Goliath would be given a rich reward. He would marry the king's daughter and his family would be honoured. But, as Saul expected, there were no takers.

And so, every day, morning and evening for over a month, the defiant boasting and challenging went on. And the morale of the army of Israel sank lower and lower.

Bethlehem was about twenty miles from the Valley of Elah, where the two armies were drawn up face to face for battle. Jesse was a prosperous citizen of Bethlehem. He had eight sons. The three eldest, Eliab, Abinadab and Shammah, were soldiers in the Israelite army. The youngest son was David, and his job was to mind his father's sheep.

We need to remind ourselves that there had been a strange incident in the life of David some time before this. The great and elderly prophet, Samuel, had come to their house with the news that one of Jesse's sons was to become the king of Israel. The sons had paraded before Samuel, beginning with the eldest. They were all fine, strong, handsome men. But Samuel kept saying, 'No, not this one,' until he came to David and recognised him as God's chosen one. He anointed David and said that he would become king. Of course, Saul was the actual king at the time, but David never forgot what had happened, what Samuel had done. It was stored safely deep in his memory and in his heart.

We now return to the battle. David would have loved to have joined his elder brothers and been a soldier in the army of King Saul. He was a confident young man – and ambitious and courageous. Being a shepherd wasn't a soft job. It meant facing bears and wolves, lions and jackals, predators who would have liked to have made a meal of part of the flock. It also meant facing less obvious, but equally dangerous creatures like snakes and scorpions. David was, and he needed to be, an expert with the sling, to protect his flock and himself.

It was all Jesse could do to keep David away from the army, and what David imagined to be the excitement and glory of battle. From time to time, to try to work it out of his system, Jesse sent David to the camp to take food to his brothers and to bring back news to their anxious father.

Delighted to be going, David found someone to look after the sheep, prepared provisions for his brothers and a suitable present – not to say a bribe – for the officer who was in charge of them. As he arrived at the camp and started to search for his brothers, Goliath appeared.

'Choose your man to fight me!' he roared. 'If he kills me, we shall be your slaves. If I kill him, the Israelites will be our slaves.'

It was the same boring but frightening message.

David could not help but notice the quietness which came over the camp of Israel when the Philistine bully roared out his challenge. No one said a word.

'What's going on?' asked David. He hadn't found his brothers yet – or perhaps they hadn't found him.

The soldiers nearby said, 'The king has promised that whoever kills the giant, will receive a rich reward. He will marry the king's daughter and his family will be honoured.'

'Oh,' said David, and moved along to a different group of soldiers.

'What would happen if someone killed the giant?' he asked them.

They told him, 'Whoever kills the giant will receive a rich reward. He will marry the king's daughter and his family will be honoured.'

'Oh,' said David.

Just then his eldest brother, Eliab, appeared and he clearly knew quite a lot about his clever, ambitious youngest brother. 'What are you up to?' he said. 'You're here to interfere; I know you.'

All innocence, David said, 'Oh no. I was only asking a question.' And he turned to a third group of soldiers and said, 'All I was asking was what would happen to the man who killed the giant.'

They said, 'Straightforward. He will be given a rich reward. He will marry the king's daughter and his family will be honoured.'

'Well, just fancy that,' said David and obediently followed his brother.

David had outwitted Eliab. He had, ever so innocently, wandered up and down the ranks of Israel, carefully avoiding his brothers, and had made himself known to everyone by his repeated question. And word was taken to Saul that there was a possible volunteer to take on the giant.

'Bring him here,' said Saul, full of hope.

He must have been bitterly disappointed when he saw David. He was a fresh-faced youth, when what was needed was a skilled and battle-hardened warrior. And it is greatly to Saul's credit that he gently said, 'You cannot go and fight with this Philistine. You are only a lad.'

But David was not to be put off. He'd seen Goliath, and coldly and calculatingly he had weighed him up and knew what he could do. David was clever. He knew what he was capable of and what the rewards were going to be. He also remembered that fateful visit of the prophet Samuel, when he had been anointed and told that he would be king of Israel. David had thought much about that during the quiet hours of minding sheep, and he had now started to work out his plan to make the prophecy come true. He had made himself known to virtually the whole army. He was sure he could become an instant hero, and in the end his offer to fight Goliath was not intended to help Saul. The real intention was to replace Saul and become king himself. David was a clever young man and ambitious and, let us not forget, very brave indeed to take on Goliath.

Saul looked at David and saw that he was about the same age as his own son, Jonathan, and he immediately liked the boy. 'You can't fight this Philistine,' he said. But David had his answer ready. You get the feeling that David had planned and rehearsed every step. He had thought it out carefully in those long hours he spent by himself, minding the sheep.

'I'm a shepherd,' he told Saul. These are his words in the Bible: 'When there came a lion, or a bear, and took a lamb from the flock, I went after him and smote him and delivered it out of his mouth; and if he arose against me, I caught him by his beard, and smote him and killed him. Your servant has killed lions and bears; and this uncircumcised Philistine shall be like one of them...'

It sounds rehearsed and it was probably wildly exaggerated. But they were brave words, and Saul gave in. 'All right then, if you're sure. But you'd better wear my armour; it's the best there is.'

David was helped into Saul's armour, and he couldn't move. It was all far too big, far too heavy. It would have made David a sitting duck.

David knew that all along. He didn't want the armour; he didn't need the armour. Putting it on was just a step in his plan to kill the Philistine, claim the rewards and, in the end, become king himself.

The armour was laid aside and David walked out to meet the Philistine. Just imagine Goliath. He was at least ten feet tall. (Look at the wall or door frame and work out ten feet.) His armour was impressive. On his head a helmet of bronze. The plate armour covering his body weighed 5,000 shekels. That is fifty-three kilogrammes or 117 pounds or over eight stones, whichever you find most helpful. His spear was a great shaft of wood with an iron head weighing six kilogrammes, nearly another stone. He had bronze leg guards, a bronze dagger, a sword (probably of iron), and a great shield. His armour all together weighed about eighty kilogrammes, very nearly twelve stones, the weight of an average man. And not only was it heavy; it was awkward.

Goliath was rather like a great armoured tank – but one without an engine. He couldn't move; or at least he would move very slowly. And David knew that. He was agile, mobile and he could literally run rings round Goliath and keep slinging stones for as long as was necessary. He had carefully noted that they would fight by a stream, and so he would have an endless supply of pebbles as ammunition, should he need them. But he didn't need them. What do you do to while away the hours as a shepherd? You practise with your sling until you can hit a beetle from thirty yards.

David's first stone went home, and the giant, falling forward unconscious, crashed to the ground. Even if he had regained consciousness he could never have regained his feet with that weight of armour on him. He lay there helpless and David, taking his time so that everyone would see and remember this moment, approached the fallen giant. He took Goliath's sword and, not without difficulty, beheaded him.

The silence which had hardly lifted since the giant's first challenge was shattered. Shouts of triumph and jubilation from Israel; disbelief and dismay from the Philistines. And then the noise of the Philistine retreat, the dropping of weapons and the sounds of fear as they fled. And the Israelites, bellowing their war cry, pursued and slaughtered.

And David had taken a giant step toward his ambition, which was also God's will that he should become the king of Israel.

David and Saul

The death of Goliath and the rout of the Philistines had been a triumph for King Saul and the army of Israel. They returned home to be welcomed as heroes. But for Saul the sweetness of victory was quickly soured. Women, young and old, singing and dancing, came out to meet the returning soldiers. But what was it they were chanting? Was Saul hearing it correctly? Yes, he was! His ears didn't deceive him. They were chanting 'Saul has slain his thousands – and David his ten thousands.' As the Bible says, 'Saul eyed David from that day on.'

David had been brought to the notice of Saul and into his court not only through his challenge to Goliath. Those close to Saul knew that he was not always well, not always stable. As the periods of depression became deeper, more frequent and more noticeable, some of his courtiers suggested that music might soothe and help him. David was known as a skilled musician and he was brought to court to play when Saul was depressed and unpredictable. Sometimes it worked, and Saul was grateful and treated David almost as a son. On other occasions his jealousy would flare.

There was good reason for that. Part of the biblical narrative suggests that before he joined the court of Saul, David had been a successful freelance bandit. He had surrounded himself with thirty picked men and brought terror to many of Israel's enemies – and reputation to himself. As far as Saul was concerned he was a threat to his own leadership and his throne. Saul was jealous of David's popularity and he certainly didn't approve of his close friendship with his own son, Jonathan.

What was Saul to do with this gifted young man who oozed charisma? Sometimes his moods answered for him, and on more than one occasion he had flung his spear at David, his diseased imagination thinking he would pin him to the wall. But David was far too clever for that, and slipped away unharmed. Saul then tried a trick, which, later and much more ruthlessly, David himself would use. He promoted David in the army and made him the commander of 1,000 men. Perhaps the fortunes of war would help, and the Philistines would do what Saul was failing to do – get rid of David.

Nothing was going right for Saul. It was as if God, who had chosen him, had now deserted him. He continually made wrong decisions, and the promotion of David was one of them. In contrast, everything David did was successful. As a commander in the army he harried the Philistines and was never defeated. He made sure he was widely known among all the tribes of Israel and he built up an enviable reputation as a gifted leader.

Saul resorted to other schemes. He offered first one and then a second daughter in marriage to David, saying that all he required from David as a marriage payment was one hundred Philistine foreskins. That meant killing one hundred men, and in doing that David stood a good chance of losing his own life. But the pattern of Saul failing and David effortlessly succeeding continued, and David doubled the stakes and presented Saul with two hundred foreskins, and so married into the royal family.

Jonathan, now David's brother-in-law as well as his friend, tried to reason with his father, saying how much David had done for the nation and that he had never tried to set himself up against Saul. Saul, in quieter mood, agreed that what Jonathan said was true, and he promised not to seek David's life. But beyond reason, there was Saul's instinct that David was his rival, undermining his authority. And the moods and rages returned and when David was playing the lyre Saul again tried to pin him with his spear, and David was forced to run away.

Saul sent men to assassinate David in his bed. But Michel, David's wife and Saul's daughter, tricked the men. She told David to escape and then padded his bed so that the men thought that he was there. One has to feel sorry for Saul. He was carrying the responsibilities of royal leadership; he was battling with severe depression; he was being undermined by a clever rival and, on top of all that, his own children were working against him.

Jonathan would dearly have liked to heal the rift between his father and his best friend. He met David secretly and promised that he would try to discover just what Saul's intentions were. For David and Jonathan to meet again might be dangerous, so they agreed upon a silent but effective way of passing on the necessary information.

Jonathan returned to court to see if Saul's moods and opinions had changed. They hadn't. So he went out into the field, pretending to practise archery. He shot several arrows and sent his servant to gather them. As the boy got near to where the arrows had fallen Jonathan shot another, far beyond him, and told him it was farther on. 'Make haste,' he shouted, 'do not stay!' The message was not for the boy; it was for David who was hidden close by.

David was on the run, and Saul committed a great deal of thought, time and manpower to the pursuit of him. David, gathering an increasing force around him, found it comparatively easy to elude the ageing king whose powers were failing and whose men had no real heart for the chase.

He had fled empty-handed and unarmed, and a man like David, who lived largely by the sword, must have felt naked. So one of the first things he did was to go to the sanctuary where the sword of Goliath was kept. He claimed the sword for himself, and no one had a stronger claim. He then made approaches to Achish, the Philistine king of Gath. With Saul as a common enemy, they might have made good allies. But David heard Achish reminding his people of David's military prowess and the possibility of deception. What if this were an Israelite trick to get David and his men inside the Philistine city as a fifth column? In the end it was all too risky for both sides. David wanted to get out of the alliance as much as Achish, and he decided that pretending madness might help. It suited Achish, who was glad to be rid of him and who said, cynically, that he had enough madmen of his own without importing more from Israel.

David made the cave of Adullam his headquarters. Many who had complaints and grievances joined him, and soon his followers numbered 400. No wonder Saul wanted him dead. He pursued David relentlessly but unsuccessfully. David and his men were far more skilled at the guerrilla warfare that was being carried on. Twice David could have killed Saul. On one occasion Saul went into a cave to relieve himself. Unfortunately he chose a cave in which David and some of his men were hiding. David stealthily cut off some of Saul's robe as proof that he could just as easily have cut off his life. When Saul left the cave and was a safe distance away, David called after him, showing the piece of cloth he had cut off and telling Saul that he could have killed him, but did not. He would never lift his hand against 'the Lord's anointed', he said.

This was a generous act on David's part, but like so many of David's actions, it was carefully calculated and clever. He, too, was the Lord's anointed, and he was instilling into his own men a loyalty which he hoped would protect him in days to come. Saul recognised the force of what David said. He knew his own days as king were almost over and that David, not his own son Jonathan, would succeed him. Not entirely lacking in guile himself, he used this moment of truce to extract from David a promise that when he came to power he would not wipe out all Saul's descendants. David readily gave his promise.

On a second occasion Saul was asleep in his camp, surrounded by his personal guards and the rest of his men. With great skill and daring, David and one of his men crept into the camp and reached the spot where Saul was sleeping. David would not allow his companion to kill the king. Instead they stole Saul's spear and cup of water. They crept out of the camp, and having reached a safe distance, in a shouted conversation, David taunted Saul's right-hand man, Abner, and then spoke to Saul himself, again protesting his loyalty and arguing that Saul should stop hunting him. In response, Saul paid tribute to David's generosity and spoke again of his future greatness.

Because Saul would not call off the hunt, David had to move out of his territory to get some respite. For over a year he allied himself with the Philistines. He again approached Achish, king of Gath, and this time he and his men were welcomed as an additional force for carrying out raids on neighbouring tribes. Achish made David head of his personal bodyguard and gave him the city of Ziklag as his base. David and his men settled there for a year and four months, carrying out raids on nearby towns and villages. He was fortunate in that he was not called upon by the Philistines to carry out raids against any Israelite city, because that would have damaged David's standing with the very people whose loyalty he was trying to win, and over whom he intended to rule in the future.

Returning to Ziklag after a raid, he found that the city, which he had left undefended, had been sacked by the Amalekites. No one had been killed, but women had been carried away to be sold as slaves. David's credibility as a successful leader was in question. The people even spoke of stoning him. His career, and perhaps his life, was on the line.

David always believed he was guided and directed by God. So he asked a priest for advice. Should he pursue the Amalekites or not? He was told very clearly that he should pursue: 'You shall surely overtake and shall surely rescue.'

As the oracle had promised, the campaign was a total success. The captives were freed and booty was recovered, not only from the raid on Ziklag, but from many other raids the Amalekites had made over the years. With typical astuteness, David rewarded all who had fought with him. He also sent gifts to many cities of Judah. On the face of it, this was compensation for earlier losses, but it was also a reminder to them that David was their protector and benefactor.

At this moment of triumph for David, Saul was on the threshold of his final downfall. He staggered from mistake to mistake and from misfortune to misfortune. In the days of his greatness he had banned witches and wizards, sorcery and spiritism from his kingdom, so that he and his people could worship Yahweh without superstition. But with David a continual thorn in his side and his campaigns against the Philistines going badly, Saul, in the depths of despair and fear, consulted a witch at Endor. She conjured up the spirit of Samuel, whose message to Saul was that his time was over. He had forsaken God and so God had forsaken him. On hearing the oracle, Saul collapsed. He had to be helped up and given food before he could return to his camp.

The end had come for Saul, and it came with dignity. Despite his rejection by God, despite his fears and forebodings, like the brave soldier he was, he went out at the head of his army and engaged the Philistines in battle. It was a conclusive Philistine victory and Saul, mortally wounded, took his own life by falling on his sword. He preferred that to the shame and torture that would result from his being taken prisoner. Jonathan and two other sons of Saul also died in the battle.

The victors took Saul's body, beheaded him, and hung his remains on the gates of Bethshan. His armour, as a trophy, was placed in one of their temples. Perhaps all this was some indication of how formidable an enemy Saul had been. The people of Jabesh Gilead, remembering Saul's defence of them at the beginning of his reign, went at night and removed his body and those of his sons. They buried their bones with dignity and fasted in mourning for them.

Saul, the Lord's anointed, was an honourable, brave and honest soldier. But the task which had been laid on him was too much for him. His weaknesses became critical and his story became a tragedy. Saul had taken Israel on its first crucial step into monarchy, and in spite of his failings he had been an honourable first king of Israel.

David Becomes King

David is remembered as the greatest king of Israel. The historians of the Bible count him as great because of his faith in Yahweh, the God of Israel. He was close to God, and even when his behaviour was immoral or despicable David was ready to admit it and he repented with real grief and remorse. Throughout his life he believed that he had been chosen by God and was being led by God – an instrument in the working out of God's plan.

A classic expression of David's devotion to Yahweh is in Psalm 89, where we read of a new covenant made between God and David. This was not to supersede the covenant which God had made with Abraham and renewed with Isaac, Jacob and Moses. It stood alongside it. In Psalm 89 God says, 'I have sworn to David my servant ... He shall cry to me, "Thou art my Father, my God and the Rock of my salvation."'

David was a strange mixture: a musician, poet and man of prayer. He is believed to have written some, if not all, the Psalms. He was also an ambitious, scheming politician, a fine soldier and military leader, and sometimes he was a man who could not resist the strength of his own passions.

After the death of Saul and Jonathan, David enquired of God whether he should attempt to assume the kingship of Judah. The oracle gave clear encouragement. So David, with his two wives, and his men with their families, went to Hebron, and there he was anointed King of Judah. He was thirty years old.

David's ultimate ambition to rule over all the tribes of Israel as Saul had done before him, was still a long way off. The Philistine victory in which Saul perished was not as complete as the narrative suggests because Abner, Saul's right-hand man, arranged for Ishbaal, a young son of Saul, to be anointed king over his father's territory. Ishbaal was young and inexperienced, and he was a mere puppet king. The real power lay with Abner, and Abner was David's real rival.

Civil war continued, with the Philistines no doubt looking on with approval as the two factions in Israel attacked and damaged each other. It was by no means a full-scale and continuous war, and there were periods of calm and cooperation, but beneath the surface old hatreds and jealousies burned. This was evident when a planned military exercise, involving both David's and Abner's men, turned into a vicious battle with heavy losses on both sides. But the general trend of events was clear. As the Bible says, 'There was a long war between the house of Saul and the house of David; and David grew stronger and stronger, while the house of Saul became weaker and weaker.'

Part of the weakness of the house of Saul was due to a split between Ishbaal and Abner. Both became overconfident of their strength. Abner felt strong enough to take for himself a woman who had been Saul's concubine. This may have been a simple matter of the attraction between a vigorous man and an attractive woman, as Abner claimed. It may also have been some sort of political manoeuvre and statement of power, as Ishbaal thought. At this time Ishbaal felt strong enough to rebuke Abner. Abner's response was to say that Ishbaal continued in power only because of his support. He threatened to hand over to David all the tribes of Israel that he controlled.

It was no idle threat. He enquired of the various tribal leaders if they were prepared to accept David as king, and then he went to David to make an offer. David worked honourably with his old enemy, but during the negotiations Joab, David's commander, killed Abner in blood vengeance for Abner's killing of Asahel, Joab's young brother, when the military exercise got out of hand. David did not approve of this murder and mourned Abner as a great man in Israel. This showing of respect, though no doubt sincere, also presented David in a favourable light to the tribes loyal to Abner.

With Abner dead there was anarchy in Israel. Two men, seeking personal gain, tricked their way into the king's house and murdered Ishbaal. They thought that they would be welcomed by David for removing the last obstacle to his kingship, so they mutilated Ishbaal's body and took his head to David. David was outraged at such treachery and condemned the men as murderers and had them executed.

Now no one stood in David's way. The preparations made by Abner bore fruit, and the elders of the tribes of Israel came to David in Hebron and invited him to be their king, their 'shepherd and prince'. So David was again anointed at Hebron and became king of all the tribes of Israel, as Samuel had predicted so long ago.

Two things remained. The first was to claim as his capital the outstanding fortress of the territory, Jerusalem. It was held by the Jebusites, who claimed that it was so strong that it could be held by the blind and the lame. Perhaps that was true against a conventional, frontal attack, but the Jebusites had not counted on David's guile and courage. He called for volunteers to climb the water shaft that led into the city, to surprise the minimal garrison and open the city gates. Joab was among the volunteers and the city was taken. David immediately strengthened the city's defences and made it his capital.

The final thing that remained before David could feel himself settled as king takes us back to his relationship with God. The Ark of the Covenant, the sacred symbol of the presence of God, had, in Saul's day, been captured by the Philistines. Its presence had caused them trouble and illness and they had sent it away. It was eventually kept at Kiriath-jearim. David decided that it ought to be kept in Jerusalem and he went with a large company of soldiers to escort it in triumph. There was singing and dancing as the Ark made its triumphal procession.

A strange incident took place which put an end to the merry making and convinced David that he was not worthy to be the guardian of the Ark in Jerusalem. One of the oxen pulling the cart which carried the Ark stumbled. Uzzah, a soldier in the escort party, put out his hand to steady the Ark and as he touched it he immediately fell dead. It was as if the Ark was too holy to be touched. The shock of this death amid so much optimism and rejoicing made David anxious and frightened. He doubted his own worthiness and decided that for the time being the Ark must again be kept away from Jerusalem. A local man named Obed-edom took the Ark into his house and it remained there three months.

After three months David was told that Obed-edom had prospered since the Ark had been in his house. That was a sign to David that the anger of God, or whatever had caused the death of Uzzah, had now passed, and it was safe to take the Ark to Jerusalem. Again there was a great celebration and procession. As the Ark moved away from the house of Obed-edom, David made a sacrifice to God, and then he danced before the Ark as it was brought in triumph to rest in Jerusalem.

David and Uriah

David ruled over all Israel from Jerusalem. The Bible, possibly making the most of a good thing, records his victories over the Philistines, Moabites, Edomites, Ammonites and even as far afield as Syria, where he established armed outposts. Also recorded are two stories which reveal what a complex person David was, what a mixture of strength and weakness.

Feeling secure as king, particularly with Abner out of the way, David revealed the tender side of his character by making enquiries to see if there were any descendants of Saul still alive. He wished to show them kindness in memory of Jonathan and his friendship for him. A man who had been a servant in the house of Saul said that one son of Jonathan survived. He was called Mephibosheth and was a cripple. David sent for Mephibosheth, and we can imagine with what fear he came into the presence of the man who sat on the throne that might have been his father's.

David was relaxed and generous. He assured Mephibosheth that he need not be afraid, that he intended only good for him because his father had been a very dear friend. He invited Mephibosheth to live in court at the king's expense and he restored to him the lands that had traditionally belonged to the family of Saul. He also appointed servants to care for all his needs. In doing this David revealed one side of his character which we can only find admirable.

But there was another side. One afternoon, after resting, David walked on the flat roof of his palace. From there he saw a woman bathing. She was very beautiful. David had at least three wives, and in his position as king could have access to as many beautiful women as he might want. He made enquiries about the bathing woman and was told that she was called Bathsheba and was the wife of Uriah the Hittite, one of David's soldiers. Caring only to satisfy his lust, he sent for Bathsheba and had intercourse with her.

David's sin was not that he was attracted to the woman; he had no choice in that. It was that after being told that she was the wife of another man, he still had to have her. He abused his power and position as king to get what he wanted – like a spoilt child. Worse was to come.

It wasn't long before David received a message from Bathsheba telling him that she was pregnant. The implication was clear: David must be the father because her husband was away with the army at the time of conception. David descended a further rung on the ladder of deception and sin. Like many people with power who are accustomed to getting their own way, David thought he could cover things up.

He sent for Uriah, who returned from the battle lines. David pretended that what he wanted from Uriah was a report on the campaign. Such a task, reporting personally to the king, may have led Uriah to believe that he was being considered for promotion. Nothing was further from David's mind. His clever and well-practised guile was now being used to get himself out of an embarrassing situation. After receiving Uriah's report, David sent him home, expecting that the soldier on leave would gladly take the opportunity to spend the night with his wife. Bathsheba's pregnancy might then be taken to be the happy result of this unexpected leave.

David had not reckoned on the discipline, loyalty and devotion of Uriah. Far from taking advantage of the situation, Uriah spent the night in the palace headquarters, to demonstrate solidarity with his fellow soldiers in the front line by trying, as best he could, to share their hardships. When David discovered what had happened, that his plan had not worked, he invited Uriah to stay a little longer. Uriah could only obey. David invited him to a meal and forced drink on him until the soldier was drunk. But even in that condition Uriah kept to his militarist discipline. He did not stagger home and sleep with his wife as David expected, but again stayed with other soldiers in the palace area.

By now David had lost all reason in trying to deal with his self-made problem. He wrote a letter to Joab, commander of the army of Israel. The letter ordered Joab to ensure that when next an assault was made on the city they were attacking, he must see to it that Uriah was in the front line and that he got killed. The words of David were, 'Set Uriah in the forefront of the hardest fighting, and then draw back from him, that he may be struck down and die.' It was brief and to the point. And to make matters worse, David used Uriah as the messenger to carry his own death sentence.

As an able and loyal commander, Joab carried out David's orders, and Uriah was killed. A report was taken to David, including specific mention that Uriah was dead. David told the messenger to tell Joab, 'Do not let this matter trouble you, for the sword devours now one and now another.'

Bathsheba knew nothing of David's plots and deceptions, but she must have had suspicions when she heard that her husband had returned from the battle and had been in conference with the king. The wives of all soldiers know that their husbands might be killed, but the timing of Uriah's death must have troubled Bathsheba. She mourned for her hero husband, and when the time of mourning was over she became David's wife. The child was born and was a boy.

In this story we see the weaker, crueller side of David, the clay feet of this great man. But the story isn't over yet. David may have covered up his sin with more and greater sins, and he may have hidden his guilt from most people, but it could not be hidden from God. The Bible says, 'The thing that David had done displeased the Lord.'

At that time Nathan was the court prophet. He had, in some ways, taken the place of Samuel as the conscience of the nation, though he had nothing like the wide influence of Samuel. Nathan was there to advise the king and his cabinet and to try to ensure that God's law was observed in the way they lived and governed. He had the right to speak plainly and, if need be, critically to the king.

Nathan was clever, too. He pretended to be reporting to David a trivial incident of injustice that had come to his notice and which he thought the king might be interested in. He said that there were two men who lived in the same city, but in very different circumstances. One was rich, with many flocks and herds. The other was very poor, with only one young female lamb. The poor man was particularly fond of his lamb. He had reared it himself and it was almost regarded as a member of the family; it was petted and shared the family's food. A traveller, a friend of the rich man, had come from a distance to stay with his friend. The rich man left his own large flocks and herds untouched and callously took the poor man's one pet lamb, killed it and served it as a meal for his visitor.

The story made its impression on David and he was furious. He declared that whoever had been so cruel and callous deserved to die. Also, fourfold reparation should be made. Nathan listened to David's raging and then said, 'You are the man.' He went on to say that David's behaviour was not only wicked but was also base ingratitude after all that God had given him and done for him. A violent future for his family and descendants was promised. Whether Nathan meant that that would be the punishment God would inflict, or simply that the violence in David's character would inevitably be passed on to his children, we cannot tell. Perhaps the two are not really different.

David admitted his guilt and was told that though he would not suffer personally, the child with whom Bathsheba was pregnant would die. Sure enough, shortly after birth the child became ill. David was desperate. He threw himself on God's mercy. He prayed, he fasted, he kept vigil. His servants and friends tried to break him out of his self-inflicted suffering and to get him at least to eat something. But David did nothing by half measures, and his remorse and self-punishment were intense and painful to see. After a week (and what a long week that must have been), the child died. David's servants were afraid to tell him. They had seen what he did to himself while the child was ill. What might he do when he knew that the child was dead?

David soon realised that something had happened. He saw the servants whispering together and behaving oddly. He asked them if the child were dead and was told it was so. David got up from the ground where he had been lying. He bathed and cleaned himself up, changed his clothes and went into the place where the Ark of the Covenant was kept. There he prayed. Then he went to his palace and had the first meal he had taken in days.

The servants found David's behaviour strange. But there was a logic to what he did, as he told them. It was right that he should fast and weep and pray while the child lived, for there was a chance that God would forgive David and allow the child to recover. But now that the child was dead, God's decision was final and there was no point in David pleading any more.

Though David's relationship with Bathsheba started in the worst possible way there seems to have been genuine love between them. Bathsheba became pregnant again and in due course gave birth to another son, whom they named Solomon.

David in Old Age

The twelve tribes of Israel had never really been united since they entered the Promised Land. They each had their own territory and their own concerns. For most people, life was about settling, surviving and trying to get on with your neighbours. There wasn't much time for remembering that generations ago they were related to the other invaders and that the founders of their tribes had all been sons of one man, Jacob, if not the sons of one mother. David had been a remarkable king in uniting for a time all twelve tribes under his rule. It was so unusual, so surprising, that for ever afterwards people looked back to it as a golden age, a time of strength and prosperity, of peace and unity.

The bond that held the Israelites together under David was always fragile. As he grew older and his sons matured, jealousies and rivalries began to show themselves. One son, Absalom, was ambitious for the throne. He set out to gain people's favour and, when he thought the time was ripe, had himself proclaimed as king. His challenge was so effective that David had to leave Jerusalem. Absalom entered the capital and, in a calculated action, publicly took his father's concubines, which effectively declared that he had also taken the crown.

Those who remained faithful to David, under the ever-loyal Joab, tried to win back the kingdom for their master. The outcome rested on chance. Absalom was riding a mule and passed under a tree with low branches. It may have been that he was too proud to lower his head. Whatever it was, the outcome was that his hair, famous for its luxuriance, was caught in the branches. The mule went on and Absalom was left hanging, helpless.

When Joab learnt that Absalom was helpless he could not understand why his men had not killed him. He was told that David had given clear orders that if Absalom's forces were defeated

Absalom himself should be treated with mercy and not harmed. Joab was a practical and battle-hardened soldier. He did not have David's ties of kinship and he knew how much damage Absalom had done to the kingdom. Without hesitation he thrust three daggers into the heart of the trapped Absalom. The rebellion was over.

The victory and the re-establishment of his rule meant nothing to David when he heard that his son was dead. A man of the deepest feelings and never one to hide them, David's lamentation for Absalom is among the most moving stories in the Old Testament. 'And the king was deeply moved, and went up to the chamber over the gate, and wept; and as he went, he said "O my son Absalom, my son, my son Absalom! Would I had died instead of you, O Absalom, my son, my son!"'

As David grew older, the question of the succession became more pressing. Eventually an armed struggle broke out between two of his sons, Adonijah and Solomon. Scheming and plotting raged around the bed of the dying king.

Adonijah, another handsome and spoilt son of David, proclaimed himself king. He invited only those he knew would support him to be present when he seized power. The other major party was Solomon's. He had the powerful support of Nathan, the court prophet, who had admonished David for his behaviour toward Uriah, but had since been unfailingly loyal to David and Bathsheba. Bathsheba herself was David's old love, the woman he had murdered for. She was still his queen, and though older now, was still a power in the land.

It was reported to Nathan than Adonijah had claimed the throne. He went to Bathsheba and said, 'Do you not know that Adonijah has become king, and David is not even aware of it?' He suggested that there was still time to do something about it. He outlined his plan. Bathsheba accepted it and they acted it out to perfection. This is how they did it.

Bathsheba went in to see the old, dying king, her husband. She went straight to the point. 'Did you not swear to me that our son, Solomon, would succeed you on the throne? And yet, without your approval, without your consent, even without your knowledge, Adonijah has proclaimed himself king. The people don't know who to follow. They wait for your word.'

Before David could answer Nathan came in, the old, wise and trusted adviser and man of God. Nathan said, 'Are you aware, my Lord King, that Adonijah has made himself king? Was this on your instructions and have we simply not been told?'

It was a cleverly worked plot. David didn't know that Nathan and Bathsheba had planned it, though he had made enough plots in his life to have had his suspicions. David acted quickly, as he always did. 'Send for Zadok the priest and go with him and anoint Solomon.'

So they did, and as Handel has immortally told us, 'Zadok the priest and Nathan the prophet anointed Solomon king. And all the people rejoiced.' Adonijah came to Solomon and pleaded for his life. Solomon was cautious and told him that if he behaved he would live, and if he didn't he wouldn't.

And Solomon's reign began, engineered by a prophet-led conspiracy.

Solomon's Story

(The Prophets and Politics 2)

Solomon's reign was one of great show, of surface success with gathering anger and dissatisfaction beneath. Undoubtedly he was a great builder. He built great houses – one for himself, the king's palace. He built the House of the Forest of Lebanon, he built the House of Pillars. He built the Hall of Judgement and another similar building for the daughter of Pharaoh, one of his many wives. But the greatest of all his building enterprises was the House of God, known throughout history as Solomon's Temple. No expense was spared, and the temple was a marvellous example of the principle that nothing but the best is good enough for God.

So Solomon's reign looked magnificent. There were his great buildings, all done by skilled craftsmen, backed up by thousands of slaves. There were his many wives. The Book of Kings says, 'He had seven hundred wives, all princesses, and three hundred concubines.' The writer of the Book of Kings clearly disapproved of this aspect of Solomon's life, but it was not because it was judged immoral; it was because the wives were foreign women, married in political alliances, who brought with them their own foreign gods, drawing Solomon and the people of Israel away from the worship of Yahweh, God of Israel.

So Solomon had buildings and women – and wisdom. Solomon was renowned for his wisdom, which seems to have been a mixture of prudent understanding of how to get on in life and a knowledge of the natural world, a sort of early science. Buildings, wives and wisdom. The Queen of Sheba had heard of the greatness of Solomon and she came to see him for herself. It was probably called 'a fact-finding tour' and paid for by her long-suffering subjects. When she saw Solomon's display of wealth and the way things were done in Israel she was astounded. She said, 'The report was true which I heard in my own land ... I did not believe the reports until I came and my own eyes had seen it, and behold the half was not told me. Your wisdom and prosperity surpass the report which I heard.'

It was all very impressive, but it was done at a cost, both in financial and human terms. To finance Solomon's grandiose schemes, free Israelites were sold into slavery, taxes were crippling, and with so much foreign influence through Solomon's wives, the country was losing its direction. It was losing its moral foundations. Above all it was losing its devotion to Yahweh, the God of Israel, the only God. And so it was the business of a prophet, a man of God, to do something.

Solomon had a son called Rehoboam who, it was expected, would succeed to the throne on his father's death. There was in the kingdom another young man of much the same age who was distinguishing himself with his ability and quality of leadership. His name was Jeroboam. So impressive was this man that Solomon promoted him. To quote the Book of Kings, 'The man Jeroboam was very able, and when Solomon saw that the young man was industrious, he gave him charge over all the forced labour of Joseph.' ('Joseph' is another way of saying 'Israel'.)

This was a mistake on Solomon's part, because it gave this able and industrious young man close experience of the oppression of the ordinary Israelite caused by Solomon's selfish and extravagant policies. It also gave Jeroboam the chance to help those oppressed people and to win their trust.

By this time Nathan had retired or died and his place as court prophet had been taken by Ahijah. It was now Ahijah's responsibility to promote and protect the worship of Yahweh and to keep the king and the nation as loyal as possible to the God of Israel.

Ahijah had noticed Jeroboam and arranged to meet him in secret. There was a dramatic piece of prophetic action as Ahijah took off the new cloak that he was wearing and tore it into twelve pieces. He then gave ten pieces to Jeroboam and said, 'Thus says the Lord, "I am about to tear the kingdom from the hand of Solomon and will give you ten tribes."' This tearing away of the kingdom from Solomon was punishment for forsaking Yahweh. But Jeroboam was promised ten tribes, not twelve. David's faithfulness to Yahweh was rewarded by God by the tribe of Judah being left to the house of Solomon.

The odd mathematics of this prophecy and its fulfilment is due to the fact that the twelve tribes were always more of an ideal than a reality. The tribe of Levi, which was becoming more and more a sacred guild, with duties in the temple, had for all practical purposes been incorporated into the tribe of Judah.

How history repeats itself! It had been the prophet Samuel who had anointed David, undermining Saul while Saul was still on the throne. In the end that had led to civil war and to Saul's vindictive pursuit of David. In a similar way the threat posed by the plotting between Ahijah and Jeroboam was discovered by Solomon, and Jeroboam was forced to flee for his life to Egypt, where he stayed until the death of Solomon.

When Solomon died he was succeeded by his son Rehoboam, as was expected. With a new king on the throne it was now the time for people to try to throw off the yoke of oppression which Solomon had imposed on them. A deputation went to the new king and put their case to him. 'Your father made our yoke heavy. Now therefore lighten the hard service of your father and his heavy yoke upon us, and we will serve you.'

We can perhaps hear an unspoken threat there.

Rehoboam played for time. 'Give me three days to think, and then return and you shall have your answer.' He consulted his advisers. First he spoke to the older men, who had seen service in the court of Solomon, and some perhaps under David. They were clever men, accustomed to the lies and half-truths of political life. They advised that he should promise a lighter touch in his rule, even if he didn't mean it. 'If you will be a servant to this people today and serve them and speak good words to them when you answer them, then they will be your servants for ever.'

Then he asked his younger courtiers, the men with whom he had grown up, and who saw their friendship with the king as their opportunity to do well for themselves. Perhaps they were also unsure of themselves and felt that a tough beginning was their best chance for success. They advised a harsh answer.

After three days the deputation returned. They got their answer. 'My father made your yoke heavy, but I will add to your yoke; my father chastised you with whips, but I will chastise you with scorpions.'

It was a foolish answer, and Jeroboam's moment had come. In frustration and anger, ten tribes turned their backs on Solomon's son and on the house of David, and made Jeroboam their king.

Ahijah's prophecy came true. The chosen people were divided into two kingdoms. The northern kingdom under Jeroboam had ten tribes and Samaria became its capital. It retained the name Israel. The smaller southern kingdom, still loyal to Rehoboam, had Jerusalem as its capital and consisted almost entirely of the tribe of Judah – the Jews. As so began a division which has never been healed. In St John's Gospel we read, 'Jews have no dealings with Samaritans.' That famous hatred began in the days of Rehoboam and Jeroboam. The division caused bitterness, even war. And it was inspired and planned by prophets. What drove the prophets to be involved in this way was their personal loyalty to Yahweh. They wanted to see the nation keeping the Covenant, worshipping only Yahweh and living by the Law, which demanded justice and compassion for all people. That was God's plan and that is what the prophets sought; but they found loyalty to God and justice for men scarce commodities in Israel.

The Divided Kingdoms

David's remarkable talents had enabled him to bring together all twelve tribes of Israel, and for forty years he held them in an uneasy unity under his rule. His son Solomon succeeded him and he too ruled over a united Israel. Solomon's reign was remarkable for its extravagance and luxury. He made a fine impression on those outside but he was not wise enough to care for his own subjects. His lavish lifestyle and ambitious building programme caused hardship for ordinary people, and by the time he handed over to his son, Rehoboam, the nation was ready to fall apart.

Encouraged by the prophet Ahijah, Jeroboam led a revolt which resulted in ten tribes submitting to his rule, leaving Rehoboam ruling over the tribes of Judah and Benjamin. It is at that point that the history of Israel enters the period of the Divided Kingdoms, North and South, Israel and Judah.

Before this time, the name 'Israel' meant all twelve tribes descended from Jacob; after the division it meant only the northern kingdom with its capital at Samaria. Judah was the southern kingdom and retained Jerusalem as its capital.

The Books of Kings (with a roughly parallel account in the Books of Chronicles) record the history of the divided kingdoms. They follow the history of the northern kingdom, Israel, until it was defeated by the Assyrians in 721 BCE. In that catastrophe the people were deported and were swallowed up by, and integrated with, the nations around them. From that time the northern kingdom ceased to exist.

The history of Judah, the southern kingdom, is also recorded in the Books of Kings until its defeat by the armies of Babylon in 586 BCE. The people of Judah were also taken into exile – in their case into Babylon – but they retained their identity and eventually returned to their own land. So their history went on, and still goes on. We shall look at the exile and the return later.

The kingdom of Israel lasted about 200 years as a separate

nation. Judah lasted some 350 years before Babylon defeated it. During those years there were many kings, judged good or bad by the writers of the Bible. There were also many prophets who continued to proclaim the word of God, whether it was popular or not. Some of the books of the Bible bear the names of those prophets, such as Amos who prophesied in the northern kingdom, and Isaiah and many others who worked in the southern kingdom. Their books contain their teachings and sometimes record their actions. There were also other prophets who do not have a book bearing their name. It is to one of the greatest of these that we now turn – Elijah.

Elijah's Story

In a Time of Drought

The prophets who succeeded Nathan and Ahijah and who proclaimed the message of God in the divided kingdoms found that nothing much had changed. The king and the people were still attracted to the worship of other gods, and justice and compassion were still in short supply.

We are going to look at the life and work of Elijah, a prophet in the early days of the divided kingdoms. He was eventually succeeded as Yahweh's spokesman by his disciple, Elisha. Their names are easily confused, and the writers of the biblical stories themselves seem to have confused some of their exploits.

Elijah burst onto the scene in the reign of King Ahab, about twenty-five years after the time of Jeroboam I. We know nothing of his early life nor are we told how he became a prophet, nor what his qualifications were. We are not even told the name of his father, which is unusual in the Old Testament. He is simply known as Elijah the Tishbite, that is, from the village of Tishbeh in Gilead. It may be that Elijah was a title or nickname rather than a personal name because it means 'Yahweh is my God', and that was always the most important thing in Elijah's life and work.

Elijah announced that a drought that had brought great suffering to the kingdom of Israel was God's punishment for apostasy – for forsaking the true God and worshipping the gods of other nations, the *baals*. Elijah himself survived the drought because God told him to go to the Wadi Cherith, a seasonal river that was still flowing. Most versions of the Bible say that Elijah settled himself beside the brook, and twice a day ravens brought him bread and meat. We have no need to doubt God's power nor his care for Elijah, but a slight alteration to the Hebrew text makes it Arabs – Bedouin – who were the bringers of food to the prophet. Perhaps this makes better sense, especially as the story goes on to tell of the kindness of a foreign woman. Anyway, whether it were ravens or Arabs, Elijah survived by the brook Cherith until it, too, dried up.

God then told Elijah to go to Zarephath, a Phoenician village, where a widow would feed him. We might think it odd that God should sent him to a widow, and one who had a son to care for. That little one-parent family, with no male provider, would be among the most needy at any time, and particularly in the hard times of a drought. God seems to have chosen her to highlight the virtues of generosity and compassion. Elijah found the woman collecting wood for a fire. He asked for a drink and she immediately went off to fetch one. He called her back and asked for some food as well. Only then did she tell him that she was gathering fuel to cook a final meal for her son and herself. She had already accepted that after the meal she and her son would slowly starve to death.

Elijah believed that God would not have sent him to the woman unless he and the woman and her son were going to survive the famine. He told her that her meagre supplies would not run out until the drought was over. And events proved him right; the grain and the oil seemed to be divinely renewed.

Elijah was able to repay the widow's kindness when her son fell desperately ill. All the life and energy seemed to have gone out of him. Like many a parent with a sick child, the woman felt that her son's suffering was probably the result of some shortcoming in herself. Elijah ignored her real but futile anxiety and moved the boy to a more airy room. He prayed and, the Bible says, 'stretched himself upon the boy three time'. Whether this was a sort of 'kiss of life' is hard to say, but whatever it was – fresh air, Elijah's prayer or his actions – the result was that the boy recovered. A very similar story is told about Elisha.

The Bible tells of a meeting between Elijah and Ahab, the king. They clearly did not like each other, and Ahab's greeting, 'Is it you, you troubler of Israel?' suggests that they had met and disagreed before. Elijah was just as unflattering in his reply, telling the king that the long drought was of his making, because he did not worship only Yahweh, but followed the *baals* as well. He wanted to prove to the king, and indeed to all the people of Israel, that the *baals* were nothing, and the worship of them was futile. He challenged Ahab to arrange a competition between himself, who would be on the side of Yahweh, and 450 prophets of Baal. The contest was to be carried out as publicly as possible – all the people of Israel would be invited to watch.

The people and the prophets gathered, as arranged, at Mount Carmel. Elijah was confident despite being so heavily outnumbered. He had his own experience of the power of Yahweh and he believed that he could demonstrate once and for all that Yahweh was the only God. He fully expected to convince both king and people. 'How long will you go limping with two different opinions?' he asked. 'If Yahweh is God, follow him; but if Baal is God, then follow him.'

Elijah outlined the details of the competition. Both he and the prophets of Baal were to build an altar and prepare two bulls for sacrifice. They were to make all the usual preparations, except they were not to light the sacrificial fire. They were each to pray to their god to send fire from heaven to consume the sacrifice. He invited the prophets of Baal to try first.

They prayed, they chanted, they danced, they cut themselves, but from early morning until after midday nothing happened. Elijah taunted them. 'Shout louder,' he said, 'perhaps your god is asleep or has gone out for a short time.' Eventually the exhausted prophets of Baal gave up.

It was Elijah's turn. In full view of all the people he carefully built his altar. In fact what he was doing was rebuilding an old one because the prophets of Baal had made the mountain a place of worship for their gods and the ancient altar of Yahweh had been damaged. He repaired that altar and dug a trench around it which he filled with water. He then poured water over the kindling wood. This was done three times. We might wonder, Why this terrible waste of water in a time of drought? For Elijah it was a demonstration that Yahweh was lord of earth and heaven; he could send both fire to kindle on the altar and water to end the drought if he so wished. Also, there was going to be no suggestion that any fire was the result of a lucky spark.

Elijah prayed. He asked Yahweh to demonstrate that he was indeed the only God. Fire came and consumed not only the wood and the two bulls on the altar, but also the stones of the altar, and it dried up all the water in the trench. It was fire from heaven and a clear demonstration of the power of Yahweh. No one even suggested that lightning might be the beginning of a dramatic change in the weather.

There was no doubt that Elijah had made his point, and the people acknowledged it. They fell down, faces to the ground, worshipping, and they shouted, 'Yahweh, he is God! Yahweh, he is God!' Elijah seized this moment of pro-Yahweh fever and incited the crowd to kill the 450 prophets of Baal.

It must have been a terrible and memorable day; all that fervour, all that violence. And then came the clouds, small at first but getting bigger and darker. And the rain fell in torrents and the drought was over.

Elijah in Danger

Ahab may have disliked Elijah and felt uncomfortable when he was around. But he accepted Elijah's right to speak for Yahweh and to criticise whoever he thought deserved it, even the king himself. Perhaps that was due to Ahab's awareness of the history of Israel and his acceptance of the traditional role of God's spokesmen, men like Samuel and Nathan and Ahijah, all of whom criticised the king of their day. Ahab's wife, Jezebel, had no such background. Like Elijah, her name proclaimed her devotion. Jezebel means something like 'Where is Baal?' and was probably a phrase used in the worship of her god. She was a foreign princess, from Sidon. She was married to Ahab to encourage or cement a political alliance. With her background she could see no reason why Elijah or any prophet should interfere with affairs of state. She was appalled to hear how he had instigated the massacre of the prophets of Baal, who were her men. She was determined to be rid of Elijah once and for all. Foolishly, as it turned out, she threatened him before acting, and Elijah had the opportunity to flee.

He escaped south to the desert regions near Beersheba. He

was exhausted, disheartened and afraid. He had had enough. The people's enthusiasm for Yahweh, so fervent at the moment of victory on Mount Carmel, was short-lived, and with his life under threat he felt that he was completely isolated, the only person still loyal to Yahweh. He had done his best and it wasn't good enough. He had failed and he was tired of trying; he was tired of life. He asked God to let him die. In response, God sent a messenger or an angel with food, telling Elijah that he would need food to give him strength for the journey he must make.

The journey took him to Horeb, the mountain of God, a mountain with a history. Sometimes called Sinai, it was the sacred spot where Moses had met God at the Burning Bush. It was the mountain where the Law had been given to Moses amid terrifying sights and sounds, earthquake, thunder and lightning. It was where Moses had hidden in a cave and seen the back of God as he passed by. It was to this sacred spot that Elijah was sent.

He reached the mountain and sheltered in a cave. God asked him what he was doing there. Elijah replied that he had been fanatically loyal to Yahweh, but no one else seemed to care. The people of Israel worshipped the *baals*, they had destroyed the altars of Yahweh and killed his prophets. Elijah remained alone, and his enemies sought his life.

He was told to go out of the cave and stand on the mountain and Yahweh would pass by. Everything that had happened to Moses in this place must have been clearly in the mind of Elijah. And all the things traditionally associated with Yahweh at Horeb took place. First there was a great wind that shook the mountain and shattered rocks. Great winds had always been associated with the spirit and power of God, but despite that, despite all the traditions connected with Moses, Elijah knew that Yahweh was not in the wind.

Then the mountain was shaken by an earthquake, and despite knowing that the mountain quaked when God gave the Law to Moses, Elijah knew that Yahweh was not in the earthquake. Then it was fire, and Yahweh was not in the fire.

Then there was silence, profound silence. And Elijah trembled with awe as he realised that he was in the presence of God.

Again he was asked why he was there on the sacred mountain,

and he replied as before: his work as a prophet, a fanatic for Yahweh, had failed and he was fleeing for his life. Then God spoke, and the meaning of Elijah's experience became clear. No longer was God to be found only in the spectacular extravagances of nature – storm, wind and tempest. He would be found in quietness and in the ordinary things of everyday life. He would be worshipped by the keeping of the Law – that is, by the worship of Yahweh as the only god, and by a life of harmony and justice with nature and with all human beings.

God's concern about loyalty and justice was then spelt out. Elijah was instructed to do three things, all of which would have a profound effect on the future of the people of Israel. First he was to anoint Hazael as king of Syria. Hazael would be Yahweh's rod, and the damage inflicted in the wars between Syria and Israel would be God's punishment on Israel for its apostasy. Secondly, he must anoint Jehu as king of Israel. That action will signal the end of the rule of the house of Omri, Ahab's father. Like Samuel and Ahijah, Elijah was to encourage a rebellion by anointing a new king while the present king reigned. He was to place on the throne a man known to be fanatically loyal to Yahweh. Thirdly, he was to commission Elisha to be his successor as the prophet of Yahweh.

In practice it was only the third that Elijah personally carried out, though all three commissions were accomplished. Hazael did indeed become king of Syria. He caused much suffering by waging war against Israel, and it was in battle against the Syrians that Ahab himself lost his life. The second commission was carried out by Elisha, continuing the work of Elijah. He anointed Jehu, and by doing so initiated a revolt which violently disposed of Queen Jezebel and ended the rule of the house of Omri.

We may question whether these acts, done in the name of God, produced any lasting good, or whether movements born in violence always continue and end in violence. We may believe that the end never justifies the means, and that people, especially people who believe that they are led by God, should be very cautious in claiming that God has spoken to them, lest they hear their own desires and mistake them for the voice of God.

Naboth's Vineyard

Reassured by his experience on Mount Horeb, Elijah returned to Samaria and soon found himself involved in a question of justice and the abuse of power. Next to Ahab's palace in Samaria was a small vineyard which belonged to a man named Naboth, who lived in Jezreel. Ahab wanted to buy the vineyard and he intended to turn it into a vegetable garden. It was conveniently situated and he was willing to give Naboth a better vineyard in return or pay the full market price. What could be the problem? The problem was that the vineyard meant more to Naboth than its market value. It had been in his family for generations, and another piece of land, however wonderful, simply could not replace it. So Naboth refused to sell.

Ahab was used to having his own way. He went home, threw himself on his bed, turned his face to the wall and sulked. Jezebel found him in this condition. She was a good deal tougher and nastier than her husband and she scornfully asked him who was king in Israel. She told him to leave it to her. She would see about Naboth and his precious vineyard.

She set to work. She wrote, using the king's name and seal, to the elders of Jezreel, and told them to proclaim a feast day and to make Naboth the chief guest. Instructions were given that at the height of the festivities, two men were publicly to accuse Naboth of cursing God and king – blasphemy and treason. The elders might not have wanted to carry out these orders. Perhaps they suspected they came from Jezebel rather than from Ahab, but knowing the vindictiveness of the queen, they did as they were told.

The feast took place, Naboth was accused, and in the heightened emotions of the feast and perhaps inflamed by wine, the crowd became a mob, neighbours became enemies, and Naboth was dragged out of the city and stoned to death. Jezebel was told that her orders had been carried out, and triumphantly she went to her husband and said, 'Naboth's vineyard is yours, and you don't have to pay for it; Naboth is dead.' And the weak and greedy Ahab took the vineyard he so coveted.

When Elijah heard of this appalling injustice he stormed into

Samaria and confronted Ahab. Ahab knew that this time it was a more personal matter than when they had met during the drought and he had called Elijah 'the troubler of Israel'. This time he knew that he had sinned and that Elijah was bringing the judgement of God. He knew there was nothing friendly about this visit and his greeting to Elijah was, 'Have you found me, O my enemy?'

As Ahab expected, Elijah declared God's judgement. The injustice and abuse of power that had taken place could not go unpunished. Every male descendant of Ahab would be slain, ending the reign of his dynasty. As for Jezebel, the violence she had brought upon Naboth would return upon herself. Elijah said, 'The dogs shall eat Jezebel within the bounds of Jezreel.'

This gruesome prophecy was fulfilled when Elisha anointed Jehu, who swept to power and ordered queen Jezebel thrown down from an upper storey window in Jezreel. She died immediately. Her body was left where it fell. It was trampled by the soldiers' horses and dogs came and licked up the blood.

Elijah's 'Death'

Elijah's life was almost over. He had fought and worked tirelessly to proclaim the sovereignty of Yahweh. All he wanted was that the king and people of Israel should acknowledge Yahweh as the only God, and keep the Covenant by living in accordance with the Law. He had made some difference, but the job was nowhere near finished. He had chosen Elisha and made him his companion and helper so that he could take over when Elijah had gone.

His going – for we hesitate to call it his death – was unique. Elijah seemed to be well aware that his work was done and his life almost over. Elisha seemed to know this too, as did various groups of prophets who were loyal to Yahweh and who had followed and supported Elijah. Elijah wanted to be alone, perhaps alone with God, when he died. But his friends, particularly, Elisha, had other ideas. They wanted to be with him to the very end. It is the natural instinct of friends. Elijah's first attempt to slip away by himself was when he and Elisha were walking together to Gilgal. Suddenly Elijah announced a change of plan for himself. 'The Lord is sending me to Bethel,' he said. 'You stay here.'

Elisha would not hear of it and insisted on going with him to Bethel. At the shrine the resident prophets busily told Elisha what he already knew and what he dreaded, that he was going to lose his master. Elisha told them that he knew well enough, and that they should be quiet about it.

Then Elijah announced that God was sending him to Jericho, and he would go alone. But again Elisha insisted on going with him. At Jericho the resident prophets told Elisha that he was going to lose his master. Elisha, who was not known for his patience, told them that he already knew it, and that they should keep quiet.

While at Jericho, Elijah said that God was sending him to the Jordan. He told Elisha to remain in Jericho. But no, Elisha insisted on going with him. Together they reached the mighty barrier of the river. In the history of Israel two great leaders – two great servants of Yahweh – were associated with the miraculous crossing of water barriers. Moses had crossed the Red Sea and taken all Israel with him. And Joshua had taken all Israel across this very River Jordan before the triumphant capture of Jericho. Elijah took off his prophet's cloak, rolled it up and struck the water. The water divided and Elijah and Elisha crossed as if on dry ground.

It was the time for Elijah to hand over the work to Elisha. He asked the younger man what last thing he might do for him. Elisha said, 'Give me a double measure of your spirit.' He wasn't being greedy, he wasn't asking for twice the inspiration that had guided and driven Elijah. He was asking for an elder son's share of an inheritance, twice as much as a younger son. Elisha was asking to be treated as Elijah's closest spiritual descendant, so that he might worthily continue the work of God.

As they walked on together, something amazing and spectacular happened. The story tells of a chariot and horses of fire. It speaks of a whirlwind that carried Elijah away into heaven. Whatever it was, Elijah was seen no more, and his work, like his cloak, was left in the hands of Elisha.

It was this strange departure of Elijah which gave rise to speculation that perhaps he was not really dead; perhaps he was around somewhere and would return when he was needed. The speculations and the legends grew, and in the penultimate verse of the last chapter of the last book in the Old Testament we read, 'Behold, I will send you Elijah the prophet before the great and terrible day of the Lord comes.' So Elijah was expected to return before the day of the Lord, before the Messiah came.

For Jews the wait goes on, and a chair is set for Elijah at the Passover *seder*, the ritual meal, in the hope that he will return and usher in the Messianic age. For Christians he returned in the person of John the Baptist. John dressed like Elijah; he was a stern and fierce champion of the Lord, a critic of royalty and of the abuse of power. And Jesus said of him, 'If you are willing to accept it, he is Elijah who is to come.' What an example of commitment Elijah left.

The Written Prophets

A traditional way of classifying the prophets of the Old Testament has been to speak of the three Major Prophets and the twelve Minor Prophets.

The three Major Prophets are Isaiah, Jeremiah and Ezekiel. They are major because of the importance of their teaching. They are also major because of the length of their books. Isaiah (though it contains the work of three prophets under one name) contains sixty-six chapters. Jeremiah contains fifty-two chapters, and the five chapters of the Book of Lamentations are sometimes attributed to him. Ezekiel contains forty-eight chapters. We therefore have a large portion of the teaching of these prophets, which has been recorded either by themselves or by their disciples.

The twelve Minor Prophets run from Hosea to Malachi in the Old Testament table of contents. Most of them are short books. This may be because the prophet's ministry was brief or because he said little. Perhaps only the most important teaching has been recorded and preserved, or perhaps much of what they said has been lost.

The prophetic books do not contain much narrative. They are books of teaching, containing prophecies, oracles, poems, visions, parables – both spoken and acted – all the devices used by the prophets to try to drive home their message. Because there is very little narrative, it makes the telling of their story rather difficult.

What never changes is the role of the prophet. He is always a man called by God to proclaim God's word to his own generation and carry forward the working out of God's plan. He is concerned with every part of life, with what goes on in the home, in the marketplace and in the corridors of power, as much as what goes on in the temple.

Whenever God's justice and truth were flouted, the prophet spoke out demanding that the offender, whether king or commoner, hear the Word of the Lord, and change their ways.

We shall see how, because of their fervour for Yahweh, the prophets were constantly involved in politics, economics and matters of justice.

The Book of Amos

(The Written Prophets 1)

God sometimes calls the most unlikely people to be his messengers and to do his work.

The eighth century BCE was a prosperous time in Israel, though the peak of prosperity had passed and economic depression was beginning to affect all but the very rich. On the throne was King Jeroboam II. He was harshly judged by the writers of the Old Testament. The second Book of Kings records his reign in a mere seven verses, and the verdict is, 'He did what was wrong in the eyes of the Lord.' But the writer cannot avoid recording that 'he reigned for forty-one years'. In those days, as in these days in unstable parts of the world, anyone who reigns for forty-one years is a very successful ruler, whatever judgement the biblical writers might pass on him.

The historian of the Book of Kings passed his judgement on Jeroboam because he allowed and encouraged the people of his kingdom to worship gods other than Yahweh, the God of their ancestors, the God of Abraham, Isaac, Jacob, Moses, David and Elijah. That was Jeroboam's sin, and no matter how successful his armies were in making the land safe for the people, no matter how successful his economic policies were in making the country prosperous and peaceful, no matter how happy the citizens of Israel were, in the eyes of the biblical writers he was a bad king because he did not promote and enforce the worship of Yahweh, the one true God.

The political situation was that the collection of tribes over which David had reigned had split up in the reign of David's grandson, Rehoboam. The division of the tribes was not precise. Roughly speaking, Judah and Benjamin remained loyal to the house of David. They formed the southern kingdom known as Judah. The other ten tribes broke away and formed a separate kingdom in the north. This bigger kingdom was called Israel (or sometimes Ephraim), and it was from its capital, Samaria, that Jeroboam II reigned.

We can imagine that the view from his palace in Samaria was a pleasing one. The king lived in considerable luxury, and his friends – the courtiers, military leaders, politicians and civil servants – also enjoyed a high standard of living. They were rich, they were secure and they were complacent. They seemed to be unaware, or they didn't care, that the majority of their fellow Israelites lived in far poorer conditions, some in terrible poverty.

We might see similarities between life in Samaria in the eighth century BCE and life in developed Western countries today. There are differences, of course, and perhaps the greatest is that at the moment we don't seem to have an Amos. Samaria did. Amos burst upon the scene, disturbing life in Samaria, a gadfly who believed he had no choice; he had to sting people.

The irony was that Amos wasn't even an Israelite. He didn't belong to the northern kingdom. He came from the village of Tekoa in Judah. Nor was he a professional religious expert, a priest or a member of a school of prophets. He was a prosperous farmer who kept sheep and grew figs. But he was so filled with the conviction that God had sent him to Samaria that he thundered out his message paying no regard to whether he upset people or not. The vigour and the force of Amos's preaching reflected the power of the message which God had given him to deliver. He said, 'The Lord roars from Zion and thunders from Jerusalem.' And Amos was ready to do as much roaring and thundering as might be necessary to deliver God's word.

His opening message may not have been unacceptable or displeasing to the people of Samaria. He began by condemning their rivals and their enemies. First he condemned Syria, with its capital, then as now, at Damascus.

'Thus says the Lord, "For crime after crime of Damascus, I will grant them no reprieve."' Then he condemned the Philistines, the traditional enemies: 'Thus says the Lord, "For crime after crime of Gaza, I will grant them no reprieve."' Then it's 'crime after crime of Tyre; crime after crime of Edom, of Ammon, of Moab'. And then, and probably particularly enjoyable for the Israelites to hear, 'For crime after crime of Judah...' How good to hear that arrogant, self-satisfied southern kingdom condemned by God! 'For crime after of Judah I will grant them no reprieve.'

But Amos was saving up the worst for last. 'Thus says the Lord, "For crime after crime of Israel I will grant them no reprieve."' And he spelt out the sins, the crimes for which the people of Samaria were condemned: God will grant them no reprieve because they sell the innocent for silver and the destitute for a pair of shoes. They grind the faces of the poor into the earth and brush the humble out of their way.

The sins of Israel are the sins of an unjust society, in which the rich were getting richer and more complacent, and the poor were getting poorer and more hopeless. The catalogue of sins which Amos lists is very graphic and it shows how carefully he had observed the way of life in Samaria, how detailed his knowledge was. He had wandered about the markets and the streets. He had visited the rich suburbs and watched the rich at play, and he had spent time in the squalor of the backstreets and watched the poor in their misery.

His message was that the people of Israel had forgotten God and his laws. They might go through many of the motions of religious practice, but their behaviour revealed that it was simply lip service. They flouted God's laws by despising and belittling their fellow men and women.

He spoke out against the rich, lazy women of Samaria who sprawled on ivory couches and called their servants to bring drinks, while they feasted on veal and were entertained by musicians.

He spoke out against the traders who, wanting to be like the rich, would stop at nothing to make a profit. They mixed dust and husks in the grain to make it go further. They fixed their scales to give short measure. They longed for the Sabbath to be over so that they could get back to their trading and their cheating.

As a true prophet, Amos never flinched. He never drew back from delivering an unpalatable message, however unpopular it might make him. He said that God was revolted by the way the poor and helpless were being treated. Even the regular observance of religious festivals didn't please God; it didn't compensate for their oppression of the poor. God said, 'I hate, I spurn your pilgrim feasts; I will not delight in your sacred ceremonies ... Spare me the sound of your songs; I cannot endure the music of your lutes. Rather, let justice roll on like a river, and righteousness like an ever-flowing stream.' That was what God wanted – justice and righteousness.

It is not surprising that Amos was reported to the authorities. It was Amaziah the priest who dutifully told the king what was going on. We are not told what the king's reaction was, but we do know that Amaziah went back to Amos and rather scornfully told him to get out of Israel and go back to Judah and do his raving and prophesying there. He seems to have assumed that Amos was a professional prophet who earned his living by his fierce, but possibly insincere, outbursts.

In reply Amos said that he was no prophet. He was a shepherd and a farmer. The words he used suggest that was a man of independent means. He did not need to see visions and spout prophecies in order to earn a living. He did not choose to come to Samaria; God had sent him. He explained, 'The Lord took me as I followed the flock and said to me, "Go and prophesy to my people Israel."' For Amos there was no choice, no decision to make. It was God's doing: 'The lion has roared; who is not terrified? The Lord has spoken; who will not prophesy?'

He poured scorn on those who fancied themselves to be religious and told their friends they were looking forward to the day of the Lord. They thought the day of the Lord would be a time when Israel would become the greatest of the nations and they, the people of Israel, would be rulers on earth, with their security, their comfort and their luxury guaranteed.

'You don't know what your are talking about,' said Amos. 'The day of the Lord will bring judgement on you; you are foolish to look for its coming.' In the words of the Bible – 'Fools who long for the day of the Lord, what will the day of the Lord mean to you? It will be darkness and not light.' And the darkness and judgement of that day will be inescapable. 'It will be as when a man runs from a lion, and a bear meets him, or turns into a house and leans his hand on the wall (thinking he is safe) and a snake bites him.' Man's inhumanity to man deserves punishment, and God's judgement is inescapable.

The punishment that would come would be military defeat and political overthrow, with all the suffering that would entail. God would use other nations as his rod. Samaria would be destroyed and its people would be the slaves of a foreign people. What could be worse for those who considered themselves God's favourites?

But Amos's message, like that of all the prophets, was not unrelieved gloom and doom. Though God's judgement lay over the land, not all would be destroyed; a remnant would be saved. Amos spoke from his own experience. 'As a shepherd rescues out of the jaws of a lion two shin bones or the tip of an ear, so shall the Israelites who live in Samaria be rescued.'

God does not want to punish and destroy, but justice must be done. And when the price has been paid and the sentence has been served, then God will be able to restore Israel. '"A time is coming," says the Lord, "when I will restore the fortunes of my people Israel ... Once more I will plant them on their own soil, and they shall never again be uprooted."'

Amos was right about the punishment. The Assyrians attacked Israel. They destroyed Samaria and took many people into captivity. Other defeated peoples were settled in Israel, and through intermarriage the identity of the nation as descendants of Jacob disappeared. It was Amos's own nation, the people of Judah, who experienced both the punishment he foresaw and the restoration he hoped for. His stern words, which are the words of God, continue to ring in the ears of Jews and Christians alike, challenging and warning. 'Let justice roll on like a river and righteousness like an ever-flowing stream.'

The Book of Isaiah

(The Written Prophets 2)

It is generally agreed by scholars that the biblical Book of Isaiah contains the prophecies of *three* separate men. There are good reasons for this opinion. The literary style of each section differs. If we were to connect together passages from the writings of Charles Dickens, Thomas Hardy and Salman Rushdie, experts (and many who are not experts) would know that the whole was not written by the same person. So it is with the Book of Isaiah. Another, and perhaps more powerful, reason is that the historical settings of the three parts of the book are quite different. They fit more comfortably into three distinct periods – the eighth century monarchy in Judah, the sixth century exile in Babylon, and the fifth century period of reconstruction in Jerusalem after the return from exile. (All these dates are, of course, BCE.)

The three divisions of the Book are:

Chapters 1–39 First Isaiah – also called Proto-Isaiah.

Chapters 40–55 Second Isaiah – also called Deutero-Isaiah.

Chapters 56–66 Third Isaiah – also called Trito-Isaiah.

We are now going to look at the ministry and teaching of the First Isaiah. He is sometimes called Isaiah of Jerusalem, or the States-man Prophet. As we shall see, he continues the prophetic task of proclaiming God's word and will to his own generation and by doing so involves himself fully in the social and political life of his country.

Besides the book that bears his name we can find brief parallel information about Isaiah in the Second Book of Kings, Chapters 18 and 19, and he gets the briefest of mentions in II Chronicles, Chapter 32.

The Historical Setting

It is a sad fact of history and of human experience that the so-called 'great powers' use their strength to dominate and terrorise weaker nations. Sometimes they claim to be bringing the benefits of their own 'superior' way of life, but generally their desire for power and loot is undisguised. Their leaders hang on to power by promising prosperity and security, and if they don't deliver, the people will get rid of them and find another leader. The change might be accomplished by ballot, by heredity, by coup or by assassination. The 'great power' in the days of Isaiah of Jerusalem was Assyria, and they had just changed their leader.

Tiglath-pileser III was the new man. He was ruthless and ambitious, and in 745 BCE, when his weak predecessor was assassinated, he seized the throne. His aim was to restore the strength of Assyria and extend its empire over all the nations of the Middle East. He sought timber, mineral riches, loot and tribute from the smaller nations. He also wanted access to Egypt, his only real rival for power.

The ambitions of Assyria created a time of political turmoil throughout the Middle East, and the divided kingdoms of Israel and Judah couldn't help but be deeply involved. Israel, the larger northern kingdom had been warned by the prophet Amos that its days were numbered. The decline and fall he promised were mirrored in the fortunes of the Israelite monarchy. King followed king in rapid succession – five in fifteen years. Death was usually by assassination, and the assassins who gained the throne usually lost it in the same way. The death throes of Israel were presided over by Hoshea, a puppet king, holding his throne by courtesy of the Assyrian superpower. In the end, thinking an alliance with Egypt would free him from the Assyrian yoke, Hoshea rebelled. Assyrian reprisals were swift and decisive. The cities of Israel were attacked and destroyed, and in 721 BCE Samaria was besieged, captured and sacked. Many of the people were deported, and conquered peoples from other lands were settled among the survivors in Samaria. Over the years, intermarriage took place, and those people of mixed race who lived in Samaria became the Samaritans despised by later generations of Jews. To all intents and purposes, the year 721 BCE marked the end of the northern kingdom of Israel; it became no more than an unimportant outpost of the Assyrian empire.

With all that happening in the northern kingdom it was inevitable that Judah, the southern kingdom, would also be greatly affected by these events on the international scene.

Isaiah's Story

The Call

Just about the time that Tiglath-pileser seized power in Assyria, another event of perhaps greater importance happened in Jerusalem. Unlike the Assyrian monarch's high-profile coming to power, what happened in Jerusalem probably had no witnesses. A man named Isaiah, the son of Amoz, had an encounter with God. Recording the event much later, he wrote, 'In the year of King Uzziah's death I saw the Lord.' This experience set Isaiah on a course of proclaiming God's will for the nation during the reigns of three subsequent kings – Jotham, Ahaz and Hezekiah. Isaiah's was a long ministry, and it plunged the prophet into all the political events of his time. His responsibility, placed on him by God, was to advise the king of God's will, and to try to get him to follow it rather than to take what might seem to be the most obvious, the most shrewd or the most politically advantageous course.

Because of his close involvement in matters of state and his easy access to the kings he served, Isaiah has sometimes been called the statesman prophet. Certainly he seemed comfortable in the best society of Jerusalem. He was quite at home in the great houses and royal palaces of the city, and he must have been a frequent visitor and worshipper in the temple. His familiarity with the temple, its furnishings and rituals helped to shape his life-changing encounter with God.

Isaiah's account of the experience is very moving but also rather confusing. The immediate impression he had was of the greatness of God. He doesn't try to describe God; to do such a thing would come close to making a word idol, and offending against the second commandment. Like Moses, Isaiah knows that he cannot look on God with safety, and his eyes drop to the hem or skirt of God's robe. Even that seems to fill the temple, so overwhelming was the impression of the presence of God.

Then he sees the seraphim. Perhaps in Isaiah's mind there is a picture of the court of heaven, where God sits as Judge, surrounded by the members of the heavenly court – seraphim, cherubim, angels and archangels. Or it may be that in his state of heightened awareness many of the things that he saw daily in the temple took on a special significance. He mentions the fire and tongs which were used in the sacrificial ritual. He mentions the threshold over which he must have stepped many times. It may be that the seraphim were the carvings of winged creatures which formed a part of the furnishings of the Holy of Holies.

The seraphim exist to praise God, and they sing of God's nature, his holiness and his majesty. Many, many times Isaiah must have heard the holiness of God praised in the temple, but never before had it made such a profound impression on him. It is a shaking, shattering experience, and in his vision he feels the foundations of the temple shake. The foundations of his own life and of the life of the nation are also being shaken. The smoke of the altar fills the temple and God is hidden, saving Isaiah from the danger of looking on God. He is in the presence of God, just as the Israelites had been when the pillar of cloud led them in the wilderness, and when God was present in cloud and smoke on Mount Sinai. Isaiah was being taken deep into his own and his nation's past.

He cannot join in the seraphim's hymn of praise. Startlingly alive to the holiness of God, Isaiah is painfully aware of his own impurity. He is no different from his fellow countrymen. He dwells 'in the midst of a people of unclean lips'. He is bowed down by guilt.

At the command of God, one of the seraphim takes a coal from the altar fire, using the tongs set there for the purpose. With it he touches Isaiah's mouth, symbolically cleansing his lips and making him fit to speak with God. Forgiven and purified, Isaiah hears the voice of Yahweh telling the court of heaven that there is a task to be carried out on earth, and asking for a volunteer. 'Whom shall I send, and who will go for us?'

Isaiah is not yet sure what the task will be, but he has been so overwhelmed by the vision of God's greatness, and feels so free from the burden of his guilt that he dares to make a human voice sound in the court of heaven. 'Here am I. Send me.'

His offer is accepted. Only then does he discover the discouraging fact that his message will be proclaimed to people who have strayed so far from God that they will be incapable of hearing and obeying God's word.

Isaiah's task will be twofold. First, he is to teach the rulers and politicians of Jerusalem how God wants them to act when under threat from foreign powers. Secondly, he is to speak to the people of Judah about their moral behaviour and their religious practices. He will tell them of God's plan for the city and for the nation, both in the immediate future and in the long term. But they will not understand; they will not obey until 'cities lie waste without inhabitant, and houses without men, and the land is utterly desolate'.

So Isaiah was called and commissioned by God to a thankless task. His message was to be one of gloom shot through with brilliant shafts of light and hope. No matter how obstinate and disobedient God's people might be, God himself is faithful and his power and mercy are such that he will save the people of Judah despite themselves.

The Task

The first political crisis in which Isaiah had to speak out was in 734 BCE, when Assyria moved its army down the Mediterranean coast to attack the cities of the Philistines. It overstretched itself and, for the first time since the accession of Tiglath-pileser, it began to look vulnerable. Syria and Israel saw this as an opportunity to free themselves from Assyrian rule. They decided to rebel and they invited Ahaz, king of Judah, to join them.

Isaiah advised Ahaz, 'Take heed, be still, do not fear.' He promised Ahaz that the kings of Syria and Israel were like smouldering torches; they would quickly be extinguished. No action was necessary to deal with them. All Ahaz needed to do was to trust God. Isaiah promised that God would give a sign which would signal the brevity of the alliance between Syria and Israel. The words he used have become well known and very important to Christians as predicting the birth of Jesus. Isaiah said, 'A young woman shall conceive and bear a son, and shall call his name Immanuel ... Before the child knows how to refuse the evil and choose the good, the land before whose two kings you are in dread will be deserted.'

The name to be given to the child is Immanuel, which means 'God with us'. It stresses the grounds for the trust in God which Isaiah calls Ahaz to show. And before the child is old enough to know what is right and what is wrong, Syria and Israel will be defeated.

Despite Isaiah's comforting words and signs, Ahaz was desperately afraid of the power of Assyria. He informed his Assyrian overlords about the Syrian-Israelite alliance and tried to guarantee Judah's continuing safety and independence by paying tribute. Isaiah thought that was a mistake. Ahaz should not have paid because, once started, it would never end. Ahaz should have kept still, done nothing, except to trust in Yahweh:

> ...for thus says the Lord God, the Holy One of Israel,
> in returning and rest you shall be saved;
> in quietness and in trust shall be your strength.

Like other prophets, Isaiah was ready to use any method to drive his message home. When Sargon, king of Assyria, was attacking the coastal city of Ashdod, Isaiah was told by God to go about Jerusalem naked and barefoot. He did this for three years. It was a sign that in such a shameful way will the king of Assyria lead off into captivity the rulers of Egypt and any other nation foolish enough to rebel against him.

When the inevitable happened and Samaria fell, Israel became part of the Assyrian empire. This meant that Judah's northern boundary was Assyria's southernmost boundary. The king of Judah knew of Assyria's ambitions, and that it would need to conquer Judah before marching on toward Egypt, the final goal. What should he do?

Isaiah was shrewd. He drew lessons from the fate of the northern kingdom. He said that even when Samaria was in ruins, the delusions of grandeur of the citizens made them think that they were safe and that prosperity would return. They had said,

'The bricks may have fallen, but we will build with expensive stone; the common sycamores may have been cut down, but we shall have time to grow splendid cedars.'

How arrogant, how unrealistic, and how stupid! What a failure to see God's hand and God's judgement, said Isaiah. Judah should learn from Israel's failures.

But kings are political creatures. On the boundaries of empires, subject nations are constantly trying to free themselves from the shackles of their overlords. When Judah was threatened from the north it was natural to look to the south for help. That meant looking to Egypt. But in Isaiah's time, Egypt's days of power were a memory rather than a reality. He knew there was no real help to be found there, and again he counselled trust in God rather than frenzied human activity, whether diplomatic or military. He said that the Egyptians were divided against themselves, their famous sages were fools, their men were as weak as women. There was no help or safety to be found in Egypt.

In the year 705 BCE the great Assyrian king, Sargon, was succeeded by Sennacherib. As power changed hands, the nation was vulnerable. At that time Assyria's close neighbour, Babylon, was growing in strength and took the opportunity to rebel. While Sennacherib was occupied with putting down the Babylonian revolt, Hezekiah, the new king of Judah, disdaining Isaiah's advice, joined an alliance with Egypt and Philistia. Their rebellion took the form of ceasing to pay tribute. But they had misjudged and underestimated Sennacherib. He soon dealt with Babylon, and by 701 had invaded Judah. Many cities of Judah were taken or destroyed and Jerusalem was besieged.

Isaiah described the situation: 'Your country lies desolate, your cities are burned with fire; in your very presence aliens devour your land, it is desolate...' As always he advocated trust in God. Human help and alliances cannot be trusted: 'Woe to the rebellious children ... who set out to go down to Egypt without asking for my counsel ... The protection of Pharaoh shall turn to your shame.'

Jerusalem was taken but it wasn't destroyed. The Second Book of Kings tells a remarkable story. As the Assyrian armies approached Jerusalem, having wrought havoc elsewhere in Judah, Isaiah said that God's word in this situation was:

> He shall not enter this city
> nor shoot an arrow there,
> he shall not advance against it with shield
> nor cast up a siege-ramp against it.
> By the way on which he came he shall go back;
> this city he shall not enter.

They were brave words and seemed in the circumstances quite unrealistic. But as events worked out it seemed as if some plague or terrible epidemic struck the camp of the Assyrians, and the next morning they were gone – as Isaiah had prophesied.

Some damage had been done. The treasures of the temple were looted or perhaps they were used to buy off Assyria and save the city from being sacked. And so Isaiah's worst fears were not fulfilled. Certainly there was plenty of chaos and disaster, but it was never the last word; always there was hope. Ever since his vision of God in the temple, the overwhelming conviction that inspired Isaiah was of the power and holiness of God. He was sure that God's will could not be denied; it would be accomplished however much people rebelled against him. The Holy One of Israel had a plan, a destiny, not only for the chosen people but all people, and that plan would be worked out in God's own time. The vision had showed Isaiah that the justice of God called for justice among men. So, rather like Amos, he spoke out against the oppression of the weak and the perverting of justice. He criticised the rich for their thoughtless luxury and greed. He stressed that God wanted obedience, not the formal practice of rituals:

> What to me is the multitude of your sacrifices?' says the
>   Lord;
> I have had enough of burnt offerings of rams
> and the fat of fed beasts;
> I do not delight in the blood of bulls, or of lambs, or of
>   he-goats...
> cease to do evil, learn to do good;
> seek justice, correct oppression;
> defend the fatherless, plead for the widow.

Because he had seen God's power and majesty, Isaiah proclaimed that however often Israel might break the Covenant, God would always be faithful and there would always be a small group – a remnant, Isaiah called them – who would keep the faith: 'In that day the Lord will extend his hand yet a second time to recover the remnant that is left of his people.'

Hope for the Future: an Ideal Ruler

Because God's power and holiness cannot, in the end, be denied, people can be sure that God will not forget or forsake the Covenant that he made with Abraham, Isaac, Jacob, Moses and David. The promise is made that God will act. He will send his Anointed One, who will be of David's line. He will be filled with the Spirit of God and will overflow with God-given gifts.

> The Spirit of the Lord shall rest upon him,
> the spirit of wisdom and understanding,
> the spirit of counsel and might,
> the spirit of knowledge and the fear of the Lord.
> And his delight shall be in the fear of the Lord.

The coming of the Anointed One, the Messiah, will bring about an age of unprecedented blessings for the world. There will be no violence, no predators, no victims – instead universal harmony and peace. It may sound unrealistic, but as a picture, a vision to inspire hope, it has few equals.

> The wolf shall dwell with the lamb,
> and the leopard shall lie down with the kid,
> and the calf and the lion and the fatling together,
> and a little child shall lead them.
> The cow and the bear shall feed;
> their young shall lie down together;
> and the lion shall eat straw like the ox.
> The sucking child shall play over the hole of the asp,
> and the weaned child shall put his hand on the adder's
>   den.

> They shall not hurt or destroy in all my holy mountain;
> for the earth shall be full of the knowledge of the Lord
> as the waters cover the sea.

Throughout his working life, Isaiah was close to the royal family of Judah, especially to King Hezekiah. He had seen the weakness of even the best of human rulers. He knew the frailty of every human being and the snares and temptations of power. Believing that it was God's nature to be Immanuel – 'God with us' – Isaiah came to believe that God would send his own representative to rule on earth and he would embody all the qualities of a perfect ruler. He would be:

> Wonderful Counsellor, Mighty God,
> Everlasting Father, Prince of Peace.
> Of the increase of his government and of peace
> there will be no end,
> upon the throne of David, and over his kingdom,
> to establish it, and to uphold it
> with justice and with righteousness...

It is this Messianic hope, this conviction that God will come among his people, that makes the writings of Isaiah of Jerusalem so precious to Christians. Often he seems to paint a picture of God's Anointed One whom Christians see fulfilled in Jesus, through whom God's plan would finally be carried forward.

The Bible does not record how Isaiah's ministry ended, nor how he died. Tradition says that he was a martyr, put to death in the reign of King Manasseh. Whether that is true or whether he died in honourable and peaceful old age, he stands as one of the great prophets of the Old Testament, a man who had met God and whose life was changed for ever by that meeting.

The Book of Hosea

(The Written Prophets 3)

The Book of Hosea is unique because it is the only surviving prophecy directed to Israel by a citizen of the northern kingdom. Amos had prophesied in Samaria, but he was himself from the south.

Hosea's call to prophecy was not by an overwhelming vision of God as it was for Isaiah and Ezekiel. He had no conviction, as Jeremiah did, that he had been born for the task. Hosea's call to be a prophet came in the form of a command from God to get married.

What happened in his marriage, how his love was strained and tested, how he still loved his unfaithful wife, all became for Hosea a mirror of God's love for Israel. Israel was an unfaithful wife to Yahweh. Could she be brought to her senses and return to the God who loved her? Hosea begs and pleads. He offers God's love and forgiveness freely; but people have a habit of despising and undervaluing anything that is free.

In reading Hosea (and other books in the Old Testament) it is helpful to be aware that the name Ephraim is often used instead of Israel. The names are interchangeable, rather like Great Britain and the UK.

References have been included for those who want them.

Hosea's Story

We must start with Hosea's private life, because that is what he starts with. It is the sort of tale of adultery and marital breakdown that is today the common theme of television soap operas. For Hosea, his disastrous marriage and his task as a prophet were inextricably intertwined.

We know a little about the married lives of several prophets. Isaiah seems to have been happily married and had a family. Ezekiel tells us about the death of his beloved wife – 'the delight of his eyes', he calls her. Jeremiah quite deliberately chose not to be married so that he would have no one to comfort him, just as the nation would have no comforter when it collapsed and was taken into exile. But no prophet tells us as much about his married life as does Hosea.

His life as a prophet began when God said to him, 'Go, take to yourself an adulterous wife.' (1:2) We cannot be certain that Gomer was a known adulteress when Hosea married her, or whether that came later. Whatever her reputation, clean or tarnished, Hosea obeyed God's command and married her.

They had a child, a son. God said, 'Call him Jezreel.' (1:4) Why Jezreel? Jezreel had been the site of a massacre, where Jehu had Jezebel thrown out of a window to her death, and where the remaining members of the royal house of Israel had been wiped out. Jehu was the great-grandfather of the king on the throne of Israel in Hosea's day, Jeroboam II. So Hosea's king belonged to a dynasty founded on blood and maintained by violence. Because of that, God says that it will also end in blood. And Jezreel, the name given to Hosea's first child, was to be a constant witness to what was coming.

There was a second child and this time it was a girl. Perhaps by this time Gomer was cheating on her husband and going off with other men. Whereas the Bible says of the first child that 'she bore him a son', – the 'him' being Hosea – when she had her daughter, it does not mention Hosea. God again told him what name the child was to have. She was to be called Lo-Ruhamah, which means 'not comforted'. If the girl was the child of another man, then perhaps Hosea felt unable to comfort Gomer as she recovered from childbirth. We don't know. What we do know is that Hosea again saw the thoughts and intentions of God in the name of the child. Israel was God's child. He had brought his child out of Egypt. He loved it. He helped it to walk, he led it, taught it, healed it. (11:1–4) But Israel had grown away from God. She shows no gratitude and does not return God's love. So God is at the end of his tether; no longer will he comfort Israel. And so Hosea's daughter was called Lo-Ruhamah.

The third child is another son. He is given the name Lo-Ammi, which means 'not my people'. Again it could mean that Hosea was not the father. It certainly means that God has passed judgement on Israel and abandoned the covenant that held them together. The words 'my people' was a time-honoured and very important description of Israel. When God spoke to Moses at the Burning Bush he said, 'I have seen the misery of "my people" in Egypt ... so now go, I am sending you to Pharaoh to bring "my people" the Israelites out of Egypt.' (Exodus 3:7,10) And what was Moses' constant plea to Pharaoh? 'Let my people go.' It wasn't Moses' people, but God's people. (Ex. 8:16) But all that had changed. By their selfish lives and by their disregard of God they had forfeited their position as God's people. And so Hosea's second son was named Lo-Ammi, 'not my people'.

So Hosea was a man with three children and a wife he couldn't trust. After the birth of the third child, Gomer gave up any pretence that she was a faithful wife and mother. She went off to 'enjoy herself'. She found many men who were willing to satisfy her thirst for sexual variety. She sank low, and may have become a concubine or even a slave.

It is a story of remarkable love and patience on the part of Hosea, and we don't know the end of the story. We are never told whether Gomer settled down and eventually realised what a remarkable husband she had.

Hosea pondered about what had happened to him and what

he had done about it. As he thought about it he recalled God's words to him when he had been told to take the extraordinary step of paying to get his own wife back. Those words had sunk deeply into his mind. God had said, 'Love her as the Lord loves the Israelites though they turn to other gods.'

The trouble with the people of Israel in Hosea's day was that they thought they were religious; they thought they worshipped Yahweh the God of Israel. And they thought they must be doing things right because most of them were comfortable and prosperous. Jeroboam II had been on the throne a long time. He ensured peace for his country by paying tribute to Assyria, buying them off. Life seemed secure; there was an ease about everything. They lived in an affluent society.

They were quite sure that their prosperity was a sign of God's favour, just as misfortune would have been a sign of his displeasure. To them, that was common knowledge, the accepted theology, and it was enshrined in many of their proverbs. So they knew they were enjoying God's favour. In reality they were like a fruit, shiny and healthy-looking on the outside, but rotten on the inside. Hosea knew that; and he longed to persuade his fellow countrymen to look at themselves and come to know themselves, and admit their failings, because only then could they begin to put things right.

Hosea realised that his own painful and humiliating experiences were a reflection of God's experiences with Israel. They had been chosen by God and had entered a Covenant with him – 'You shall be my people, and I will be your God.' But when the northern kingdom separated from the south after the reign of Solomon, they began to worship Yahweh in the form of a bull, 'the calf of Samaria'. (8:5) This had been done as a political manoeuvre, to try to consolidate the independence of the northern kingdom. It was intended to provide a substitute for the worship of Yahweh in the temple in Jerusalem, to stop people's eyes straying to that holy city whenever they thought of God. But God had said, 'Thou shalt not make graven images,' and to worship him in the form of a calf could only be hateful to him. Hosea realised that.

There was more wrong with the religious practices of the

people of Israel. They let themselves be influenced by the religion of the farming communities among whom they lived. These people of the land had long worshipped fertility gods. The male gods they called *baals*, which means 'lords' or even 'husbands' – and that word must have struck Hosea strongly. The *baals* were thought to be married to the local land, and that marriage ensured the fertility of the crops and livestock. Alongside the *baals* they often worshipped goddesses, whose symbol was a tree or wooden pole. The *baal* was married to her too, and worship at their shrines often involved intercourse with temple prostitutes. It was supposed to promote the abundance of nature. Some of Hosea's countrymen worshipped such goddesses alongside Yahweh.

To Hosea, the parallel was blindingly obvious. Just as Gomer had left him and gone off with other men, so Israel, Yahweh's chosen bride, had gone off with other gods. The trouble was that they were so sure of themselves that they were unaware of their faults. They could not see that they were bringing disaster on themselves. God said, 'A people without understanding will come to ruin.' (4:14)

There were so many things wrong in the fabric of the nation. Its people were promiscuous, they were greedy, they were cruel. So cruel that he can compare them with a story in the Book of Judges (Ch. 19), in which the mayhem included rape and murder. And it was not just the common people; even the priests and the prophets 'stumble'. (4:4,5) They try to ensure survival by making political alliances, now with this country, now with that. They are like a silly dove, fluttering about, not knowing where to go. (7:11) They are so corrupt that God himself pushes them toward the edge. He is like a moth eating away a garment, like mildew spoiling it. Hosea loves his similes. God says, 'I will be like a lion to Ephraim, like a great lion to Judah. I will tear them in pieces and go away; I will carry them off with no one to rescue them.' (5:14)

Israel is just like Gomer. How hurt Yahweh must be! In a lovely poem in Chapter 2, Hosea pours out some of the pain he feels, knowing that God must feel it too. How he has been hurt, and wants to hurt in return! So he will curtail Gomer's freedom and will expose her to ridicule. (2:6,10) But despite his humiliation and pain, despite everything Gomer has done to him, Hosea realises that he still loves her. He wants her back. More than anything he wants her to realise how much more he loves her than any of the other men she has been with. He wants her to say, 'I will go back to my husband as at first, for then I was better off than now.' (2:7) He wants to begin all over again. He will woo her again: 'I am now going to allure her; I will lead her into the desert and speak tenderly to her.' (2:14) They will have a new start together: 'I will betroth you to me for ever; I will betroth you in righteousness and justice, in love and in compassion. I will betroth you in faithfulness, and you will acknowledge the Lord.' (2:19,20)

Hosea puts all his feelings of love for Gomer into this poem, and then he realises that he is not speaking his own thoughts and words, but the words and thoughts of God. God loves Israel more perfectly than he could ever love Gomer. Despite their unfaithfulness, God cannot abandon his people: 'How can I give you up, Ephraim? How can I hand you over, Israel? My heart is changed within me; all my compassion is aroused.' (11:8) If Hosea's love endures, how much greater than man's love is God's! 'I will not carry out my fierce anger, nor will I turn and devastate Ephraim. For I am God, and not man – The Holy One among you.' (11:9)

What Hosea discovered about the steadfast love of God teaches us that there is always hope, always. Even at the end, just before Samaria fell to the invading Assyrians, Hosea called to Israel to change its way and go back to God, like an unfaithful wife who has come to her senses and returned to her husband. Listen to this heart-rending plea: 'Return, O Israel, to the Lord your God. Say to him, "Forgive all our sins and receive us graciously…"' (14:2) If only they knew how God longed for them. He waits only for their response so that he can heal them and give them new life and an assured future. (14:4–7)

From the depths of his own bitter experience, Hosea learnt of God's pain when his people forsake him. He learnt from his own ability to love and forgive that God loves and forgives for ever. It is all undeserved. It is grace, free to all who want it. It only has to be accepted. Sadly, God's grace is often rejected; the free gift of love is thrown back in God's face. That is what happened in Hosea's Israel. Still believing that they were right, they saw their city sacked and their nation disappear from history.

The Book of Jeremiah

(The Written Prophets 4)

It is not easy to tell the story of Jeremiah. The book that bears his name is long and complex and is in no way a biography of the prophet. It is more of an anthology, a literary patchwork quilt. It contains poems, some probably spoken or written by Jeremiah himself, others remembered, collected or composed by his disciples and admirers. There are also snippets of narrative material describing what happened to Jeremiah, and some of these stories are told twice. There is editorial material in which unknown editors use the words, ideas and reputation of Jeremiah in support of their own concerns about God's people, about how the Jews, after their return from exile in Babylon, should worship Yahweh and practise their faith.

The last four chapters of the Second Book of Kings provide the background to Jeremiah's life. But to uncover the story of Jeremiah, the man and the prophet, we have to move about in the book which bears his name, using material when it seems clear which part of his life and ministry it belongs to. With some passages this is fairly straightforward; with others it involves a certain amount of guesswork. But complex and jumbled though the Book of Jeremiah is, it is a collection of such richness that out of the uncertainties and difficulties emerges the picture of a man of unshakeable faith, whose ministry altered the faith of his own people for ever, and laid the foundations on which a religion of personal devotion to God could be built – in both Judaism and Christianity.

Because we have to jump about in the text so much, references have been included in case you want to look things up. But it should be possible to read 'the story' ignoring and omitting the references.

Jeremiah's Story

Call and Comission

Jeremiah lived from about 645 until about 580 BCE. It was the time when the kingdom of Judah was crumbling to defeat and exile, and Jeremiah had the sad task of being a prophet to a dying nation. His message was the unpopular one that his country's fate was unavoidable because it was Yahweh's punishment for the sin of unfaithfulness.

Jeremiah was a member of a priestly family from the quarrying village of Anathoth, a few miles north-east of Jerusalem. (1:1) The family was ancient and could probably trace back its priestly status for generations. As a priest Jeremiah would officiate at the local shrine or 'high place' in Anathoth, and he would have grown up steeped in the traditional faith of Israel. Yet it is not as a priest that Jeremiah is remembered, but as a prophet.

His call to be a prophet happened, he tells us, during the reign of King Josiah. Jeremiah didn't 'see' God, as Isaiah had done, but there was a very clear 'hearing' of the voice of God, who told him that he had been chosen from before his birth to be God's spokesman, 'a prophet to the nations'. (1:5) Like Isaiah and Moses, his immediate reaction was to feel that the task was too great for him. He told God that he was only a child. (1:6) In fact, he was probably about twenty years old. But God ignored the excuse and reassured Jeremiah that he would be with him. (1:8) Then Jeremiah experienced what he believed was the touch of God on his mouth, giving him the words of God to speak:

> I have put my words in your mouth.
> See, I have set you this day over nations and kingdoms,
> to pluck up and to break down,
> to destroy and to overthrow,
> to build and to plant. (1:10)

Jeremiah accepted his commission and began a ministry that was to last for almost fifty years, extending through the reigns of Josiah, Jehoahaz, Jehoiakim, Jehoiachin, Zedekiah and Gedaliah.

In the course of his ministry he would be misunderstood, hated and imprisoned. He would renounce marriage so that, like his nation, he would be without comfort, help or consolation when the dreadful events he foresaw took place. He would be denounced as a traitor, and attempts would be made on his life. Perhaps he had guessed what was in store for him when he tried to refuse God's call!

Like all the biblical prophets, Jeremiah believed that it was his task to speak to his own and, if necessary, other nations about how God saw and judged their behaviour. He looked at the political events of his day and vividly saw the hand of God in them, saving one nation, punishing another.

His ministry began as the great Assyrian empire, which had attacked, defeated and destroyed the northern kingdom of Israel, was in decline. More acute and better informed than most people, Jeremiah was aware that rising in the far north was another mighty power, the Scythians.

Early in his ministry Jeremiah composed prophetic poems or oracles, warning of the coming of the Scythian hordes. In a vision he had seen a boiling pot tilted over so that its contents would pour southwards, burning and destroying everything in its path. 'Out of the north disaster shall break out...' (1:13,14) The reason for the coming disaster was Judah's failure to obey God:

> Your ways and your doings
> have brought this upon you.
> This is your doom, and it is bitter;
> it has reached your very heart. (4:18)

But at this early stage of his ministry Jeremiah still hoped that the nation might repent and God be persuaded to change his mind and avert the disaster. But he didn't hold on to the possibility of salvation for very long. Jeremiah's deep pessimism about the future of his nation sprang partly from his understanding of the history of his people, with their persistent failure to live according to God's Law, and partly from his own relationship with God and his growing belief that every single individual might have a close, personal relationship with God, regardless of the faith or failure of the nation.

Jeremiah was born in the reign of 'bad' king Manasseh of Judah. Judging by ordinary, worldly standards, Manasseh was extraordinarily successful. He reigned for fifty-five years. He had managed such a feat by astute political manoeuvring, by appeasement, by accepting the overlordship of the Assyrians, so that they would not do to Judah and Jerusalem what they had done to Israel and Samaria. Such a policy inevitably involved the acceptance of foreign influences in many matters, including religion. This is why the biblical historians of the Book of Kings judge Manasseh so harshly: 'He did what was evil in the sight of the Lord, following the abominable practices of the nations.' (II Kings 21:2)

After Manasseh's death, his son Amon succeeded him and maintained his father's policies. Perhaps a reaction was building up in the nation. Whether it had or not, Amon didn't reign for long. He was assassinated after being on the throne for a mere two months. He was succeeded by his eight-year-old son, Josiah.

Josiah's Reform

Josiah's reign is remembered for his reform of religious practice in Judah. The reform was set in motion, when Josiah had been on the throne for eighteen years, by the discovery of 'a book of the law'. (The story of this discovery is in II Kings, Chapter 22). The book came to light during building repairs in the temple. Josiah was quickly told of the find, and the book was read to him. He was appalled by what he heard, and gave orders that the divine commands contained in the book should be carried out. It seems very likely that the book was at least a part of the present biblical Book of Deuteronomy. A question comes into our minds as to whether the book was 'planted' and the young king persuaded to carry out reforms by a religious and political pressure group that may also have been behind the assassination of king Amon.

Whatever the origin of the Book of the Law, it brought about a sweeping reform of the religion of Judah. All foreign cults were rigorously removed. Jerusalem was recognised as the one true sanctuary of Yahweh. Local shrines, like the one at Anathoth, were closed down, and the priests given compensation for the loss of their work. It may well be that the young Jeremiah welcomed the reforms and perhaps saw hope of repentance for a nation led by an enlightened and godly king.

But as time passed Jeremiah realised that the reforms had affected only the outward features of the nation's religion. They had not touched inner, personal faith. It's possible, too, that Jeremiah might have been sickened by the violence that accompanied some of the purges in the reform. In the end he realised that even after the reforms people were unchanged, still selfish, still greedy. The religious leaders merely said what they thought people wanted to hear, rather than proclaiming the real and often uncomfortable word of God:

> For from the least to the greatest of them,
> every one is greedy for unjust gain;
> and from prophet to priest,
> every one deals falsely.
> They have healed the wound of my people lightly,
> saying, 'Peace, peace,'
> when there is no peace. (6:13,14)

Time passed, and the Scythians never came to Judah. Jeremiah had been wrong. They had advanced as far as Egypt, sweeping all before them. He had seen that accurately enough. But their chosen route was by the Mediterranean coast, which meant that they avoided Judah. Do we have to say that Jeremiah was a false prophet because he got this wrong? He certainly said that about others. And the Book of Deuteronomy tells us that only if a prophecy is fulfilled can we say that the prophet spoke the word of God. (18:21,22) But the question about true and false prophecy is a good deal more complicated than that. In the case of Jeremiah, he was right about the advance of the Scythians. He was also right about the state of his own nation, its apostasy and corruption. And in the end his words were fulfilled. Destruction did come from the north; but it was Babylon, not Scythia, that was God's rod to punish Judah. Jeremiah's words of doom, at first unfulfilled, eventually came true.

King Josiah, after a reign of thirty-one years, died of wounds received fighting against Pharaoh Necho of Egypt at the battle of Megiddo. He was succeeded by his son, Jehoahaz. But the triumphant Pharaoh Necho was the real master, and he deposed Jehoahaz and replaced him with his brother, Jehoiakim, who was to be a puppet king, with Pharaoh holding and pulling the strings. So once again the nation was under foreign influence with all the inevitable dangers to the true worship of Yahweh.

The Disloyalty of Jeremiah

Jeremiah cried out against the apostasy that left Yahweh shut out of the nation's thoughts and actions. He stood at the temple gate and proclaimed God's message. 'Amend your ways and your doings, and let me dwell with you in this place.' (7:3) His countrymen cherished a widespread and naïve belief that the nation would never be defeated because in Jerusalem stood the holy temple, the dwelling place of God. 'How can God's house be destroyed?' they said. Jeremiah knew that such beliefs were no more than superstition. They could go on repeating the phrase, 'The temple of the Lord, the temple of the Lord', as if it were a magic charm. But it was self-deception. The temple was a building. They should go to Shiloh, at one time a great sanctuary of God, and see what Yahweh had allowed to happen there. It is easy to imagine how distasteful and treasonable such preaching would seem to the proud and patriotic people of Jerusalem.

It was probably about this time that Jeremiah performed one of his prophetic actions. Instructed by God, he bought an earthenware jug. He then collected together some of the elders of Judah and some of the priests. He led them to one of the city gates and there he delivered his uncomfortable and unwelcome message. 'Thus says the Lord of Hosts, "I am going to bring such disaster upon this place that the ears of everyone who hears of it shall tingle ... I will make them fall by the sword before their enemies ... I will give their dead bodies for food to the birds of the air and to the wild animals of the earth. And I will make this city a horror, a thing to be hissed at.'" (19:3,7,8) He then reinforced his words by action. He smashed the pot and said, 'So will I break this people and this city, as one breaks a potter's vessel, so that it can never be mended.' (19:11)

Jeremiah must have known what sort of impact his words and actions would have. We can understand it if we imagine what impression someone would have made speaking like that during the London Blitz. Not only did he appear unpatriotic, undermining the morale of a nation under threat from its enemies. It was worse than that. He would be seen as guaranteeing that the disasters he foretold came true. The words of a true prophet were the words of God, and it was believed that once the word of God was spoken, it must happen. We can find this way of thinking in many places in the Old Testament, but none more clearly than in Isaiah. (55:10,11)

> For as the rain and the snow come down from heaven,
> and return not thither but water the earth,
> making it bring forth and sprout,
> giving seed to the sower and bread to the eater,
> so shall my word be that goes forth from my mouth;
> it shall not return to me empty,
> but it shall accomplish that which I purpose,
> and prosper in the thing for which I sent it.

So once Jeremiah had said, in God's name, that Jerusalem would fall and the nation would be defeated, he had ensured that it would happen.

Despite the prestige that attached to every prophet, the authorities could not allow Jeremiah to go on unchallenged. They wanted to silence him. A priest called Passhur had Jeremiah arrested, beaten and put in the stocks for the night. Uncomfortable though that was, it certainly did not stop Jeremiah. As he was being released he denounced Passhur and prophesied that the king of Babylon would loot the treasures of Jerusalem, slaughter many of the people and take others, including Passhur and his family, into exile. (20:1–6)

It may have been the confrontation with Passhur that caused

Jeremiah to be banned from the temple and from speaking there. (36:5) But he wasn't going to be silenced; God's word must be heard. So, four years into the reign of Jehoiakim, he dictated the prophecies he had delivered up to that time, using Baruch as his assistant and secretary. He instructed Baruch to take the scroll to the temple area and read the prophecies to the people. The writing must have taken a long time, because Jehoiakim was in the fifth year of his reign when Baruch publicly read the prophecies. But though long in the writing, they were short in the reading. They were read three times in the same day.

The authorities were soon aware of what was going on, and Baruch was ordered to bring the scroll and read it again to a gathering of the leading men of Jerusalem. They heard it and enquired about its origin, and when told, advised Baruch that he ought to leave quickly and go into hiding, taking Jeremiah with him. When they had given this kindly advice they went to the king and reported what had been happening.

It was winter. The king was in his winter apartment with a brazier burning near his chair. He listened as the elders read the scroll and he contemptuously tore up each section as it was finished and threw it into the fire. Jehoiakim had no time or respect for the troublesome Jeremiah.

Jeremiah learnt that the scroll had been destroyed and simply set about dictating a second version and adding prophecies against Jehoiakim himself. 'I will punish him and his offspring for their iniquity; I will bring on them and on the inhabitants of Jerusalem and on all the people of Judah, all the disasters with which I have threatened them – but they would not listen.' (36:31)

The disasters Jeremiah predicted were not long in coming. Nebuchadrezzar, King of Babylon, advanced on Judah with his all-conquering army. Sensibly, Jehoiakim surrendered, buying time. For three years the people of Jerusalem and Judah lived in an uneasy peace. Then, foolishly, Jehoiakim felt confident enough to stop paying tribute. Nebuchadrezzar, disdaining to send his full army, dispatched bands of mercenaries to harry and raid the cities of Judah. It was in the middle of this period of uncertainty and fear that Jehoiakim died. He was buried honourably in the family tomb, which was not at all what Jeremiah had predicted. He had said, 'With the burial of an ass he shall be buried, dragged and cast forth beyond the gates of Jerusalem.' (22:19) That certainly didn't happen. And again it seems as if some of the small print of Jeremiah's prophecies was off the mark.

Jehoiakim's son, Jehoiachin, succeeded to the throne and, as might be expected, all sorts of hopes and expectations gathered around the new king. Would the new reign bring peace and prosperity? Not as far as Jeremiah was concerned. For Jeremiah the king might be new, but nothing else was. The nation was still corrupt and far from God. His predictions of disaster continued. In God's name he prophesied that Jehoiachin (or Coniah as he was sometimes known) would be taken into exile. No son would succeed him on the throne, so he could be counted as childless. (22:30)

The First Deportation

In the year 597 BCE Nebuchadrezzar made himself master of Jerusalem. The elite of the city – the king, the princes and military leaders, the craftsmen – were taken into exile in Babylon, and Zedekiah, a son of good King Josiah, was put on the throne to rule as Nebuchadrezzar's puppet. Jeremiah could see nothing good in the new situation. All his hopes and sympathies were with the exiles. In a vision he saw two baskets of figs. One basket held figs of the highest quality, the other figs that were inedible. For Jeremiah the exiles in Babylon were the good figs; those who remained in Jerusalem under Zedekiah were the useless figs. (24:1–10) He saw God's hand in all that had happened. The exile was a punishment for past sin, but it was also a preparation for a better future. So sure was Jeremiah of this that he wrote a letter to the exiles encouraging them to make the best of their lives in Babylon. They should make Babylon their home. That was God's will and plan for them. They must build houses, plant gardens, marry and prosper. They must work for the good of Babylon, for their own well-being depended on it. (29:4–7) Their exile would not be for ever. After seventy years their preparation would be complete and they would be ready to return to Jerusalem. 'For I know the plans I have for you, says the Lord, plans for welfare and not for evil, to give you a future and a hope.' (29:11)

While prophesying hope and optimism for the exiles in Babylon, Jeremiah continued to prophesy gloom and destruction for the king and people of Jerusalem. In another acted prophecy he wore a wooden yoke, the kind used to yoke oxen together. (27:2) It was a symbol of the yoke that Nebuchadrezzar would place on the nation. When a rival prophet, who would be regarded as much more loyal and patriotic than Jeremiah, removed the yoke and smashed it to pieces, saying that in the same way God would smash the yoke of Babylon, Jeremiah simply fashioned a metal yoke, unbreakable and inescapable – like the power of Babylon. What a thorn in the flesh of the authorities Jeremiah must have been! As far as they were concerned he was preaching treason.

After nine years of submission, Zedekiah and his advisers judged that it was safe to rebel. They were wrong, and soon Jerusalem was under siege, a situation that lasted for two and a half years. It was while the city was under these siege conditions that Jeremiah called upon the king to surrender and encouraged ordinary citizens to leave the city and go out to join the enemy. Something had to be done about a man who encouraged such behaviour.

Jeremiah was arrested as he left the city to go to his village, Anathoth, to conduct, he claimed, some business. (37:12) It was very reasonably assumed that he was following his own advice and deserting to the enemy. He denied the charges but was taken before the military leaders, who already knew enough about him to prejudice them against him. He was beaten and put in prison.

Though the generals and colonels had no time for Jeremiah, the king, Zedekiah, suspected that he might really be speaking the word of God. Secretly he had Jeremiah brought from his prison. He asked him if there was any word from God. Uncompromising as ever, Jeremiah replied, 'You shall be delivered into the hand of the king of Babylon.' It wasn't what Zedekiah had wanted to hear, but he accepted it and even made arrangements that Jeremiah should be made more comfortable in prison with a regular ration of bread. (37:16–21)

Worse was to come. Jeremiah was again denounced as a traitor and this time the military leaders took him to the king and asked for the death penalty. (38:4) The king said he would leave things in their hands, and Jeremiah was dropped into a cistern used for collecting rainwater. It was empty, the water no doubt having been used up during the siege. Naturally there was deep mud at the bottom. He was thrown in and left to drown in the mud or starve – certainly left to die. He would have died had not a court official, an Ethiopian called Ebed-melek, gone to the king and said that things had gone too far.

Zedekiah again acted kindly toward Jeremiah. He told Ebed-melek to get assistance and lift Jeremiah from the cistern. The story tells in detail how the rescuers threw down rags, telling Jeremiah to place them under his armpits to prevent the rescue ropes chafing as they hauled him up. (38:12)

It is worth reminding ourselves that the princes and military leaders, who were so opposed to Jeremiah, were as honest and consistent as he was. War brings such conflicts between good people. We might think of conscientious objectors in 1914 or 1939, courageous in standing up for their beliefs, but cowards in the eyes of many. Or we might think of Dietrich Bonhoeffer, a devout Christian, supporting a plot to assassinate Hitler. War brings such conflicts of conscience. The generals of Jeremiah's day were committed to fighting for their country by every means possible, and the last thing they wanted was a man of Jeremiah's stature and influence undermining their work and destroying the nation's morale. For his part, Jeremiah knew that a siege would bring dreadful suffering to everyone. Surrender would be a practical solution because the king of Babylon was God's chosen instrument, and under his rule the faith of Israel would survive and flourish. For Jeremiah, Nebuchadrezzar was God's servant. (27:6)

In the tenth year of Zedekiah's reign, when the Babylonian army surrounded Jerusalem and the future looked black, Jeremiah demonstrated his faith that the future was in God's hands by buying a field in his home village of Anathoth. It was all done with meticulous legality, with written documents and witnesses. The documents were then given to Baruch to be placed safely in an earthenware jar. It was an act of faith in the future, 'for thus says the Lord, the God of Israel: houses and fields and vineyards shall again be bought in this land.' (32:15)

A Message of Hope

So the gloomy prophet's message began to glow with hope. In fact, hope had never been totally absent. At first there was the hope that the nation might repent, be forgiven and saved from conquest and exile. Then there was hope in the Babylonian exiles, that God was preparing them for a return to Jerusalem. The darkness of the final days of Jerusalem threw into sharp relief the rays of hope that Jeremiah's trust in God gave him.

His hope was for a totally restored nation – not just Judah, but Israel, the northern kingdom as well, though it had ceased to exist more than a century before. His rapturous prophecy says, 'You shall plant vineyards upon the mountains of Samaria.' (31:5) Perhaps Jeremiah was dazzled by the brilliance of his own hopes. Certainly they were not fulfilled in the way he hoped. When the exiles eventually returned to Jerusalem, the harsh conditions and the problems they faced were quite unlike the idealised vision of Jeremiah.

But that same chapter, Chapter 31, contains Jeremiah's greatest gift to the religious development of the human race. He spoke of a new covenant that God would make with his people. The earlier covenants with Abraham, Moses and David were covenants for the nation, not for the individuals whose names they bear. In Israel and Judah, religion had always been primarily a corporate matter, something between God and his chosen people. In a sense the individual mattered only because he was a part of the nation. The briefest and best statement of the meaning of the covenant is in the Book of Leviticus: 'I will be your God and you will be my people.' (Lev. 26:12) There is a profound truth in this corporate understanding of faith and responsibility. But it is not the whole story.

It took the genius of Jeremiah to correct the balance. He looked forward to a new covenant under which each person would be responsible for their own actions, good and bad. He quoted and amended an old proverb: 'In those days they shall no long say, "The fathers have eaten sour grapes and the children's teeth are set on edge." But everyone shall die for his own sin.' (31:29,30)

This new teaching grew out of Jeremiah's own experience of God, and out of years of pondering the faith of the nation. He had come to realise that if knowledge of God was not dependent purely on membership of the nation, then it would not matter if the nation were destroyed and should disappear. Each person might know God individually. Under the new covenant, God's Law would not be written on tablets of stone, but on the heart of every person. 'I will put my law within them, and I will write it upon their hearts, and I will be their God and they shall be my people.' (31:33)

In his own lonely life, Jeremiah had discovered that though he was not accepted by his priestly companions nor by other prophets, he knew God and, more important, God knew him. He came to believe that everyone might experience such personal intimacy with God, and since his time both Jews and Christians have found in their own lives that Jeremiah was right.

The Final Days

The siege of Jerusalem went on for two and a half years, and there was terrible suffering in the city. (52:6) At last the walls were breached and Zedekiah and the military leaders fled. They had no real hope of escape and were soon captured. The king's sons were put to death in his presence and then his eyes were put out, leaving the harrowing sight of the death of his children as the last thing he saw. Zedekiah was then taken to Babylon and executed. (52:10,11)

The Babylonian army entered Jerusalem and devastated the temple, the royal palace and all the great buildings of the city. Treasures were looted and more people were taken captive to Babylon. (52:12–19) Amid the horror and confusion of the fall of Jerusalem, Jeremiah survived. He was on his way to Babylon, a prisoner among others. It perhaps came to the attention of the authorities that for many years Jeremiah had been pro-Babylon, urging the rulers of Judah to surrender. For whatever reason, he was given the choice of going on to Babylon or staying in Judah under the newly appointed governor, Gedaliah. He chose to remain with Gedaliah, who made his headquarters at Mizpah, in the countryside north of Jerusalem.

Gedaliah's brief governorship was a time of hope for Jeremiah. His confidence in Babylonian rule was being justified. Judah was allowed to get on with life, and the worship of Yahweh was not hindered. A wonderful harvest that year raised Jeremiah's hopes that some sort of kingdom, under God's care, was coming into being. But his hope was short-lived. The turmoil in the politics of Judah continued and a disaffected prince of the royal house accepted hospitality at Gedaliah's table and then, with a group of friends, assassinated Gedaliah and killed many of his supporters as well. The brief golden age was over. (41:1,2)

As so often at a time of crisis in Judah, people began to look toward Egypt for help. They decided it would be best to go to Egypt for refuge. Jeremiah, true to his long-proclaimed policy, refused to go with them, and warned that there was no safety in Egypt; the sword would pursue them there. (42:16) But he couldn't influence them nor change their minds, and they set off for Egypt and forced Jeremiah to go with them.

By this time Jeremiah must have been over sixty years of age and worn out by a lifetime of conflict and hardship. But he wasn't finished yet. Even in Egypt he acted out his prophetic message. He buried stones in the Egyptian city of Tahpanhes, to symbolise the laying of a foundation for the throne of the king of Babylon who would surely come to reign there. (42:10) At the end of his ministry, as at the beginning, Jeremiah spoke out against the worship of other gods, the apostasy of the people of Judah. (Ch.44) God might still be watching over the exiles in Babylon with plans for their welfare (29:11), but as for the people who had fled to Egypt and put their trust in politics and armies, his word was: 'Behold, I am watching over them for evil and not for good.' (44:27) Jeremiah was faithful and consistent to the end.

Exactly what the end was we do not know. There is nothing about his death in the Book of Jeremiah. Tradition says that he was stoned to death by his own people. Certainly there would be something fitting about such an end to the sufferings of this remarkable man.

Though his own people opposed him and may have killed him, Jeremiah would have been content if he knew that the lessons he taught had been learnt. When the exiles did return from Babylon to

Jerusalem there was no triumphant return and no reuniting of the two nations of Judah and Israel. However, in the most difficult circumstances, they remained faithful to their God, the only God. They also learnt that knowing God was something possible for all people. They had learnt that Yahweh was not confined to Jerusalem and its temple. He was present and active in foreign lands, in all lands. Even the loss of the temple and the daily sacrifices did not make contact with God impossible. God could always be found through prayer: 'You will call upon me and come and pray to me, and I will hear you.' (29:12) Though he was staunchly patriotic and looked for the establishing of a new covenant with Judah and Israel, Jeremiah did not rule out other nations coming to Yahweh. His prayer was, 'O Lord, my strength and my stronghold, my refuge in the day of trouble, to thee shall the nations come from the ends of the earth…' (16:19)

Jeremiah's greatest gift to all who seek to know God was his insistence that though religion is clearly a corporate matter involving all those around us, it is also a personal matter between God and the individual soul. He knew that God could be found in the solitude of suffering and pain as well as in the joy of festival and thanksgiving. More than any other prophet of the Old Testament, his personal life of suffering and being misunderstood seems to foreshadow the life of Jesus. Certainly, Jeremiah's hope of a new covenant for Israel and Judah was taken up by Jesus and enlarged. For Jesus it became a covenant for all people. (Mark 14:24) We look at Jeremiah and his disappointed hopes and are reminded of Jesus' words to the woman of Samaria as he talked to her by the well: 'The hour is coming, and now is, when true worshippers will worship the Father in spirit and truth.' (John 4:23) Jeremiah would have said 'Amen' to that.

The Book of Ezekiel

(The Written Prophets 5)

The life and ministry of Ezekiel overlapped with that of Jeremiah. While Jeremiah was in Jerusalem, suffering with the people, and then, against his will, being taken to Egypt, Ezekiel was in the first group of exiles who were deported to Babylon.

Living among the exiles, Ezekiel watched and waited for the final catastrophe, the fall of Jerusalem and the destruction of the temple. His early prophecies were gloomy. Like all the prophets, he saw the defeat and disgrace as a punishment sent by Yahweh for national apostasy and unfaithfulness, their failure to live up to their high calling to bring blessing to all people. He is also like other prophets in that he cannot prevent rays of hope shining through, and he preached a message of rebirth for the nation in his visions of the valley of dry bones and the new temple.

The Book of Ezekiel is a complex mixture of prophecies, visions, spoken and acted parables, details of his personal life, his illnesses and his bereavement. From these we can construct the 'story' of Ezekiel.

Again references have been put in to help should they be needed. They can just as easily be ignored.

Ezekiel's Story

Call and Comission

Many people have heard of the valley of dry bones. Some have heard of 'wheels within wheels'. But few know much about the man who saw those visions and wrote them down. Few know when and where he lived, what he believed, what he feared, what he hoped and what his life was like.

Ezekiel lived at much the same time as Jeremiah, though he was rather younger. Both prophets lived through some of the most terrible events in the history of their nation. Ezekiel was born in Jerusalem in about 624 BCE, when Jeremiah would have been about twenty years old. Like Jeremiah, he was born into a priestly family. He must have studied in Jerusalem preparing for his destined work as a priest, and his writings show that all his life he believed the priesthood and the worship of the temple in Jerusalem were of the greatest importance.

The Law states that a man can begin to exercise his priesthood at the age of thirty. (Numbers 4) But four years before Ezekiel reached that milestone, for which he had been preparing all his life, disaster overtook the nation. In the year 597 BCE the Babylonian army captured Jerusalem and carried into exile the cream of the population – the royal family, the civil and military leaders, many priests and most of the able citizens. Ezekiel was among them. He was taken to Babylon, and when we begin to read his book he is living in his own house on the River Chebar, not far from the city of Babylon. (1:1–3)

We need to appreciate as clearly as we can how great a disaster was the fall of Jerusalem and the taking of the people into exile. Jerusalem was not just the political capital, it was the holy city, the city chosen by God 'to place his name there'. (Deuteronomy 12:2–5) Some forty or fifty years before the time of Ezekiel, sweeping religious reforms had been carried out during the reign of King Josiah, and one of the most important features of the reforms was that they increased the importance of Jerusalem by making it the only place where sacrifice could be offered to Yahweh. Sacrifice was immensely important. It was the means by which God was thanked and praised. It was through the regular sin offering in the temple and the yearly ritual of the Day of Atonement that both the nation and individuals were forgiven and reconciled to God. So, for Ezekiel the priest, exile and separation from Jerusalem and temple worship were a terrible burden to bear.

Heavy on Ezekiel's mind was the memory of what had happened to Israel, Judah's northern sister nation. Israel had been conquered by the Assyrians. Samaria, its capital, had fallen and its people had been taken into exile. The nation had not survived. It had disappeared, swallowed up by surrounding peoples, dissolved by intermarriage and assimilation. And the question in the minds of many Judaean exiles, and certainly in Ezekiel's, was, 'How can God's people survive now that we have been separated from the temple and its worship?

It was after he had been in exile for four years that God broke into Ezekiel's life in a new way, calling him to be a prophet and changing his life completely. Ezekiel dates God's call very precisely. It seems as if the call happened when he was aged thirty. How wisely and kindly God dealt with Ezekiel. He was thirty; it was the very day on which he should have taken up his priestly duties in Jerusalem. That could not happen because he was an exile in Babylon, and therefore God called him to serve in a different way.

Ezekiel describes his call in great detail. 'In the thirtieth year, in the fourth month, on the fifth day of the month, as I was among the exiles by the River Chebar, the heavens were opened, and I saw visions of God.' (1:1) It was as if he saw a violent storm, with lightning shooting out of a great cloud. Then in the depths of the cloud shapes began to form. He saw figures; something like four-winged men, shining as if made of burnished bronze. Each had four faces; a human one facing forward, at the sides were the faces of a lion and an ox, and at the back the face of an eagle. They moved in perfect harmony, forwards, backwards, sideways, as they were impelled by the spirit of God. Between them appeared to be fire, and lightning crackled out from the fire. These figures were the guardians and escorts of God. They carried a vaulted platform, shining like crystal, on which stood the throne of God. (1:4–25) On the throne he could see something like the figure of a man. But it was no ordinary man, no man at all. From the waist upward he shone like burnished bronze, and below the waist he seemed to be of fire. A bright rainbow, always the symbol of God's mercy, framed the whole vision. 'Such was the image of the glory of Yahweh,' wrote Ezekiel, 'and when I saw it, I fell upon my face.' (1:26–28)

Like Isaiah he had seen a vision of Yahweh on his throne, high and lifted up. The experience was overwhelming and literally indescribable. Ezekiel never attempted direct description. He always says that he saw the 'likeness' or the 'image' of this or that.

The important thing is that Ezekiel had been given a glimpse of the glory of God in a foreign land. All his priestly training had conditioned him to believe that God's glory dwelt in the Tabernacle or in the Holy of Holies in the temple in Jerusalem. But this vision revealed that Yahweh was not confined or restricted. He was the God of the whole world. Exile from Jerusalem did not mean exile from God, either for himself or for his fellow countrymen. So overwhelming and awesome was this knowledge that Ezekiel fell prostrate on the ground. He was ready to listen and to obey.

'Son of man,' said God, 'Stand upon your feet.' (2:1) After the awe-inspiring vision of God's glory Ezekiel was very aware of his human weakness – just like Isaiah, just like Jeremiah and just like Moses. And the term God used to address Ezekiel – 'Son of man,' or 'member of the human race' – emphasised the distance between God's glory and purity and the fallibility and sinfulness of all human beings. Helped by God's spirit Ezekiel obeyed and stood up. God told him that he was to be his spokesman to the people of Judah. It would be no easy task. God's experience of his chosen people had not been encouraging. 'They are a rebellious people,' said God. He told Ezekiel that he would encounter opposition, contempt and injury, but he must be more hard-headed than the people. Whatever it costs him, he must declare the message of God. (3:8)

At their call, both Isaiah and Jeremiah had experienced the touch of God on their mouth as they received the commission to speak God's word. For Ezekiel the experience was even more graphic. He was shown a scroll, written on both sides, and he was told to eat it. He did, and in that way the word of God became a part of him. (2:9–3:3) So overwhelming was this experience for Ezekiel that for a week he could do nothing; he lay paralysed, disabled by what had happened to him. Then, filled with the word of God and driven by the spirit of God, Ezekiel was taken to face his audience, the exiles among whom he lived by the River Chebar.

Even after seven days Ezekiel was still unable to speak the word of God that was in him, so God told him to act out a prophecy. (Ch. 4). On a sun-baked clay tile he drew the plan of a city. Then he piled up earth into mounds and walls surrounding the city, and battering rams were positioned. Even without speech, there was no doubt that Ezekiel was depicting the siege of a city. But which city? He then lay on the ground for many days, acting out the powerlessness of a nation in exile, a nation being punished for its sins. Next, he restricted himself to siege rations, a daily ration of half a pound of poor food and less than a pint of water each day, made all the more unpleasant and revolting by being ritually unclean. Finally he shaved his head with a sharp sword, symbolising how the conqueror would denude the nation, leaving it bare and disfigured. (5:1)

After the actions came the words. The exiles were to be left in no doubt as to what it all meant.

Ezekiel spoke. 'Thus says the Lord, "This is Jerusalem."' Instead of being the holy city, a light to all nations, it had become an evil city, and must be punished. And not only Jerusalem. 'The mountains of Israel' – the Judaean countryside – must also be denounced and punished. It was in the countryside that the 'high places' flourished, where foreign and fertility gods were worshipped. Ezekiel declared God's judgement: 'I, I myself will bring a sword upon you, and I will destroy your high places. Your altars shall become desolate, and your incense stands shall be broken, and I will throw down your slain in front of your idols.' (6:3,4)

The judgement of God would bear some fruit; some people would admit their wickedness and the justice of God, and would be forgiven. But that tiny ray of light could not disperse the darkness of Judah's future. Ezekiel could see only more and worse trouble for his nation. His message was clear. The city will be destroyed, and with it the temple. Many will die by sword, pestilence and famine. (7:15) They will fall to an implacable foe and there will be no one to lead or give counsel, no prophet, no priest, no elder, no king nor prince – none will be able to help. (7:26–27)

A Vision of Jerusalem

One day Ezekiel was in his house in Babylon and the leaders of the exiles were with him. He felt himself snatched up, as if he had been picked up by the hair. He was transported, in a vision, to Jerusalem. (8:3) In his vision an angel showed him the terrible things that were happening there. Instead of repenting, its people, feeling that Yahweh had deserted them, were turning to other gods.

First Ezekiel was shown an altar to the Queen of Heaven, the goddess of sexual desire and pleasure. It had been set up in Yahweh's temple. He was appalled by this first revelation, but was told that worse was to come. He was taken through a secret door and found himself in a room where the walls were covered with painting of various creatures. This time it was an Egyptian cult, no doubt brought into the temple of Yahweh by those who wanted political and military support from Egypt. (8:7–13) That such images should be in the temple of Yahweh outraged Ezekiel – but worse was still to come.

In the temple court women were 'weeping for Tammuz'. They were involved in the cult of a Babylonian nature god, whose death and resurrection each year were believed to control the death and rebirth of nature in winter and spring. Worshippers took part in ritual mourning as their god died.

The vision continued, the angel leading Ezekiel on to see still further horrors. They reached the altar of burnt offering, which was close to the Holy of Holies, where the glory of Yahweh was believed to dwell. At the altar, instead of the properly appointed priests of Yahweh, men like Ezekiel himself, there were twenty-five men engaged in the most popular cult of Babylon, the worship of the sun god, Marduk. As they worshipped they faced the sun rising in the east, and thus offensively and literally turned their backs on Yahweh.

The vision continued. Ezekiel heard a voice. It was the voice of God, calling for the city to be destroyed. Six gigantic warriors appeared, armed and ready to kill. Their leader was not armed, but dressed in linen. Perhaps he was a priest. He had writing materials with him so that he could record the carrying out of God's commands. He also marked the foreheads of those few who had remained faithful to Yahweh, so that amid the slaughter they would be recognised and spared.

The order was given for the slaughter to begin. There was to be no mercy. Men, women and children were to perish. Ezekiel protested to God that this was too much. But God's mind was made up. He said, 'As for me, my eye will not spare, nor will I have pity, but I will bring down their deeds upon their heads.' (9:10) After the people, it was the turn of the city itself. The man in linen was ordered to take coals from the altar of incense and scatter them over the city to destroy it with fire. (10:1,2)

So great were the sins of the people of Judah, so terrible their desecration of the temple that God moved his protecting presence from the city. In his vision Ezekiel saw the glory of God leave Jerusalem. He wrote, 'And the glory of the Lord went up from the midst of the city, and stood upon the mountain which is on the east side of the city.' (11:23) This could only mean that Jerusalem had been abandoned by God. No longer could people say, as Jeremiah told us they did, 'The temple of the Lord, the temple of the Lord' – believing that God's presence in Jerusalem would ensure that it would never fall. The glory of God had gone, and the temple was just another building, and Jerusalem just another city.

With that Ezekiel's vision of a visit to Jerusalem ended, and he felt the spirit of God bring him back to Babylon among his fellow exiles.

Acted Warnings

Like many prophets before him, Ezekiel found that the warnings he had given, the words of God that he had spoken, were ignored. And the important thing for Ezekiel was not that the people were ignoring him; no, they were ignoring God. He must not give up. He was commanded to act out more prophecies in an attempt to make his fellow exiles take notice. Following God's instructions, he prepared the sort of bundle that a refugee might scrape together in the final moments as a city was being attacked and destroyed. The bundle contained the bare essentials for a long trek into exile in a foreign land. He prepared the bundle during the day and put it outside his house, expecting it to be noticed. In the evening he broke through the flimsy clay brick wall of his house, and as darkness fell he picked up his bundle, covered his face and set off walking away from his house. As he did all this he said nothing. (12:1–7)

His actions were intended to be noticed, and people were expected to ask questions. The optimists among them might have wondered if Ezekiel was showing them that they should destroy and abandon their temporary dwellings in their exiles' camp, and begin the journey back to Jerusalem. But whatever they thought, Ezekiel wasn't going to tell them what his actions meant until the next morning.

Morning came and Ezekiel was, as usual, brutally frank. 'Thus says the Lord God, "This oracle concerns the prince in Jerusalem and all the house of Israel who are in it."' (12:10) Just like a spoken prophecy, an acted one carried the consequences that once performed it must come true. So, in effect, Ezekiel was ensuring the fall of Jerusalem and a further wave of deportations into exile.

But God's warnings hadn't finished yet. God told Ezekiel to shake and shudder as he ate his food. (12:18). Perhaps the strain of his role as a prophet in such critical times was making him ill again. Whatever it was he could see in his own weakened state, a reflection of the state of the people of Jerusalem. They would quake in fear at the judgement God was bringing on them through the armies of Babylon.

Some people still mocked and said that the prophets were always contradicting themselves, and you couldn't trust any prophecy: 'The days grow long, and every vision comes to naught,' they said. Ezekiel didn't argue; he simply proclaimed God's answer, that time is short, and soon every prophecy will be fulfilled. (12:22–25).

But not all prophecies were true. In Jerusalem there were

prophets who spoke their own words rather than the words of God, who specialised in false comfort, telling people only what they wanted to hear. Just like Jeremiah, Ezekiel had to speak out against the prophets who prophesied peace, when there was no peace, who were crafty and devious, who felt at home in the dark alleys and hiding places of a ruined city. (13:4) They dealt in false comfort which had as little substance as weak walls covered with an impressive layer of whitewash. (13:10–16) Besides the false prophets were the prophetesses (or perhaps they should be called witches), who made bracelets and headdresses to carry their magic spells. They dealt in falsehood; they gave false comfort to some and created false fear in others. God would destroy them all, false prophets and witches alike. (13:20–23)

Warnings in Stories

In spite of Ezekiel's threats and warnings the people showed no sign of changing their ways. How was Ezekiel to get through to them? He had proclaimed God's word clearly by both word and action. But still they didn't listen. So, like many famous teachers, he told stories to claim people's attention.

Israel prided itself on being Yahweh's special vine, a favourite tree, chosen by him, planted in specially prepared soil, tended with the utmost care and expected to bear much good fruit. Both Isaiah (Ch. 5) and the writer of Psalm 80 used this popular image. Ezekiel used it too, but he used it to try to shake his audience out of their complacent confidence. In Ezekiel's story the vine doesn't bear grapes, so it is cut down and burnt.

In another story highlighting Israel's faithlessness, he used the image of prostitution to describe the nation's disloyalty to Yahweh and its flirting with the gods of other nations. In Ezekiel's story Yahweh tells how he found an abandoned child. The child was Jerusalem. It came of mixed ancestry and had a pagan past. (16:3) Its parents had followed the common practice of exposing unwanted children, especially daughters, and this child had been neglected and abandoned. (16:4,5) Without the care newborn children need she would have died, had not Yahweh rescued her. She grew up into a lovely young woman. And when she was at the age for marriage, Yahweh lavished attention on her and turned her into a lovely bride, renowned among the nations for her beauty. (16:8–14) All this attention was too much for her and she became promiscuous, giving herself to her many admirers. Eventually she sunk so low that she became a common prostitute, dishonouring herself and her faithful husband. Her affairs with foreign men are described, as is the way she allowed the children of her marriage to be sacrificed.

Justice had to follow. Jerusalem's punishment was carried out by her cheated lovers. All her jewels and her fine clothes were taken from her and she stood naked before them. The sentence for adultery was passed and she was stoned to death and her body hacked in pieces. (16:35–43)

Later Ezekiel told another story about two sisters who were married to the same man. The faithful husband is again Yahweh, and the sisters represent Israel and Judah. The elder sister becomes a prostitute and in the end is punished by one of the men who had used her. That was Ezekiel's picture of Israel, looking away from Yahweh to the gods of Assyria, and then being punished by Assyria. The younger sister represents Judah. She too flirts with Assyria, but then turns to Babylon for affection. The result will be disgrace, suffering and in the end, destruction by her lover.

Ezekiel was not the first prophet to use the image of marriage to describe Yahweh's relationship with Israel. Both Hosea and Jeremiah had used it. Ezekiel takes things further with detailed descriptions of the nation's sins. He also ends his parable with the death of the unfaithful wife, which seems to suggest that he expected Judah to disappear, just as Israel had, swallowed up among other nations and losing its unique identity.

Individual Responsibility

In the Old Testament the people of Israel have a well-deserved reputation for grumbling. Constantly they 'murmured' against Moses in the wilderness and, as the years and centuries passed, nothing changed. The exiles in Babylon believed that they were suffering because of the wrongdoings of previous generations. They didn't dispute that Israel had sinned in the past, but they had no personal feelings of guilt and couldn't understand why they should be the ones to suffer. It was the familiar question: 'Why us?' 'Why me?'

The fact that they made this complaint shows how far they had moved from the traditional belief that both sin and righteousness were communal rather than individual matters. The old way of thinking was there in the Ten Commandments, where it says that God will 'visit the iniquity of the fathers upon the children to the third and fourth generation'. (Deuteronomy 5:9) The defeat and disintegration of the nation had caused them to question all that. After what they had seen and experienced, they knew there might not *be* a third and fourth generation.

Ezekiel gave God's answer. First, it was not man's business to question God's judgement, however unwelcome it might be. Secondly, God's justice regards what a person does and not what his father might have done. Belonging to a righteous family will not help the son who forsakes righteousness. Similarly, a man who turns from the sinful habits of his family will be counted as right with God. Each person is responsible before God for their own behaviour, and will be judged accordingly. (18:5–20)

Ezekiel went on to speak of the grace of God, how he offers forgiveness and is willing to forget the past, however bad it might have been. With God there is no counting up of rights and wrongs, no strict statistical measurements being made. God longs to forgive. (18:27) Yahweh calls to his people and asks them to change their ways. "I have no pleasure in the death of anyone," says the Lord God, "so turn and live."' (18:32) In this way Ezekiel taught the justice and grace of God.

A Vision of the Future

In August 591 BCE, the leaders of the Jewish exiles again visited Ezekiel in his house to ask him to make an enquiry to God for them. (20:1) Ezekiel must have known or guessed that their question was about whether God approved of their plan to begin offering sacrifices to Yahweh in Babylon. (20:31) At first sight the suggestion seems a devout and worthy one. They were doubtless missing the temple and its rituals, which had brought them so much strength and comfort. Surely, to want to recommence such worship in Babylon, perhaps using the talents and technical knowledge of the priests who were with them in exile, including Ezekiel himself, surely God must approve of that. They probably expected Ezekiel to commend them for their piety and good sense. Not so. He saw in their plan proof that they were no different from their rebellious forebears. They wanted to offer sacrifice where it suited them, not in the one place chosen and sanctified by God. It also showed Ezekiel that they had abandoned hope of a return to Jerusalem, and in Yahweh's power to save.

As he thought about Jerusalem, the temple and its sacrifices, Ezekiel saw them in his mind's eye. He prophesied their total destruction by an unstoppable fire. (20:47) But his words were dismissed as mere riddles. (20:49) So he spoke again, prophesying the coming of a sword, which would destroy both good and bad alike in Jerusalem and throughout Judah. (21:3) Jerusalem, he said, is no longer the 'city of righteousness' but the 'blood guilty city'. (22:2) He couldn't speak these words as if he were a disinterested spectator. It hurt him to say such things, and he sighed and spoke with breaking heart. (21:6)

The Catastrophe

The whole of Ezekiel's ministry up to this point – all his words, all his actions, all his suffering – had concentrated on the coming catastrophe, the final destruction of Jerusalem and Judah. At last the terrible event came. The siege of Jerusalem began toward the end of 589 BCE. Hundreds of miles away in Babylon, Ezekiel recorded the date so that when the news eventually came to the exiles, the truth of the word of God he had been proclaiming would be clear to all. (24:2)

Ezekiel never preached as a detached observer, untouched by the terrible events he prophesied. His own life was bound up in the tragedy. Jerusalem was to be devastated and its people to die by sword and fire. Ezekiel himself also had to suffer. He was told by God that his wife, 'the delight of his eyes', would die suddenly. He was also told that when that terrible event happened he was not to show any signs of grief and mourning; no weeping, no going barefoot and bareheaded. Even the groans he cannot suppress must be quiet. (24:16,17) Not surprisingly, when his fellow exiles noticed his strange behaviour, they asked him what it meant. He gave them God's message: when 'the delight of their eyes' – the temple in Jerusalem – is taken from them, they too will be stricken with inexpressible grief, and all the normal standards of behaviour will be forgotten.

Ezekiel was both prophet and priest. As a priest he would publicly proclaim the Law of God at festivals, traditional words. As a prophet he delivered new words from God, words perhaps of comfort, perhaps of judgement. In both roles he stood between the people and God. So he was the first to feel the pain of God's anger, and the first to know the healing of God's grace. He tells us that God appointed him as a watchman for the nation. (33:1–9) It was his duty to watch for the approach of danger and to warn people to protect themselves. An obvious danger would be foreign armies, but a far greater danger was the approach of God himself as he came in judgement. Ezekiel the watchman had to warn people so that the wicked might abandon their evil ways, and the righteous would be careful not to slip. His task was that of a pastor, reminding people how, despite everything, God was constantly calling them into a close, loving covenant with himself.

After all the warnings, after all the pleadings, the moment came. Jerusalem had fallen. Waiting for this terrible event paralysed Ezekiel. He was unable to move his limbs or to speak. But when the news was brought to Babylon and the uncertainty removed, Ezekiel found movement in his limbs and speech on his tongue. (33:22) The crisis had passed; judgement had been carried out; the worst had happened. Now, like a parent who has had to punish the child he loves, Yahweh would come to his people offering salvation. Ezekiel would have a new task, that of preparing Israel for the future.

The Fate of the Shepherds

While Ezekiel saw himself as a watchman, he saw the political leaders of Judah as shepherds. This was no new description. It had a long history and was well understood by both leaders and people. It was common usage in the ancient Middle East. Besides Israel and Judah, rulers in Egypt and Mesopotamia had described themselves as shepherds, those who rule and lead, who care and protect. Ezekiel condemned the shepherds of Israel. They liked to exercise power and to enjoy the privileges, but in their role as protectors and providers, especially as protectors of the weak, they had failed completely. (34:1–10) They had forgotten that their position was not of their own creating; it was a gift from Yahweh, who was himself the Great Shepherd of Israel. Because of their failure, the shepherds would be dismissed and Yahweh himself would take charge of the flock. He would care for the weak, collect the scattered and find them pasture where they would be safe and where the food was good. (34:11–16)

It is not just the shepherds who are criticised. The sheep themselves are at fault. With no shepherds to control them, the strong have pushed aside the weak and when they have eaten and drunk their fill, they foul the waterhole and trample the pasture, and the weak become weaker still. All this will stop when Yahweh himself becomes the shepherd. (25:31–46)

Perhaps Ezekiel wondered how it would work out in practice, how Yahweh, the invisible and utterly unknowable God, could be the shepherd-king of Israel. Perhaps it was his pondering that led him to announce that God would carry out his promise by sending his 'servant David' to be the shepherd. (34:23) This was not some fantasy about King David rising from the dead. Nor was it political wishful thinking that the disgraced and defeated house of David would somehow re-establish a ruling dynasty. Ezekiel's hope was that God would, in his own good time, send his servant, an ideal David, to rule on God's behalf as the shepherd of Israel. This kingdom of David would be no ordinary kingdom. Unlike the kingdoms of Assyria and Babylon and Egypt, it would not be established and maintained by military force. It would be a kingdom of peace. The land would resemble the Garden of Eden, full of peace and plenty. (34:23–27) Like Isaiah (11:6–9), Ezekiel foresaw a messianic age, and Christians believe his hopes have been fulfilled in the person of Jesus.

Hope for the Future

Again God spoke to Ezekiel about the new start he was offering to Israel. They did not change, they continued to be apostate and immoral. (36:20) But God does not change either. For his own name's sake, he will restore Israel to the Promised Land. (36:24) He will cleanse them from their sins, and to ensure a complete renewal of the nation he will give them a new heart. (36:26) It will be as if a heart of stone was replaced by a living heart of flesh. There will be a new awareness of God's grace, because God will pour his spirit into each person and they will be transformed, with a longing to keep God's Law. (36:27) Once again, searching for words to convey the wonder of life lived in harmony with God, Ezekiel goes to the common mythology of the Middle East and describes the new life in terms of paradise regained, the human race readmitted to Eden. (36:35)

We can see how Ezekiel used all his powers of imagination and invention to find ways to proclaim his message and make it real and living to his hearers. The watchman, the shepherd, eagles, vines, foundlings, the Garden of Eden, a new heart, acted parables, physical illness – even his own stark grief over the death of his wife – all were, for Ezekiel, ways of revealing the words and the will of God. It was his unshakeable belief in the constancy and the grace of Yahweh that inspired Ezekiel to compose his greatest and best-known word picture – the valley of dry bones.

He was carried by the spirit of God into a valley that had been the site of a battle. (37:1–2) The fighting was long over, for the bodies of the slain were decayed, the bones dry. He was asked by God if such corpses could ever live again. It was clear that by any human standards it was impossible. But Ezekiel was aware of God's power and cautiously replied, 'Yahweh, you know.' (37:3) At Yahweh's command, Ezekiel called to the human remains. With a rustling sound the bones came together, forming skeletons. Then sinews grew, then a covering of skin. There was a semblance of human form but, as yet, no life. They looked like the newly dead. Then, just as in the creation story (Genesis 2:7) God breathed his spirit into the bodies. At once they were filled with life. They rose to their feet, a great army. (37:9)

In this wonderful picture Ezekiel gave God's answer to the despairing exiles who thought that since the fall of Jerusalem the nation was dead, dismembered and finished. Ezekiel's message was that nothing is ever beyond the power and grace of God. Even the dead can live again.

The re-creation of the people of God would be accompanied by a demonstration that Yahweh was not merely the God of Israel, but the only God, the ruler and judge of all nations. The setting up and recognition of Yahweh's universal rule is told in a complicated story of the defeat of a mythological figure, the warrior Gog, and his mighty armies. (Chs. 38 and 39) Gog's kingdom is called Magog, and this may uncover the real meaning of Gog. There are prophecies against many nations in the Book of Ezekiel, but there are no prophecies against Babylon. Perhaps that isn't surprising. After all, Ezekiel was a captive in Babylon and it might have been dangerous for him to have spoken out openly, condemning it and predicting its overthrow and destruction. Perhaps he didn't speak openly, but in code.

The Hebrew letters of the word Magog are simply MGG. If, in each case, we simply move one letter back in the Hebrew alphabet, we get LBB. And if we then turn the new word round, we get BBL – Babel or Babylon. It might be fanciful, but it might be true! And if it is true, then we have found Ezekiel's way of prophesying that even mighty Babylon will not stand if Yahweh decrees that it shall fall.

A Vision of a New Temple

In the spring of the year 573 BCE, Ezekiel was once again seized by God and, in a vision, transported to Jerusalem. (40:1) He was placed on a high hill and was immediately aware of what seemed to be a great city spread out before him. Then he realised that it was not a city; it was the new temple in the new Jerusalem. He was met by a guide, a divinely appointed surveyor, whose appearance was as if he were made of bronze.

Carrying his measuring instruments with him, the guide led Ezekiel on a detailed tour of the temple. As they went along everything was measured so that Ezekiel was in no doubt as to the size and magnificence of the building. This was no man-made edifice; this was the creation of God himself. Rising in ever higher terraces, it was a fitting dwelling for the Lord of the universe. Ezekiel was shown walls and gateways, vestibules, storerooms, changing rooms, flights of steps, kitchens, pillars, windows … everything.

The building was complete, but like the bodies in the valley of dry bones that were entire but dead until God breathed his spirit into them, so the temple was complete but empty because God was not in it. Earlier in his ministry, Ezekiel had recorded a vision in which he had seen the glory of God leaving the temple and abandoning the city. (11:23) In this new vision all that is reversed. Ezekiel wrote, 'Afterwards he brought me to the gate, the gate facing east. And behold, the glory of the God of Israel came from the east; and the sound of his coming was like the sound of many waters; and the earth shone with his glory.' (43:1–2) Yahweh had returned to his temple, and the east door by which he entered was to be shut for ever. (44:2)

Among the mass of detailed regulations about how the temple would be organised is an inspiring passage telling how the dwelling of God in the temple would be the source of life and healing for the whole world. Once again the divinely appointed guide was with him, measuring as he went. Ezekiel was shown a trickle of water coming from under the threshold of the temple. The tiny stream disappeared under the wall, and Ezekiel was taken out by the north gate and round to where the stream reappeared. They followed it, measuring its depth every half mile. Beginning ankle deep, it quickly deepened until it could only be crossed by a swimmer. (47:3–6) On the banks of the river were trees that bore fruit every month, a continual harvest. (47:12) The leaves of the trees had healing qualities. (47:12) The life-giving quality of the water was such that fish abounded, and even the Dead Sea into which it flowed was turned into fresh water. (47:8)

Again Ezekiel had turned to the mythology of paradise, the Garden of Eden, to describe what the return of Yahweh to his temple would mean. It would mean renewal for Israel and hope for every nation. God's chosen people would live again in their own land. They would worship and serve Yahweh faithfully, and their new life would be the prelude to renewal for the whole earth and blessing for all people – God's ancient promise to Abraham. It would be the triumph of God's grace and forgiveness. That is the message of Ezekiel.

Second Isaiah

Chapters 40–55 of the biblical Book of Isaiah come from a different pen than the first thirty-nine chapters, which are concerned
with the career and teaching of the statesman-prophet, Isaiah of
Jerusalem. The literary style is different and the setting is clearly
many years later, during the Judaean exile in Babylon.

We do not know the name of the prophet, but because of the
position of his writings in the Book of Isaiah, he is often referred
to as Second Isaiah or Deutero-Isaiah.

It is tempting to give him the title 'The Prophet'. There are
several reasons for this:

1. He is in the prophetic tradition of the Old Testament,
   called to proclaim the word of God to the people of his
   own time, and seeing the hand of God in the events of
   the world, in the rise and fall of nations.

2. He has a particular qualification for the title, 'The
   Prophet'. He speaks and writes a good deal about 'The
   Servant of the Lord'. In the Old Testament many people
   are called servants of Yahweh, but none more than
   Moses, who is given the title about forty times. There are
   close links between Moses and Second Isaiah. Moses led
   the people of Israel from their captivity or exile in Egypt
   to freedom in their Promised Land. Second Isaiah
   promises a second and more glorious exodus by which
   God will lead the Judaean exiles from Babylon back to
   the same holy land.

3. Just before the death of Moses, God said that he would
   raise up 'another prophet' like him. 'I will raise up for
   them a prophet like you from among their brethren and
   he shall speak to them all that I command him.'

(Deuteronomy 18:15) A prophet like Moses! We cannot claim that the author of Isaiah 40–55 was the prophet spoken of by God, but it is hard to find a better candidate – unless it is Jesus, as many Christians believe.

Certainly these chapters of Isaiah had a profound effect on Jesus. The Prophet speaks of God's servant who will save his people by his undeserved suffering. Jesus said that he had come as a servant – to serve, not to be served. The story of his sufferings, the Passion Story, seems to have been modelled in part on Chapters 52 and 53 of Isaiah.

The return from exile that the Prophet foresaw did take place, though it was not quite the triumphal procession he hoped for. Because of his inspiration to his own people in their history of suffering, and because of his influence on Jesus and therefore on the Christian faith, his writings are of the greatest importance.

Once again references have been put in for those who like to use them.

The Prophet's Story

Life Among the Exiles

Babylon was a magnificent city. Its royalty, its courtiers and its merchants lived in luxury and could feast in great magnificence every day. But like every great city it had its poor, and among the poorest of the poor were the exiles from Judah, living in their shanty towns. For them life was miserable, and most of them had lost any hope that it might improve. We hear their voice in Psalm 137: 'By the waters of Babylon there we sat down and wept, when we remembered Zion.' Zion, or Jerusalem, was a fading memory. Its people and the people of the surrounding towns and villages had been hauled off into exile when Nebuchadrezzar, King of Babylon, had attacked and defeated Judah. He had besieged and conquered Jerusalem, first in the year 597 BCE, and then again ten years later, when he destroyed the city. Each time people had been taken into exile.

Some of them had been living in Babylon for forty years. For the older exiles memories of life in Jerusalem were still strong. But younger people and children knew nothing but life in the great city of Babylon. It was a place of magnificent public buildings and royal palaces. The gardens on the roof and terraces of Nebuchadrezzar's palace were among the wonders of the ancient world, the fabled Hanging Gardens of Babylon. There were great festivals and processions, parading the wealth of Babylon, the splendour of its king and the power of its gods. The New Year festival celebrated the creation of the world by Marduk, the great god of the Babylonians, and hymns praising Marduk became familiar to the exiles, who watched with fascination the display of religious and national self-congratulation.

How depressing it was. But there seemed to be no way to argue against it. Yahweh, the God of the people of Israel and Judah, had proved powerless in the face of Marduk. His people had been humiliated and taken into exile. His holy city, Jerusalem, had been destroyed. His house, the temple, was a heap of stones. The hymns of the Babylonians were probably right; Marduk was all-powerful, and no god could be compared with him. What clearer proof could there be than the respective positions of the rich Babylonians and the Judaean exiles who were their prisoners and their pool of slave labour?

Forty years is a long time to be a subject people, and the exiles in Babylon had lost all hope. Prophets, whom some of the older exiles had seen and heard, men like Jeremiah and Ezekiel, had preached mixed messages of doom and restoration. Ezekiel, an exile himself, had looked forward to the day when Jerusalem would be restored and the temple rebuilt. But his words of doom spoke more clearly to the people of Judah than his visionary dreams of a new Jerusalem. And so hope had faded and resignation and despair had become the natural attitude of the exiles. It was in this despairing situation that the Prophet preached his message.

We know from the Book of Ezekiel that even in exile the displaced people of Judah were allowed to meet in each other's houses. They would meet for worship, when the Psalms and prayers they had used in Jerusalem would be sung and recited, keeping them in touch with their ancestral faith, and perhaps causing them to reflect ruefully on how powerless their God Yahweh seemed to be. The exiles were ready to admit that their suffering was deserved. But was there to be no end to it? The Prophet must have been present when the exiles met and reminisced and despaired. He knew how they felt. He was sensitive to their misery and aware of the way hope had seeped out and finally been lost.

A Second Exodus

It was to these hopeless, despairing people that he came with a message of salvation. He wasn't offering a vague hope; he spoke of a certainty. It wasn't a promise of salvation based on repentance and reform. Many prophets in the past had offered that. His was a new message of salvation based solely on the mercy and love of Yahweh. In his opening words, which sum up the whole of his message, the Prophet proclaimed the mercy of God and the certainty of a second Exodus.

'Comfort, comfort my people, says your God. Speak tenderly to Jerusalem, and cry to her that her warfare is ended, that her iniquity is pardoned, that she has received from the Lord's hand double for all her sins.' (40:1,2)

That was the Prophet's message: comfort and tenderness from God, the end of war, her sins punished and the punishment ended for ever. He went on to speak of the return from exile that God will accomplish: 'In the wilderness prepare the way of the Lord, make straight in the desert a highway for our God. Every valley shall be lifted up, and every mountain and hill be made low; the uneven ground shall become level, and the rough places a plain.' (40:3,4)

This time the exodus will not be a scurrying, fearful escape, their route blocked by the sea and their arrival delayed for forty years by life and death in the wilderness. This time 'you shall not go out in haste, and you shall not go out in flight, for the Lord will go with you, and the God of Israel shall be your rear-guard'. (52:12) In this new exodus the wilderness itself will be transformed. There will be no crises of drought and hunger as in the first Exodus. (41:18) This was the Prophet's vision of a second Exodus.

It will be so different from the first. This time a triumphal highway will be constructed. Yahweh will travel along the magnificent route, and it will make Marduk's progress in the processions of Babylon look paltry and mean. And when Yahweh moves in triumph toward Jerusalem, it will be witnessed, not just by the citizens of one city, but by the whole earth. (40:5)

The Prophet was ordered to proclaim this message of salvation. The voice of God told him to cry out, to preach. (40:6) Like many before him, the Prophet wondered how effective he would be. He was cautious and responded that the people to whom he must speak were neither receptive nor determined. They were weak human beings, changeable like everything else on earth.

God reassures him. Certainly the people are like grass and there is nothing stable about them, but what God is about to do does not depend on people, it depends on God. (40:8)

We don't know how this wonderful message was received – but we can guess. The fact that the Prophet had to plead with his people, that he constantly repeated his message, that he used every means he could to convince them that his message was true, is a clear sign that they did not believe him. Their despair was too deep. They had actually come to believe that Yahweh was finished, and that Marduk was the god who could do great things.

False Gods and True God

Somehow the Prophet had to break down the lethargy and dispel the despair he found all around him. At the great festivals, images of Marduk and other gods of Babylon were carried in procession through the streets of the city. Their magnificence was there for all to see. 'But just think,' says the Prophet, 'what are you looking at? Is it a god? No, of course not; it is a piece of wood or metal.' Several times he launched into derisive attacks on the man-made gods of Babylon. He pictures a Babylonian worshipper growing a tree, cutting it down, then taking part of it to make a fire to bake bread, and using the rest to make a god, which he then bows down to and worships. He says to it, 'Deliver me, for thou art my god!' (44:15–17)

'How can the exiles respect or be impressed by that?' asks the Prophet. How can they fear a piece of wood or metal? It can't do anything; it can't even move unless someone carries it. And all the Babylonian gods are like that. They are nothing and they do nothing. They didn't create the world; Yahweh did.

The Prophet composed poems celebrating the creative power of Yahweh. He invited his hearers and readers to look at the stars and wonder at the beauty of Yahweh's creation. 'Lift up your eyes on high and see: who created these? He who brings out their host by number, calling them all by name; by the greatness of his might, and because he is strong in power not one is missing.' (40:26) The Prophet praises Yahweh as creator and scorns the gods of Babylon. Far from being creators, they are themselves the creations of men. (40:19,20)

Still driving home his message that Yahweh is the only God, he asks, 'Who has measured the waters in the hollow of his hand

and marked off the heavens with a span, enclosed the dust of the earth in a measure and weighed the mountains in scales and the hills in a balance?'

The exiles know the answer because they know the Psalms that celebrate Yahweh as creator. They may even have heard the creation stories that became part of the Book of Genesis.

Yahweh is the creator, and only he. But he is more than creator. He is also Lord of history. Human beings, however powerful they may seem to be, even rulers of Babylon, are like grasshoppers. It is Yahweh who gives kings their power and he who takes it from them. (40:23,24)

The Prophet used every means he could to persuade his people. He composed a series of court hearings. The court is to decide who is the real and effective God. A public notice is issued: 'Let us together draw near for judgement.' (41:1) The gods are summoned to appear in court and asked who actually causes the events of history to happen. In particular they are asked who caused the rise of 'one from the east'. This 'one from the east' is not named, but it is clear that it is Cyrus, king of Persia. The speed of Cyrus's victories was startling the world and threatening the Babylonian empire. In court there is no reply from the gods of Babylon, so Yahweh's claim is upheld; he is the one true God, directing the course of history, determining the rise and fall of nations. (41:4)

'Fear Not'

The Prophet created such an overwhelming picture of the power of Yahweh that he had to reassure the exiles that they were not in danger from God's power. The words 'fear not' appear again and again in his message. Babylon and its rulers should fear, but Israel was Yahweh's servant, his chosen one. (41:8)

Prophets had often warned Israel of God's anger at the nation's apostasy. Their punishment, even the exile, was foretold by prophets like Amos and Jeremiah. There was a real place for fear then. But those days had passed. The God who created Israel, led it and punished it, was now its Redeemer. (41:14) This is the heart of the Prophet's message: Israel's time of fear is over, the time of redemption is here. Yahweh says, 'You are precious in my eyes, and honoured, and I love you.' (43:4)

A New Moses

The people of Israel always looked back to the Exodus from Egypt as the time when Yahweh most clearly showed his love for them. He had raised up Moses as their leader and deliverer. Then he had made 'a way in the sea, a path in the mighty waters.' (43:16) What wonderful days those had been! But the time was coming when those days of old would be considered as nothing compared with the new deliverance which Yahweh was planning. (43:19)

The exiles may have been slow to believe the Prophet's message, but when they heard how Yahweh was going to accomplish their deliverance, they were ready to laugh in derision or cry out that the suggestion was a disgrace – disloyal, irreligious and totally unacceptable. That is because the Prophet had announced that the nation's salvation would be achieved by a foreigner, Cyrus, king of Persia. According to the Prophet Yahweh had said, 'He is my shepherd, and he shall fulfil all my purpose.' (44:28)

What a shocking thing to say! Prophets like Amos, Jeremiah and Ezekiel had threatened that God would use foreigners to punish his people. But never before had it been suggested that a foreign king would be their *saviour*. The word the Prophet uses to describe Cyrus's role is 'Messiah' – the anointed one. 'Thus says the Lord to his anointed, to Cyrus, whose right hand I have grasped, to subdue nations before him … I will give you the treasures of darkness and the hoards in secret places, that you may know that it is I, the Lord, the God of Israel, who call you by your name. (45:1,3)

It is no surprise that the Prophet met opposition when he spoke like this. There were some among the exiles who said that Yahweh would simply not do such a thing – he would never use a foreigner to save Israel. 'What about the house of David?' they said. 'Surely that is where God's people should look for a saviour.'

The Prophet's response is that their complaints are like the quarrels of a pot with the potter who made it. How can Israel, God's creation, question the wisdom and the acts of the creator?

(45:9) God is a mystery, his ways are often hidden and humans must accept that there is much about God that they will never understand. (45:15)

Babylon Will Fall

In a great poem of triumph, the Prophet pictures the fall of Babylon, when Cyrus and his armies overthrow it. The city falls and its gods are shown to be powerless. Their worshippers try to save the images; they load them on to beasts and try to rescue them from the fallen city. 'Bel bows down, Nebo stoops, their idols are on beasts and cattle ... They cannot save the burden, but themselves go into captivity.' (46:1,2) Bel is another name for Marduk, and Nebo is Marduk's son. They are finished, though their worshippers try to carry them to safety. What a contrast to Yahweh. Far from being carried by his worshippers, Yahweh carried Israel as a child, and still carries him. (46:3,4) Israel should not doubt God. If they call to mind what God has promised and what he has done in the past, they will realise that they can trust him in the future. (46:12,13)

In one of the Prophet's poems foretelling the fall of Babylon, the city is addressed as if she were a great lady, 'the virgin daughter of Babylon'. Her life will no longer be sheltered and refined. She will become a slave, her clothes no longer elegant and rich, but tucked up for work. (47:1–4) Instead of being at the centre of world events, in the bright light of fame, she will be silent and in darkness. (47:5) It had seemed as if her power would last for ever, but the twin disasters of the death of her children and widowhood will come upon her. (47:7–9) Neither the wisdom of its sages nor the skills of its magicians will be able to save Babylon. The guidance of its famous astrologers will be of no avail. (47:10–13) 'There is no one to save you.' (47:15)

The Prophet is so sure that Babylon will fall that he encourages the exiles to imagine their escape. (48:20) But the exiles are not so sure. Still unable to shake off their despair, they cannot share the Prophet's optimism. They are so weighed down by their present troubles that they think his prophecies are wishful thinking. So once again he has to deal with their despair. He has heard what they say, that God has forsaken them. 'What nonsense,' says the Prophet. 'Can a woman forget her sucking child, that she should have no compassion on the son of her womb? Even these may forget, yet I will not forget you.' (49:14,15)

Others complained that Israel could have no future because her children have been taken away by death or by exile. The Prophet responds that they will have so many descendants that they will complain that there is no room for them all. What is more, the nations to whom their children have been exiled will return them at God's command. (49:22)

The exiles were still not convinced and said that his words were brave and fine, but could the things he spoke of actually happen? 'Can the prey be taken from the mighty or the captives of a tyrant be rescued?' (49:24) The Prophet understands their doubts; they are right to say that such acts are against all expectation, but Yahweh is God and his might will ensure that the promised deliverance takes place. The result will not only be the saving of Israel; the world at large will come to see the power of Yahweh. 'All flesh shall know that I am the Lord your Saviour, and your Redeemer, the Mighty One of Jacob.' (49:26)

The God of all the Earth

The Prophet let his beliefs lead him where no earlier prophet had ventured. He realised that if Yahweh is the only God then he must be the God of all the earth and of all nations. He may have chosen Israel as his 'bride' and as his 'servant', but he has done that so that through Israel all people might come to know him, worship him and receive his blessing. In one of his poems he calls Israel to understand the broadness of Yahweh's love: 'Listen to me, my people, and give ear to me, my nation; for a law will go forth from me, and my justice for a light to the peoples ... my salvation has gone forth, and my arms will rule the peoples; the coastlands wait for me, and for my arm they hope.' (51:4,5)

What the Prophet looks for is the fulfilment of God's promise to Abraham that through him and his descendants all people would be blessed.

With great beauty he describes the coming of God's salvation.

It will be announced by a messenger: 'How beautiful upon the mountains are the feet of him who brings good tidings ... who publishes salvation, who says to Zion, "Your God reigns."' (52:7) The watchmen on the city walls see the coming of the messenger and join in the celebration, and the people's response can be only to rejoice.

The Servant of the Lord

And what of the Servant of the Lord? Though the Prophet speaks of the servant many times in his poems, there are four particular passages which have become known as the 'Servant Songs'. The passages are Chapter 42, verses 1–4; Chapter 49, verses 1–6; Chapter 50, verses 4–9; and Chapter 52, verse 13–Chapter 53, verse 12.

The first Servant Song, Chapter 42, verses 1–4, is brief enough to be quoted in full:

> Behold my servant, whom I uphold,
> my chosen, in whom my soul delights;
> I have put my Spirit upon him,
> he will bring forth justice to the nations.
> He will not cry or lift up his voice,
> or make it heard in the street;
> a bruised reed he will not break,
> and a dimly burning wick he will not quench;
> he will faithfully bring forth justice.
> He will not fail or be discouraged
> till he has established justice in the earth;
> and the coastlands wait for his law.

In this poem, God is the speaker. He tells people to pay attention to his Servant. The Servant is chosen and upheld by God, who delights in him and inspires him. He has been commissioned to bring justice to the nations, and he will carry out the task with sensitivity and gentleness. The tenderest of things will not be harmed by him. Despite disappointments, he will not give up until he has carried out his task. God's description of the Servant reveals that his mission is not simply to Israel; it is awaited by 'the coastlands' – that is, by all the nations of the world. There is also a distinct and chilling hint that there is suffering in store for the servant.

In this Servant Song we are told many things about the Servant, but not who he is.

The second Servant Song, Chapter 49, verses 1–6, is spoken by the Servant himself. It tells of his call by God. Like Jeremiah, he feels that he was chosen and destined for his work even before he was born. 'The Lord called me from the womb, from the body of my mother he named my name.' After a time of preparation during which he was 'hid away', he was commissioned to speak out sharply and powerfully. Already the Servant has experienced opposition and difficulty: 'I have laboured in vain, I have spent my strength for nothing and vanity, yet surely my right is with the Lord.' The Servant sees his task as bringing Israel back to loyalty to Yahweh and making Yahweh's light shine out, drawing foreign nations to him, 'that my salvation may reach to the end of the earth'.

One additional thing needs to be said. In this Servant Song, in verse 3, we actually read the words, 'Your are my Servant, Israel, in whom I will be glorified.' Most Old Testament scholars agree that the word 'Israel' was probably an insertion, added later, and that this poem like the other Servant Songs, keeps silence about the Servant's identity.

In the third Servant Song, Chapter 50, verses 4–9, the Servant again speaks about his task of declaring God's plans and giving comfort. He tells of God's continual support and inspiration that comes 'morning by morning'. He speaks of his obedience to God's command, even though he has been violently persecuted. With the continued help of God he has withstood the ill-treatment and is confident that God will vindicate him in the end. He invites his enemies to take him to trial before God, knowing that God will be not only the judge but his defence counsel as well. His enemies may think themselves strong, but before the power of God they are tiny, weak and of no account – 'the moth will eat them up'.

Again we are told much about the Servant, but not who he is. In fact the word 'Servant' is not used in the poem. Instead of 'Servant' he uses the word 'Disciple' – one who is taught, a learner. In the poem the disciple recounts the suffering his calling has cost him. In this he is like Moses and Jeremiah and other men of the Old Testament who were called by God and suffered as they faithfully carried out their tasks. In this Servant Song we begin to see the emergence of a new and revolutionary idea in the religion of Israel, one that the whole of the Book of Job is devoted to thinking out. The common belief was that good fortune was a sign of the blessing of God, whereas ill fortune was a sure indication that God was not on your side. Here we see the beginning of a new idea that despite suffering, the Servant has been chosen and helped by God who will demonstrate that he is in the right.

The final Servant song, which spans from Chapter 52, verse 13 through to Chapter 53, verse 12, is the longest of the Servant Songs and the one that speaks most clearly of the suffering the Servant has experienced and the way people's understanding of suffering has to change. In the first part of the poem Yahweh announces the success of his Servant's mission. This has been a surprise to onlookers. At first, his suffering, which disfigured him, had been interpreted in the traditional way as indicating the displeasure of Yahweh. But in spite of suffering the Servant has been 'exalted and lifted up'. Even rulers will be startled, even politicians will be silenced by the sight of one whom they thought despised, being exalted by God.

As Chapter 53 begins we hear the voices of people who know of the Servant and his sufferings. Perhaps these are the Prophet's fellow exiles. They describe his lifelong suffering. In eight verses (2–9) his whole life is summarised. From childhood he was unattractive and, as a result, looked down on and undervalued. His suffering was seen in the traditional way as the punishment of God – 'we esteemed him stricken, smitten by God, and afflicted'. But slowly the light dawned, and they admit that they were wrong, and that his suffering had a purpose; in fact, 'he was wounded for our transgressions, he was bruised for our iniquities'.

In verse 7 the poet takes us back to the Servant's pains and the way he bore them. Though he was unjustly accused, he bore it all in silence. He was like a lamb before the slaughterer or a sheep before the shearer. He was also like the devout man of Psalm 38 (verses 13,14) who wrote, 'I am like a dumb man who does not open his mouth ... like a man in whose mouth are no rebukes.' His death was violent; he was 'cut off out of the land of the living'. And even in death he was dishonoured, buried in disgrace among criminals, despite his innocence.

The poem ends on a high note of triumph. In spite of what people saw and how they misjudged and belittled the Servant, it is now clear that everything that has happened has been in accordance with Yahweh's plan. Contrary to popular opinion 'it was the will of the Lord to bruise him'. The final result will be that the Servant will live again, he will have a family, 'he will see his offspring'. What is more, it is not only the Servant who will be rewarded for his steadfastness; because of the Servant's righteousness many unrighteous people will be saved.

The Identity of the Servant

As we reach the end of the last Servant Song we still do not know the identity of the Servant. Very often in these chapters of the Book of Isaiah we read the words, 'my servant Israel'. To say that the Servant is Israel is a very attractive interpretation. Like the Servant, Israel was chosen and called by God and given a mission. Throughout its history the nation has suffered. But the sufferings of the Servant are undeserved, whereas it is never suggested in the Old Testament that Israel's suffering is undeserved. Quite the reverse: prophet after prophet warned that Israel would suffer as a result of its disloyalty to Yahweh. Also, in the Servant Songs the Servant is told to restore Israel. A further point, a grammatical one, but still important, is that all the 'yous' addressed to the Servant are in the singular. So it seems that the Servant is a particular individual. But who?

He might have been a contemporary of the Prophet whose life and suffering were well known to the exiles in Babylon, but who is unknown to us.

Perhaps it was the Prophet himself. Like other prophets, notably Jeremiah, the Servant records his call, he records his conviction that before birth he was destined to serve God, and he records the suffering which came to him because of his proclamation of God's word. Perhaps the Prophet had learnt to interpret his own sufferings, and had come to see that out of the evil of suffering good could come. And when he speaks of death and burial, it may have been a poetic way of speaking of his own experience of life-threatening hardship and subsequent recovery. Perhaps he had been imprisoned in a Babylonian gaol, and the 'resurrection' was his experience of release. So perhaps the Prophet is the Servant.

Both Jewish and Christian thinkers have suggested that the Servant was an ideal figure who was yet to appear. There is a great deal in the New Testament to suggest that Jesus modelled his ministry on that of the Servant. Referring to himself as the Son of Man, he said that it was his destiny to suffer. (Mark 10:33,34) He said that he had come to be a servant, and that the giving of his life would provide a ransom or salvation for many. (Mark 10:45) Several times in St John's Gospel Jesus speaks of being 'lifted up' on the cross, exalted in suffering. (John 3:14 and 12:32) This echoes the words of the last Servant Song. (53:13) There is a lot of evidence to suggest that the Gospel writers were deeply influenced by the Servant Songs when they came to write the story of Jesus. In particular, in writing the Passion Story they have used ideas and phrases out of the Servant Songs (and out of Psalm 22) to explain Jesus' suffering, death and resurrection, which were so important to them and to thousands of others.

So who was the Servant? We do not know. And who was the Prophet? Again we do not know. He was an exile in Babylon, a prophet who proclaimed the word of God and who brought a message of hope to a despairing people. He promised a second Exodus, a glorious return to their Promised Land. This salvation did not have to be earned; it came as grace, a gift from God who said, 'Come, buy wine and milk without money and without price.' (55:1)

The Prophet's hopes were not fulfilled in the way he had imagined. Cyrus did indeed conquer Babylon, and the exiles, or some of them, did return to Jerusalem. But it was not a triumphal return, amazing all peoples. Even the Prophet could not see everything that God had in store. His words were undoubtedly an inspiration to Jesus and to many others who have suffered innocently, both Jews and Christians. Both the Prophet and Jesus declared with clarity and conviction the truth all people need to know, that Yahweh alone is God, that his love does not have to be earned but simply accepted, and that he does indeed bring good out of evil.

The Books of Ezra and Nehemiah

The Return from Exile

It seems sensible to look at these two men and their work together. Their careers overlapped and their work had the same threefold aim:

1. The rebuilding and reconsecrating of the of the holy city Jerusalem;

2. The establishment of the proper worship of Yahweh in the rebuilt and reconsecrated temple;

3. The consolidating of the returned exiles as a nation, the covenant partner of God.

The two books of Ezra and Nehemiah cover a period of about one hundred years, but exact dates are rather difficult to establish. The story begins when Cyrus was king of Persia. In 539 BCE he captured the city of Babylon, where the Jews were prisoners in exile. By royal decree he allowed and encouraged the exiles to return to their own country and begin to rebuild Jerusalem. The story of the return and the difficulties encountered occupy the Books of Ezra and Nehemiah, and take us through to about the year 430 BCE when Nehemiah was governor of the Province of Judah for the second time.

There are difficulties. The Persians had several kings named Artaxerxes, and because it is not always clear which king of that name is referred to we cannot be sure about the timing of the work of Ezra and Nehemiah. We do not know whether Ezra's ministry came before Nehemiah's, or whether they overlapped, or whether Nehemiah came first. As the Bible puts Ezra first, that is how we shall look at their stories. We shall make only one exception, and that is to put Chapter 8 of the Book of Nehemiah (which is the account of Ezra's reading of the Law) between

Chapters 7 and 9 of the Book of Ezra, because that is where it must have been originally.

The biblical Books of Ezra and Nehemiah continue the narrative of the two Books of Chronicles. The four books together comprise a history of the people of Israel up to the re-establishment of the Jews in Judaea after the return from exile. After lists of individuals (beginning with Adam), races, tribes, kings, priests, Levites, musicians, doorkeepers etc. in the first nine chapters of I Chronicles, there follows a history roughly parallel with the narratives found in the Books of Joshua, Judges, Samuel and Kings. The whole of 'the Chronicler's' narrative judges people and events from the point of view of post-exilic orthodoxy. Perhaps the writer or editor was a priest or a Levite writing in the third century BCE.

Ezra's Story

Jerusalem had been sacked by the armies of Babylon in 586 BCE. The city walls had been broken down, royal palaces and other private and public buildings had been destroyed and, deepest tragedy of all, the holy and magnificent temple had been reduced to rubble. Its altar had been smashed and its treasures looted. The royal family, descendants of David, had been humiliated and put to death. The leaders among the people – priests, politicians, generals and businessmen, along with their families – were driven into exile and forced to settle as refugees in the poorer parts of the city of Babylon.

The prophet Jeremiah both predicted and lived through these terrible times. He saw the exile as God's punishment on a faithless nation. He also predicted that when the nation had served its sentence God would bring it back to its own land. The prophet Ezekiel was himself one of the exiles. He, too, accepted the misery of the exiles as part of God's plan, and he, too, looked forward to a return to Jerusalem, the rebuilding of the temple and the restoration of the worship of Yahweh. The unnamed prophet generally known as Second Isaiah, also an exile, taught that God had punished his people. They had paid for their sins. Now Babylon would fall and the exiles would return home in triumph.

There was a return but it was not a triumph. Ezra and Nehemiah were the two practical and courageous men who, in spite of opposition and disappointment, saw the prophet's hopes come to a painstaking and difficult fruition.

The Babylonian Empire came to an end when Cyrus of Persia captured Babylon in 539 BCE. Cyrus's policy was to repatriate prisoners. It was a way of gaining the support of the various national groups within his growing empire. Decrees were published, and the one that affected the Jews read as follows:

'Thus says Cyrus, king of Persia: "The Lord, the God of heaven, has given me all the kingdoms of the earth and he has charged me to build him a house at Jerusalem, which is in Judah. Whoever is among you of all his people, may his God be with him, and let him go up to Jerusalem, which is in Judah and rebuild the house of the Lord, the God of Israel – he is the God who is in Jerusalem; and let each survivor, in whatever place he sojourns, be assisted by the men of his place with silver and gold, with goods and with beasts, besides freewill offerings for the house of God which is in Jerusalem." (Ezra 1:1–4)

There must have been surprise and relief among the exiles. Some of them remembered the words of Jeremiah. He had said that they would return after seventy years. (Jer. 29:10–14) Their time in Babylon could now be seen as an episode in the history of God's people, a Sabbath rest – and now that rest was over. The winding up of businesses, the selling of houses and property acquired over seventy years, all had to be done. As we might expect, not everyone wanted to leave Babylon. Many had been born there, and to them the city was home. Even so, large numbers accepted that this opportunity to return to Jerusalem was sent by God, who was using Cyrus as his servant to bring good to Israel, just as earlier he had used Assyria and Babylon to punish his people.

It was like a second Exodus. Their neighbours, who were perhaps the Jews who didn't return, gave gifts of gold and silver and livestock, all of which were going to be vital as they tried to begin life from scratch in a devastated Jerusalem. Cyrus also returned all the sacred vessels which had been looted by Nebuchadrezzar when he sacked Jerusalem. (Ezra 1:6)

Some 50,000 people returned under the leadership of Sheshbazzar, who seems to have been appointed as the first governor of the restored province of Judah. Sheshbazzar had a supporting council of twelve men, among whom was Zerubbabel who was important because he was a descendant of David. There may well have been plans that he should eventually become king, and the house of David re-established in Judah. We can read about these Messianic hopes that centred around Zerubbabel in the Books of Haggai and Zechariah, and it is strange that it all came to nothing. Perhaps the Persian authorities thought he might become too strong, too great a threat to the king of Persia, and so he had to be removed. But we don't know; we can only guess.

Under the well-organised leadership of the governor and Council of Twelve were priests, Levites, singers, gatekeepers and temple servants, all of whom would be vital for the re-establishing of the proper worship of Yahweh. But there was no temple. The first temple had been a royal gift, the Temple of Solomon, and in keeping with this tradition, Cyrus made a very generous donation. Also, in Solomon's time the people had contributed to the building of the first temple through taxation. This time it was more democratic, and people made voluntary offerings as their contribution to the restoration of the temple and its worship. (Ezra 2:68)

The first, decisive step in the whole programme of restoration was the setting up of the altar. It was placed on precisely the same spot as the altar in Solomon's temple, and just as David had offered sacrifice on the altar before the temple had been built, so it happened in Ezra's day. Also, copying the first temple practice, the Feast of Tabernacles was celebrated after the dedication of the altar. (Ezra 3:1–6)

So a start had been made. From now on daily sacrifices were offered, but there was a great deal of work still to be done. Again following Solomon's example, they began ordering materials for the rebuilding of the temple and employing masons and carpenters. Serious work began in the spring with the promise of months of good building weather before them. Levites supervised the work, and building began on what remained of the foundations of the old temple. (Ezra 3:7,8)

This important step toward restoration was accompanied by a solemn act of worship. The Book of Ezra says, 'When the builders laid the foundation of the temple of the Lord, the priests in their vestments came forward with trumpets, and the Levites, the sons of Asaph, with cymbals, to praise the Lord, according to the directions of David king of Israel; and they sang responsively, praising and giving thanks to the Lord, "For he is good; for his steadfast love endures for ever toward Israel."' (3:10,11) It was such an important and moving occasion that the vast crowd which was present 'shouted aloud for joy', though some of the older people who had known Solomon's temple wept as well.

It wasn't all plain sailing. There were people living around Jerusalem who did not want the city rebuilt and Judah restored as a thriving nation. Their opposition began at this time and continued until all the work was completed. These 'people of the land' as the Bible calls them, wrote a letter to the king of Persia, warning that a rebuilt and strong Jerusalem would rebel against Persia. The king took the warning seriously. His reply stated that he had searched the archives and discovered that it was indeed true that Jerusalem had a record of rebellion and sedition. He therefore decreed that work on the walls and fortifications should stop until he issued further orders. This opposition, very effectively delaying the work of restoration, continued through the reigns of several kings of Persia. (Ezra 4:1–23)

Eventually work recommenced under the inspiration of the prophets Haggai and Zechariah, and under the leadership of Zerubbabel and Joshua. (Ezra 5:1,2) But it didn't last for long. Tattenai, the governor of a nearby province, intervened and ordered the work to stop. He was told that permission had been given many years ago by King Cyrus. Tattenai made a note of all this and wrote to King Darius. Darius had the archives searched and they found the decree of Cyrus that authorised the return and the rebuilding of Jerusalem. Darius's reply to Tattenai read: 'Now you, Tattenai, governor of the province Beyond the River … keep away; let the work on this house of God alone; let the governor of the Jews rebuild this house of God on its site…' To rub salt into the wound, Darius went on to order Tattenai and his associates to make financial contributions to the work of rebuilding, and to supply bulls, sheep, wheat, salt, wine and oil for the sacrifices which were offered daily in the temple. (Ezra 6:6–12)

Whatever he felt about this, Tattenai obeyed without dissent or question, and the work on the temple recommenced with great vigour and was soon completed. This was in the year 515 BCE, and the temple was dedicated with great solemnity, and vast numbers of animals were sacrificed. The dedication of the temple was followed by the solemn observance of the Festival of Passover. 'With joy they celebrated the festival of unleavened bread for seven days; for the Lord had made them joyful.' (Ezra 6:13–18)

This rededication of the temple marked a great turning point in the history of Israel. The dark days of exile were over, and the Passover, the festival celebrating freedom from Egypt, was the most appropriate way of celebrating their new God-given freedom. (Ezra 6:19–22)

Some fifty years passed and a new wave of returning exiles numbering about 5,000 left Babylon. Ezra was among them. He is described as 'a scribe skilled in the Law of Moses that the Lord, the God of Israel had given'. (Ezra 7:6) Ezra seems to have been a civil servant attached to the court and a resident of Babylon. He is also described as a priest. (Ezra 7:11,12). Among this new wave of returnees were more priests, Levites, musicians, gatekeepers and temple servants, all of whom would be required for the proper functioning of temple worship. Ezra organised the journey so that it resembled a second Exodus.

The king, one of those named Artaxerxes, had furnished Ezra with a letter outlining his responsibilities, and giving him the authority he would need. The letter gives permission for any Jews still living in Babylon to return to Jerusalem if they wish. It instructs Ezra to conduct an enquiry into how the Law of Moses is being observed in Judah. The gifts to be taken to Jerusalem are listed, and instructions are given to other areas under Persian rule to make contributions to help the re-establishment of life and worship in the city.

Carrying this important document, Ezra arrived in Jerusalem. He marked the beginning of his work with a public reading of the Law. It was a solemn declaration of intent; that the life of the restored nation would be governed by the Covenant made by God with their ancestors.

The Solemn Reading of the Law (Nehemiah Chapter 8)

The people gathered in the square beside the Watergate and Ezra, assisted by Levites and lay assistants, read the Law. They were reading the Torah Scroll, the books of Genesis, Exodus, Leviticus, Numbers and Deuteronomy. The people stood. The Levites, who are named, 'read from the book, from the Law of God, clearly; and they gave the sense, so that the people understood the reading'. (Neh. 8:8) What were they doing? Perhaps they were there to explain and interpret the Law to the people. If so, they were beginning a long and still continuing tradition of rabbinical comment on, and interpretation, of the Law. Or perhaps it means simply that they read clearly so that everyone could hear.

The whole occasion was one of joy and celebration. The people were told to be happy. There is no place for sadness now that God's will can be done. 'The joy of the Lord is your strength.' (Neh. 8:10)

Once again the Feast of Tabernacles was kept in accordance with the Law. The branches of myrtle, citrus, palm and willow were gathered to make the booths which would remind them of their ancestors' days in the wilderness and their more recent exile to Babylon. All who had returned from Babylon took part, and again happiness was the dominant feeling. 'There was very great rejoicing.' (Neh. 8:17)

But life cannot be lived in a permanent state of joy and celebration. Ezra knew that. Not long after the highlights of the solemn reading of the Law and the joyous celebration of the Feast of Tabernacles, it was reported to Ezra that flagrant disregard of the Law was going on right under his nose. Some of the Jews, even the leaders, even the priests, had contracted foreign marriages. (Ezra 9:1–2) They had taken wives from among the surrounding peoples who neither worshipped Yahweh nor acknowledged the authority of the Law of Moses. To make a foreign or mixed marriage was tantamount to acknowledging the reality of other gods. Ezra was appalled. He tore his clothes and pulled hair from his head and beard to act out his horror. Then he sat in shocked silence for several hours, leaving the people wondering what action he would take when he came out of shock. (Ezra 9:3)

Ezra could certainly not condone these marriages and he prayed fervently for guidance. The matter had become public knowledge and the people gathered to see what would happen. In solidarity with Ezra many of them wept for the nation's disgrace. Ezra's reactions had made his position quite clear and he must have been relieved when the men involved offered to send away their foreign wives. They even found themselves urging Ezra to act firmly: 'Arise, for it is your task, and we are with you; be strong and do it.' (Ezra 10:4) There is no mention of what the dismissed wives thought, said or did about all this!

The people of Jerusalem were called together and those who lived outside the city were brought in to join them in the taking of a solemn oath. Attendance was compulsory, and anyone disobeying would be punished by the confiscation of property and by being cut off from the community. The threats were unnecessary. Everyone attended and met in an open space in front of the temple. Vows were taken to obey the Law, especially in the matter of foreign marriages. It was winter, and even in the Middle East the weather was atrocious, cold, with heavy rain. (Ezra 10:9) Someone sensibly suggested that the public meeting should be abandoned and a committee appointed to see that the Law was observed. Ezra agreed; but you can't help thinking that he knew enough about human nature to realise that once the matter was in the hands of a committee, there must be a serious doubt as to whether the work of administering the oath would ever be completed.

At this point in our Bibles, the Book of Ezra ends and the Book of Nehemiah begins. We ought to be aware that this is rather an artificial division, and that in the Greek translation of the Old Testament the two books are regarded as one.

Nehemiah's Story

Back in the Persian Empire, in the great city of Susa, which was the winter residence of the royal family, an able and clever Jew was employed as cup-bearer to the king. This was a job for a very high-ranking civil servant, a man who was utterly trustworthy. It was a position of great influence. He constantly had the ear of the king and knew his moods and his likes and dislikes. This close and privileged adviser was Nehemiah. (Neh. 1:11)

One day a report was brought to the court in Susa. It told of new trouble for the returned exiles in Jerusalem. The official who brought the report was Hanani, Nehemiah's brother and another high-ranking civil servant. The report spoke of 'great trouble and shame; the wall of Jerusalem is broken down, and its gates have been destroyed by fire'. (Neh. 1:3) Nehemiah was deeply shocked by the news and prayed and fasted for several days, hoping for guidance from God.

It seems as if he thought things out and made careful long-term plans. It was three months before he let the king see how worried he was. He chose his time carefully. It was probably one of the special feasts at which it was the king's custom to grant requests. Nehemiah put on a glum face and, sure enough, the king asked what the problem was. Nehemiah didn't even mention Jerusalem by name. He gave the impression that his chief concern was to repair the tombs of his ancestors. He certainly didn't mention that he wanted to rebuild walls and other fortifications around Jerusalem. (Neh. 2:1–3)

It is unlikely that Artaxerxes was taken in by all this, but he liked Nehemiah and trusted him not to act disloyally. So he granted Nehemiah's request and gave him wide powers, making him governor of Judah. The wily king had also had three months to think about the situation and enquire further into it, and perhaps he had decided that a stronger Judah would be useful in keeping Egypt, the furthest part of his empire, in submission. (Neh. 2:6–8)

Whatever the real or hidden reasons both men may have had, the outcome was that Nehemiah, accompanied by an armed escort befitting his status, set off for Jerusalem. (Neh. 2:9) As he drew toward the end of the journey and was passing through Samaria he felt the first stirrings of opposition. Sanballat, the governor of Samaria, and Tobiah, the governor of the Ammonite region of the empire, registered their opposition to any strengthening of Jerusalem. Nehemiah noted the opposition and moved on. He arrived in Jerusalem in the year 445 BCE.

After three days' rest the energetic new governor began work. He wanted to have a good look at the city and see what sort of state it was in. Only then could he plan the work of repair and rebuilding. He knew that it wouldn't be plain sailing, and that Sanballat and Tobiah had spies in Jerusalem. They would know everything that went on in the city. So, with a small group of carefully selected assistants he began a survey of the city – and he did it by night. (Neh. 2:12–16) Once the survey had been completed he called the people together and told them that for their own self-respect they should not live in a city in ruins, and so the walls must be rebuilt. He made sure in his public announcement that everyone was reminded that they had royal permission to do this. (Neh. 2:18)

No sooner had the announcement been made than Sanballat and Tobiah – now joined by Geshem, who was spokesman for the Arabs – began to object, saying that Judah was strengthening itself in order to rebel against Persian rule. It was obvious that they would make their objections heard in the royal courts of Persia. Nehemiah replied that God had commanded the work to be done, and anyway they had no right to interfere in the affairs of Judah. This was a claim to independence and a political statement of the greatest importance. No wonder Sanballat, Tobiah and Geshem were worried. (Neh. 2:19–20)

Work on the walls began. It was very carefully planned. Reconstruction began at the Sheepgate and they worked in an anticlockwise direction right around the city walls. They were organised in forty-one working groups and most able-bodied people were involved, including priests, Levites, temple workers, tradesmen and women. The walls had not been touched for about

150 years, not since they were smashed down by the invading army of Babylon. So some work was repair and some was total rebuilding. (Neh. 3)

As the work continued the opposition also continued, trying to undermine the morale of the people of Jerusalem. As the first stage of the building was completed, with all the gaps sealed and the walls completed to half the planned height, Tobiah mockingly suggested that it would all fall down as soon as the first fox jumped over it. (Neh. 4:4) When ridicule failed, plans were made to attack the builders. Nehemiah responded by arming some of the people and delivering a stirring speech to build up morale. 'Remember the Lord, who is great and terrible, and fight for your brethren, your sons, your daughters, your wives, and your homes.' (Neh. 4:14)

So the work continued. To step up security, Nehemiah devised a system of shift work in which building and guarding alternated. Also the builders were armed, wearing a sword at their side as they built. In this time of hard work and fear Nehemiah didn't just pray and plan and issue orders. He and his family set a personal example: 'Neither I, nor my brethren nor my servants nor the men of the guard who followed me, none of us took off our clothes; each kept his weapon in his hand.' (Neh. 4:23)

Things got worse. Famine threatened and the harsh conditions in Jerusalem looked like getting very much harsher. Part of the problem was that the Jews who lived in the countryside surrounding Jerusalem, and who normally produced the food for the city, had been brought into the city to help with the urgent work on the walls. The harvest had not been brought in and the farmers were having to let their children be sold as slaves. Some had had to mortgage their land in order to pay their debts, and they were having to borrow money to pay the taxes imposed by Persia. All this came on top of what all the people were paying to support the sacrificial worship of the temple, and to pay the priests. There were serious grievances to be dealt with. (Neh. 5:5)

Nehemiah called a public meeting to consider the problems and to get popular support for the decisions made. He suggested that the crisis might be met by the calling of an extraordinary year of Jubilee. (Neh 5:10) That would mean that all debts would be cancelled and all slaves freed. It seemed a good suggestion and there was general agreement. Perhaps the truth was that they had little choice; after all, Nehemiah was governor. He got everyone to agree and required them to take an oath binding them to keep the covenant. To make quite sure they knew how serious he was, Nehemiah shook out his robe as a threat of excommunication for anyone who broke the promises they had made. (Neh. 5:13)

Sanballat and his allies did not slacken their efforts to prevent or at least to delay the work. When they heard that the repairs were almost completed they suggested a meeting with Nehemiah in a village outside Judah. Nehemiah wasn't going to be drawn out, nor was he going to expose himself to possible danger. He probably enjoyed sending his reply, which said that he couldn't attend the meeting because he was too busy rebuilding the walls. (Neh. 6:2,3)

He was probably wise not to go, because having failed to prevent the rebuilding of the city and its defences, Sanballat and his allies changed their line of attack. It became much more personal. They said that they had information, leaked no doubt, that Judah was planning a revolt against its Persian overlord, and that Nehemiah had set up prophets who were to declare him king. Of course, Nehemiah replied that nothing of the sort was happening. (Neh. 6:6–9)

Perhaps Sanballat had got a grain of truth from his spies and then misinterpreted it. The prophets Haggai and Zechariah were, at about this time, trying to revive the monarchy, and they had lined up the Davidic descendant, Zerubbabel, to take the throne. Perhaps it was this that the spies had heard about. And perhaps it was due to Sanballat's vigilance that it never happened. (Neh. 6:1–9)

About this time there seems to have been a good deal of cloak-and-dagger intrigue going on in Jerusalem. A man called Shemaiah tried to lure Nehemiah into the temple alone. Did he intend to assassinate him? Or did he intend to anoint him king, as Sanballat feared? We shall never know. Nehemiah had been around too long to walk into a possible trap, and he simply said, 'I will not go.' (Neh. 6:10–13)

In spite of all the problems, the work on the walls was completed. It had been an amazing feat, completed in only fifty-two days, and ending in mid-August, the hottest time of the year.

How the workers must have sweated as they made the finishing touches and cleared away the scaffolding and the building materials. Even the nations around, who were not happy that Judah was again a force to be reckoned with, had to acknowledge that God must have had a hand in it. (Neh. 6:16)

Completion and Celebration

The reconstruction of the walls was completed by the hanging of the gates and the appointment of gatekeepers. Nehemiah's brother, Hanani, was made head of security. This, along with his job as commander of the citadel, made him in effect military governor of Judah, working alongside his brother, the political governor. What a powerful family they were! (Neh. 7:1–2)

So now the temple had been rebuilt and the walls had been rebuilt. The gates were in place and the guards vigilant. But where were the people? Jerusalem had been a ghost city for 150 years, ever since the Babylonians sacked it. Even after the exiles had returned, few lived in the city because there was no housing fit to inhabit. Most houses in the city were still rubble. So the returned exiles had gone mainly to the towns and villages where their families had lived before the exile. Nehemiah ordered a census to be taken so that he could know the size and shape of the problem he was dealing with. (Neh. 7:4,5)

As a preparation for measures to repopulate Jerusalem, a solemn service of penitence was held, with the people in sackcloth and ashes. The Law was read, as it had been in the time of Ezra. A great prayer, reviewing the nation's history and asking for deliverance from the yoke of Persia, was offered, and the people swore an oath to keep the Covenant. Certain matters were mentioned as being of particular importance – the prohibition of foreign marriages, the keeping of the Sabbath and the paying of the annual temple tax. These were put in writing and signed and sealed by leaders of both priests and people.

The life of the community was to be regulated by the Torah. Everything was to be done 'as it is written in the Law', (Neh. 10:36) although in practice the regulations about foreign marriages were much more rigorous than in the Law of Moses.

It was now time to deal with the repopulation of Jerusalem. It was achieved by what might be called a tithing of people. One in ten of those living in surrounding towns and villages were required to move into the city. Volunteers were welcomed and highly esteemed. (Neh. 11:1,2) Such an arrangement must have been accompanied by a programme for rebuilding houses.

Nehemiah's work was almost done. The walls of the city, so vital for the safety of the people and for the peaceful functioning of the worship of the temple, had been completed, but they had not been dedicated. A ceremony of dedication would express thanks to God for his help, and would place the walls, and thus the whole city, under his protection.

A great occasion, which would be both religious and secular, was planned. Musicians and Levites were brought in from the towns and villages to ensure that it would be as grand an occasion as possible. (Neh. 12:27,28) All who were to take part were purified. (Neh. 12:30) Two great columns of procession were formed. Ezra was at the head of one column and Nehemiah at the head of the other. Each procession had its own choir. They set off in opposite directions, moving along the top of the wall, singers singing, musicians playing. They circled the city completely, placing it totally in the care of God. The two processions met at the temple. Sacrifices were offered and the sound of jubilation could heard for miles around. (Neh 12:43)

Such great public occasions are useful for convincing people that they live in a successful and stable society, and that their lives and their future are secure. But when the processions are over, the choirs disbanded and the bunting taken down, behind the scenes the leaders still have their hands full of complaints that have to be looked into, problems that have to be solved. It was like that for Nehemiah.

After the great ceremony of the dedication of the walls was over, Nehemiah returned to Persia. (Neh. 13:6) He may have been recalled by the king, or he may have felt that he had done the job he had been sent to do and was now ready for a change – and even readier for a rest. But just as news of problems in Judah had taken him there in the first place, so new reports of problems caused him to return.

He moved more quickly than some people expected. His old enemy, Tobiah, had made friends with one of the priests in Jerusalem and somehow had acquired for himself a flat in the temple precincts. Nehemiah wasn't going to tolerate that and, as he says, 'I threw all the household furniture of Tobiah out of the chamber. Then I gave orders and they cleansed the chamber.' (Neh. 13:8,9)

Another problem was the breaking of the Sabbath. Nehemiah discovered that farmers and smallholders were treading out grapes on the Sabbath and were bringing their goods into Jerusalem and selling them on the Sabbath. Amos had complained about similar abuses in Samaria some 300 years earlier. But people don't change, and again traders were so keen to buy and sell and make a profit that they had set up a Sabbath market. Nehemiah closed the market and forbade traders hanging about the city gates waiting for the Sabbath to end, so that they could rush in and trade at the earliest possible moment. (Neh. 13:15–22)

Like Ezra, Nehemiah was very concerned about foreign marriages. Whatever people had said when Ezra had raged against their mixed marriages, the problem hadn't gone away. Some men obviously did not send away their wives as they said they would. Others must have married foreign girls since Ezra's outburst. One of Nehemiah's concerns was that the children of such marriages would grow up speaking not Hebrew, the covenant language, but only the language of their foreign mother. Both Ezra and Nehemiah were trying hard to establish a national identity for Judah, and language is important in doing that, as the Basque, Irish, Welsh and many others will tell you. Nehemiah raged and cursed the men who had married foreigners. He pulled out hair and, unlike Ezra, this was their hair, not his own. Nehemiah wasn't afraid of drama if he wanted to make a point. (Neh. 13:25)

Nehemiah tried desperately hard to do his duty. Pleasant or unpleasant, it had to be done. If it made him unpopular, if it put his life at risk, it didn't matter. It was his duty to keep the lines of communication open between God and Israel. The worship of the temple must be maintained. The Law must be observed. Nehemiah didn't look for thanks from his people; he simply tried to do what he believed God had called him to do. He had done his best, and the book ends with his simple prayer, 'Remember me with favour, O my God.'

A Glance into the Apocrypha

The story which follows breaks the boundaries originally set for this collection of Old Testament narratives because it comes from that rather shadowy section of the Bible known as the Apocrypha.

The word 'Apocrypha' means 'the hidden things' and it is a collection of twelve books that appear in the Greek version of the Old Testament and were regarded as holy Scripture by Greek speaking Jews in the time of Jesus. The twelve books do not appear in the Hebrew Old Testament and were not regarded as sacred by Aramaic speaking Jews. Some of the books are additions to or continuations of books in the Hebrew Old Testament.

Until the fourth century AD, the books of the Apocrypha were regarded as sacred writings by the Christian Church. After that time a distinction was made between those books in the Hebrew Old Testament and those in the Greek version, preference being given to the Hebrew writings. At the Reformation, the books of the Apocrypha suffered a further relegation as the reformed churches tried to purge the Church of any medieval traditions. In its Thirty-Nine Articles, the Church of England says that the books of the Apocrypha are useful for 'example of life and instruction in manners'.

Despite this chequered history, the books of the Apocrypha are of the greatest importance in understanding the history of God's people, the Jews. There is a gap of some 150–200 years between the end of the Hebrew Old Testament and the beginning of the New Testament. The books of the Apocrypha do not bridge the gap in any formal way, but they do provide important information about the life of the Jews during that period, when the world had been changed by the conquests of Alexander the Great. Greek influences were pressing on the Jews as they struggled to find religious and political independence in their own land. Some of them wanted to stick firmly to the old ways; others were ready to compromise so that their country would benefit from what they saw as the advantages of Greek influence and culture.

The story which follows is taken from the early chapters of the First Book of Maccabees. It is a story of heroic resistance to foreign power. It tells of a determination to preserve their own land, religion and customs. It is a story which echoes down the centuries and gives inspiration to many Jews today who, rightly or wrongly, see their homeland threatened. It is the story in particular of one man who earned for himself the title of 'Maccabee' – the Hammer.

Two specific notes that help us put the Apocrypha in context:

1. We are here dealing with the Old Testament Apocrypha. There is also a New Testament Apocrypha which contains books which were not admitted to the approved selection of Christian sacred books which form the canon of the New Testament.

2. It is worth noting that the Book of Daniel, which is in the Old Testament, dates from much the same time as much of the material in the Apocrypha. It contains stories that claim to be set in Babylon during the time of exile. They are in fact coded stories about the oppression suffered under the Seleucid king, Antiochus IV. The well-known stories (which it would be impertinent to retell) of Daniel in the lions' cave, Shadrach, Meshach and Abednego in the furnace, and the writing on the wall at Belshazzar's feast, are calls to resistance, and assurances that God will not forget or forsake those who are faithful to him. These stories, like that of Judas Maccabeus, teach that through suffering, and even through death, the 'saints of the Most High' – that is, faithful Jews – will eventually triumph through the power and the will of God.

Judas Maccabeus' Story

A Brief Historical Review: The Greeks in Judah

It is best to start this story with a review of Jewish history so that when we eventually meet Judas Maccabeus we know exactly the situation he was facing and how it had come about.

The history of Israel is, to a great extent, a history of the descendants of Abraham living, suffering and surviving under the rule of different foreign nations. They seem to have been constantly at war. At a local level, there were the endless skirmishes with the people who were rivals for the very land on which they lived. These tribes or nations appear repeatedly in the Old Testament as the enemies of Israel and Judah. They are the Philistines, the Ammonites, Jebusites, Midianites, Moabites, Ishmaelites, Edomites, Amorites and others, sometimes collectively called the Canaanites. A larger and more significant enemy was Syria, away to the north, sometimes called Aram by the biblical writers. But there were still greater foreign powers and greater dangers for the people of Israel.

The kingdoms of Israel and Judah, occupying Canaan, their Promised Land, sat firmly on the commercial and military crossroads of the ancient world. Their history is therefore inextricably entangled with the history of the great powers of those days. Egypt lay to the south. To the north and east was Assyria. To the east was Babylon, and beyond that, Persia. When any of the nations to the north and east wanted to attack Egypt, or if Egypt attacked them, their armies had to travel around the Fertile Crescent, which skirted the vast Arabian desert. Armies could not cross the desert, so they marched through Israel and Judah. Usually they would devastate the country on their way through, looting whatever they could, including the gold and silver vessels from the temple in Jerusalem. They would demand tribute or safety money so that the devastation would not be repeated on the return journey. Even so, it often was.

The history of Israel and Judah is bound up with the imperial ambitions of the rulers of these great powers. Somewhere around 1500 BCE, under the leadership of Moses, Israel left Egypt. After forty years of wilderness wanderings they settled into their Promised Land, fighting, integrating, making treaties, copying the farming methods and sometimes the religion of their Canaanite neighbours. Eventually they established their own monarchy, and in a period of remarkable international calm, David united the Twelve Tribes into one nation. It didn't last long. Soon Assyria rose to power. It extended its rule over Babylon and then moved south through Syria. It attacked and destroyed the northern kingdom, Israel, which to all intents and purposes disappeared from history.

Decline and fall is the destiny of all earthly empires, and soon it was Assyria's turn to fall. Babylon was now in the ascendant. Its armies conquered Assyria and then, in moving toward the ancient enemy, Egypt, it marched through Syria and was soon at the gates of Jerusalem. In 586 BCE the city fell and its chief citizens were taken away into exile in Babylon.

Eventually Babylon fell. Cyrus of Persia captured the city in 539 BCE and issued a decree which allowed the Jews to return home to Judah. Like all other empires, at its height Persia looked invincible. But then came Alexander. He united the various Greek city states under his own leadership and moved against the traditional enemy, Persia. Nothing could stand in his way. By 333 BCE, Persia had surrendered and Palestine came under Greek rule. Alexander, still young, died in Babylon in 323 BCE and his empire was divided between four of his generals. The most powerful were Ptolemy, who ruled in Egypt, and Seleucus, who ruled in Syria. They were rivals for the nations around them, including Palestine.

By the second century BCE the Seleucids were in control of Palestine. Generally they allowed the Jews to continue their traditional worship in the temple and to observe the Torah. But Greek influences inevitably crept into Jewish life, and there was a strong body of Jewish opinion which favoured the acceptance of Greek culture.

The Greeks were and are a great and cultured people. Thinkers like Socrates, Plato and Aristotle (who has been Alexander's tutor) still influence the way we think, even if we are not aware of it. Greek drama and poetry is still recognised as great. Greek architecture is still shaping the cities we live in. Greek sculpture is still immensely pleasing to the eye. The Greeks gave us democracy, and as far as their language is concerned, its flexibility and beauty is acknowledged in the English saying, 'The Greeks had a word for it'.

It is not surprising then that there were thoughtful and educated Jews who believed that an infusion of Greek culture into their way of life could do only good. The more advanced of these progressives had a gymnasium – something very like a university – built in Jerusalem. Perhaps that was acceptable, but when they went on to advocate the abandonment of circumcision as a mark of Jewishness, and other violations of the Covenant, it was inevitable that conflict would come.

King Antiochus IV, who provokingly called himself Epiphanes, meaning 'God revealed', was not a patient man. After confirming his hold over the Middle East by his defeat of Ptolemy in Egypt, he marched back through Judah and in time-honoured fashion ransacked the temple. He followed that desecration by what probably seemed to him a constructive political move. The Book of Maccabees says, 'The King wrote to his whole kingdom that all should be one people, and that all should give up their particular customs.' (I Macc. 1:41) To implement his policy he issued orders forbidding the sacrificial rituals of the temple and abolishing the Sabbath and other festivals. It was made quite clear that disregard of his orders was punishable by death. To further enforce his policy, which is usually called Hellenisation, he built an altar to Zeus on the site of the altar of Yahweh. He destroyed all the books of the Law which could be found.

These decrees were enforced with awesome brutality. 'They put to death the women who had their children circumcised, and their families and those who circumcised them and they hung the infants from their mothers' necks.' (I Macc. 1:60,61). Even in the face of this oppression many stood firm.

Things came to a head when the king's officers tried to persuade an elderly priest called Mattathias to sacrifice on the king's altar. They said that if a respected and senior person like himself would set the example, all would follow. Then there would be peace in the kingdom and what's more, he and his sons would be honoured by the king and made rich. Mattathias firmly refused – for himself and for his family. The king's officer could hardly have expected what happened next. Another Jew stepped forward, presumably a priest with a more flexible conscience. He was prepared to do what Mattathias had refused to do. Enraged at the apostasy, Mattathias rushed forward and killed the man at the altar, and then turned and killed the king's officer. There was only one thing they could do now. Mattathias and his sons fled to the hills, leaving behind all their possessions.

Mattathias was only the tip of the iceberg. Large numbers of loyal Jews, seeking to avoid the sort of conflict that had engulfed Mattathias and his family, left their homes and went into the wilderness, taking their wives and families and livestock with them, and set up a stronghold of refuge. Learning of this, the king sent out soldiers who surrounded the camp. It was the Sabbath. When the king's officer called on the Jews to be sensible, to obey the king and save their lives, they refused and perhaps rather foolishly said that they would not obey the order nor would they profane the Sabbath. The soldiers attacked and massacred about a thousand people. There was no resistance; it was the Sabbath.

The Maccabean Revolt

When Mattathias heard about the disaster he reviewed his policy. He decided that in future it would be permissible for Jews to defend themselves if attacked on the Sabbath or, as he said, 'They will quickly destroy us from the earth.' (I Macc. 2:40) And so began the Maccabean revolt.

Many angry, devout and loyal Jews joined with the family of Mattathias, and a small armed group was formed. It was more of a guerrilla force than a regular army. They were fanatical nationalists and started their campaign by terrorising those Jews who did not stand firm against the king's orders. They tore down the pagan altars that had been set up in various parts of Judah, and they forcibly circumcised all Jewish boys whose parents had not seen to it already.

Mattathias was old, and the movement which his loyalty to God had sparked off was getting too big for him. He knew that it was time to hand things over to the next generation. He appointed his son Simon as 'father' to all in the movement, and his son Judas the military commander. Judas was already renowned for his military prowess and had been given the nickname or title 'Maccabeus' – 'The Hammer'. Mattathias's dying words were, 'You shall rally around you all who observe the Law, and avenge the wrong done to your people. Pay back the Gentiles in full, and obey the commands of the Law.' (I Macc. 2:67,68) He could hardly have imagined what heroism and glory, what misery and pain, his words and example were to create – and not only in that period of history.

Whatever role Mattathias had envisaged for his son, Simon, it was Judas who took command. His first battle was against the king's army under their general, Apollonius. Fighting with desperation and enormous courage, Judas and his men overcame the superior force of Apollonius, who was himself killed in the fighting. Judas took the sword of Apollonius and used it for the rest of his life. His action makes us wonder whether he was consciously copying David, who had taken the sword of Goliath in his first battle against the enemies of Israel.

A newly formed army, commanded by another general, Seron, set out to win revenge for the king and glory for Seron. His army so outnumbered that of the Jews that many of Judas's men doubted the wisdom of going into battle. Judas reassured them with words which, we can be sure, have strengthened and inspired many who have since gone into battle believing their cause was also the cause of God.

'It is not on the size of the army that victory in battles depends, but strength comes from Heaven. They come against us in great insolence and lawlessness to destroy us and our wives and our children, and to despoil us, but we fight for our lives and our laws.' (I Macc. 3:19–22) Judas then led his army against the Syrian army and routed it.

King Antiochus could not permit such a dangerous and successful subversive force to exist in his kingdom. In order to create an army of the size he needed to ensure that Judas and his men would be wiped out, he offered the powerful incentive of a year's wages paid in advance. He emptied the treasury and managed to mobilise an army of 40,000 infantry and 7,000 cavalry. He put them under the able command of General Lysias, while he himself set off for Persia to try to raise funds to repair the damage he had done to the nation's economy.

Judas was fully aware that Lysias' intention was nothing less than the annihilation of the Jewish army and the submission of the rest of the people to the king's policies. He addressed the men before battle, reminding them that they were fighting not only for the survival of their nation, but also for God, for his honour and his sanctuary. Their preparation was not only military but religious. They prayed, they fasted and they read the Law. Judas also organised the army meticulously, appointing leaders over thousands, over hundreds, fifties and tens. He ensured the morale of the whole army was good by sending home anyone who did not want to stay and fight, as well as those exempted by the law, those about to be married and those in vital occupations.

Lysias sent out a force of some 5,000 infantry and 1,000 cavalry to attack the Jewish camp by night. Judas learnt of this through his spies and moved his men out of camp to attack the part of the king's army left in their camp, weakened by loss of numbers. Lysias' lookouts spotted the Jewish force and he led his men out of camp and engaged it on the plain. As the battle progressed it became clear that the Jews had the upper hand, and eventually the Gentiles broke ranks and fled. Many of them were slaughtered as they ran away. Judas's army wanted to do the usual thing – ransack the camp and claim as much spoil as they could. They began this traditional exercise with enthusiasm, but Judas stopped them, saying that their work was still not finished. There were still other parts of the Gentile army undefeated.

As he was speaking, the remainder of Lysias' army appeared. What they saw was the Jewish army, exultant in victory, and beyond that they could see the smoke and ruin of their own camp. Without a fight they turned and fled in panic. Only then did Judas allow the looting to take place. He and his men returned to their camp laden with booty and praising God for their victory.

By now Judas felt strong enough to enter Jerusalem and purge the temple of its pagan altars and rededicate it so that it could once more be used for the proper worship of Yahweh. So, 'They took unhewn stones, as the Law directs, and built a new altar like the former one.' (I Macc. 4:47) They rebuilt the ruined or neglected parts of the temple and its precincts and provided new sacred vessels for use in worship. On the 25th day of the month Chislev, the exact anniversary of Antiochus' first desecration of the temple, sacrifice was once again offered to God on the altar of the temple in Jerusalem. The year was 164 BCE. This triumphant and solemn occasion was marked with music and celebration.

Amidst all the rejoicing, Judas showed himself a true leader by seeing to practical matters. He stationed a garrison in Jerusalem, strengthened the city walls against possible attack and set an outpost some twenty-five miles south of Jerusalem to guard against possible attack from that direction.

It was a wise move. Some of the traditional enemies of the Jews, the local tribes and nations who had been their rivals for centuries over matters of land and power in the area, were not pleased to see Judas and the Jews once more in control of Jerusalem and most of the land of Judah. They heard with dismay of the dismantling of the pagan altars and the rededication of the temple. A strong and independent Jewish state was the last thing they wanted. So they began to persecute the Jews who lived among them, and so began, as the Book of Maccabees says, 'the work of massacre and extermination among the people.' (I Macc. 4:61)

Judas and his brother Jonathan mounted punitive expeditions in Edom, Ammon, Gilead, Tyre and Sidon, inflicting terrible casualties. The campaign had the desired effect. It put an end to the persecution, at least for the time being.

Judas again showed his wisdom. Realising that as soon as he and his men left a neighbourhood the persecution would start again, he encouraged the Jews who lived in those dangerous areas to leave and go to live in Judah.

While these battles and skirmishes had been going on, King Antiochus was being unsuccessful in raising funds in Persia. He failed there and went back to Babylon to try his luck. It was while he was there that he received reports of the successes of the Jews under Judas, and how his grand design to Hellenise them was in tatters. He was badly shaken by the news and became ill. He took to his bed and never left it, dying in 163 BCE. He was succeeded by his son who took the name of Eupator.

It wasn't long before the Gentiles who lived in Jerusalem, and those of the Jews who did not support the Maccabean movement, petitioned the king, asking him to do something about Judas and his army, which, they claimed, terrorised them. The king could not afford to be seen to do nothing. He mustered a mighty army, bigger than anything his father had ever gathered. There were 100,000 infantrymen, 20,000 cavalry and, most mighty and terrifying of weapons, thirty-two elephants trained for battle. This great army, again with Lysias as commander-in-chief, camped near Jerusalem and began to built siege engines and towers. Brave patrols, sent out at night by Judas, burnt them. Eventually both armies were drawn up for battle.

The presence of the elephants dictated the strategy of the battle. They formed focal points for the Gentile army. Around each elephant were gathered 1,000 infantry and 500 cavalry. On the back of each animal was a tower carrying four heavily armed men. It was an impressive and terrifying sight. The Book of Maccabees says, 'All who heard the din of this marching multitude and its clashing arms shook with fear. It was a very great and powerful array indeed.' (I Macc. 6:41)

Judas and his army advanced and the battle was joined. Initially the Jews were on top, killing 600 of the king's men. The brave deed of one man in particular stood out. Eleazar Avaran, noticing that one of the elephants was arrayed in especially fine armour, decided that the king would be riding on it. With great courage he slashed a way for himself through the struggling mass of men to the animal. He ran under its belly and thrust his spear up into the soft underside, killing it. It fell, and it crushed him.

As the battle progressed the Jewish army was forced to retreat before the enemy, and soon Jerusalem was under siege. The story gives a clear impression of the power of the surrounding army. 'He set up emplacements and siege engines, with flame-throwers, catapults for discharging stones and barbed missiles, and slings.' (I Macc. 6:51) Things were going badly for the people of Jerusalem.

Food was short and there was nothing in store because it was a sabbatical year and the fields had been rested. It looked as if it was only a matter of time before they would be forced to surrender.

Salvation came in the shape of internal troubles for the Gentiles; jealousy among politicians and soldiers. Lysias heard that a certain Philip, who had been the close friend and adviser of Antiochus IV, had returned from Babylon, where he had been at the king's deathbed. He had returned to Antioch and was preparing to take over the government. It seems that ambition and personal power was more important to Lysias than finishing off the Jews, so he made peace with the people of Jerusalem, withdrew his troops and marched back to Antioch. He was to live – and die – to regret this decision.

The internal rivalries within the Seleucid kingdom led to the assassination of the king and his trusted right-hand man Lysias. Other ambitious men in the army were directly responsible, but who was behind it? Demetrius, another member of the royal family, returned from Rome and took the throne. It comes as no surprise to learn that it was he who had ordered the assassinations. With a new king on the throne it was the ideal time for various discontented groups and individuals to try to gain advantages. Some Hellenising Jews, led by Alcimus, went to the king to complain about the activities of the Maccabees. As ever there were mixed motives at work. Alcimus, who was of a priestly family, wanted the job of High Priest for himself. He told the king that 'Judas and his brothers have killed all your supporters and have driven us from our country.' (I Macc. 7:6) He asked the king to appoint a strong and trustworthy man to look into matters in Judah.

Alcimus got what he wanted. Demetrius made him High Priest and appointed a high-ranking soldier, Bacchides, to go to Judah, look into the state of things and act accordingly. Alcimus and Bacchides entered Judah and made initial offers of friendship and cooperation. At first, the loyal Jews were deceived by the presence of Alcimus. He was, after all, a priest of the line of Aaron, and would surely have the best interests of God and God's people at heart, even though it did seem strange that he was backed by a powerful Gentile army. He assured the first groups of nationalists who went to see him that he intended them no harm, and he gained their confidence. But it wasn't long before he showed his true colours and, in one day, had sixty supporters of Judas arrested and executed.

Bacchides, meanwhile, had weighed up things in Judah and returned to Antioch. Either he had been recalled by the king or he found himself sick of the hatreds and civil strife that poisoned all of life in Judah. He left and handed over all power to Alcimus. With sole and effective authority the High Priest gathered around him all who were opposed to Judas and were sympathetic to the policy of Hellenisation. When Judas saw how Alcimus' high priesthood was working out in practice, he and his men began to move around Judah seeking out and punishing the unfaithful. Alcimus realised that he could not deal with Judas without help. So again he appealed to the king. The king responded by sending one of his best commanders, Nicanor. His orders were simply to bring order out of chaos.

Nicanor's first move was to send friendly greetings to Judas, suggesting that they might meet personally and discuss matters. He said that he saw no reason why things shouldn't be resolved in a friendly way. His real intention was to isolate Judas and take him prisoner. But once again Judas's intelligence officers earned their pay. They discovered the plot and Judas refused to meet Nicanor.

Outmanoeuvred in diplomacy, Nicanor led his army against Judas, but was driven off, losing some 500 men. In a rage he went to Jerusalem. Alcimus, with other priests and members of the council, gave him a warm welcome and proudly offered to let him accompany them when they offered sacrifice in the temple on behalf of the king. Nicanor wasn't impressed. He wanted vengeance and he wanted Judas, not a religious service. He threatened that unless Judas were handed over he would destroy the temple.

Alcimus was in no position to hand over Judas. Realising this, Nicanor sent for reinforcements from Antioch to strengthen his army. They lined up for battle some seven or eight miles north of Jerusalem. Judas with 3,000 men drew up his army not far away, near Adasa, and prayed to God for help.

When the battle began, Nicanor himself was one of the first casualties. The story continues, 'when his army saw that Nicanor had fallen, they threw away their arms and took to flight'. (I Macc. 7:44) Judas's army routed them and as they fled through the Judean countryside they were harried and attacked by villagers. In the end not one of them survived. It was decided that that day of victory, the 13th Adar, would be kept as a day of celebration for ever.

King Demetrius simply could not allow such a disaster to remain unavenged. He sent Bacchides, already experienced in the affairs of Judah, and Alcimus back into Judah, backed by a powerful army. This time there was no pretence of friendship or the possibility of compromise. They pillaged as they went, inflicting heavy loss of life and undermining the morale of the Jews. Judas's army, weary after so many battles, was losing confidence. Many of his men deserted, and the small band which remained tried to persuade Judas that it would be wise to withdraw and regroup, to play for time and build up their numbers, and only then return to the fight.

Judas would have none of that. Perhaps he, too, was weary of all the campaigning, and saw honourable death in battle as the best way of gaining peace and rest or perhaps he was just like his father, Mattathias, utterly fearless when the honour of God and God's people was involved. Judas's words suggest something of the sort: 'Heaven forbid that I should do such a thing as run away! If our time is come, let us die bravely for our fellow countrymen, and leave no stain upon our honour.' (I Macc. 9:10)

Battle was joined. The fighting was fierce, and many on both sides lost their lives. But the outcome was never in doubt. Judas was slain and the remnant of his army fled. His brothers Simon and Jonathan took his body and buried it with his father, in the family tomb. So fell Judas Maccabeus, the Hammer, the champion of Yahweh and saviour of his people.

The Book of Job

The Book of Job tells us nothing of the history of Israel and is not concerned with God's choice of Israel as his chosen people, nor with the covenant he made with them. Yet it is one of the most important books in the Old Testament. It is concerned with the universal problems of God's justice and man's pain: why do the innocent suffer?

The book probably reached its present form after the return from the exile in Babylon when, under Ezra and Nehemiah, there was a sustained attempt to direct the life of the nation 'according to the Law of the Lord'. Despite that, the nation was not successful in worldly terms and it still suffered as a despised subject nation.

It is unlikely that Job was an historical person. More likely he stands, like Adam, for Everyman. It is possible that he represents the people of Israel, whose suffering seemed out of proportion to their wrongdoing. It may be that Job's experience of undeserved suffering reflects the experience of the people of Israel throughout their history, down to the present day. It may have been written in the aftermath of the Babylonian holocaust, but it is just as relevant in trying to come to terms with Hitler's Holocaust. Despite the proverbial 'patience of Job' the book could be a call to the people of Israel not to be patient under suffering, but to cry out and complain (as Job does) until God gives justice.

On the other hand it may be that the book is concerned with the suffering of the individual. It is part of that section of the Old Testament known as the Wisdom Literature, which includes the Psalms, Proverbs, Ecclesiastes and the Song of Songs. Much of the wisdom of ancient Israel is concerned with the proper ordering of the life of the individual. It is filled with advice about how to live successfully and prosperously. The story of Job faces the uncomfortable fact that, even in a world ruled by a just God, the wicked often prosper while the good suffer.

Whether Job represents the nation or an individual, he is the representative of all who suffer.

Christians may see in Job a prefiguring of Jesus, who also endured undeserved suffering. Job felt deserted by God; so did Jesus. It has been suggested that only through the experience of the incarnation did God come to understand what it was like to be Job!

The Structure of the Book

The original story of Job was current in the Middle East long before it reached the form it has in the Bible. In the literature of the ancient Middle East there is a Babylonian Job and an Egyptian Job. The man Job in the biblical book is not an Israelite, which is unusual for the hero of a book of the Hebrew Bible; he seems to be an Edomite.

The Book has three distinct sections:

1. The first two chapters, written in prose, set the scene and tell us how calamities fell, one after the other, on the unfortunate and virtuous Job. In these chapters Job displays his proverbial patience.

2. There are almost forty chapters of poetry which are the heart of the book. These contain:
   – Job's very impatient complaints against God and God's injustice;
   – The attempts of Job's friends to explain to him why he is suffering;
   – Job's angry and impatient dismissal of his friends' arguments;
   – A hymn celebrating Wisdom;
   – Advice to Job from a fourth friend;
   – God's eventual response.

3. The third section is again in prose, and tells how Job's fortunes were restored.

It may be that the opening and closing sections were the original story and were used by the poet as the setting for his own radical explorations of divine justice and human faith and suffering.

Or it could be that the poem was the first composition with its brave challenging of God. Perhaps the rabbis who put together the Hebrew Bible decided that it was too unorthodox and needed toning down. This would be done by the opening section, which removes the blame for Job's suffering from God and places it on Satan, and by the closing section which provides a satisfactory happy ending. We cannot be sure.

What we can be sure about is the greatness of the book. It contains superb storytelling and magnificent poetry. But more than that, it wrestles with the questions that still cause deep distress: why do good people suffer? Why do the wicked prosper? Is God responsible? Does God care?

Job's Story

No one was better than Job. Even God admitted that. In fact it was God who said, 'there is none like him on the earth, a blameless and upright man, who fears God and turns away from evil.' (1:8) A cynic might have said, 'Of course Job is good. He has every reason to be. He's rich and successful. His wealth, counted in flocks and herds, is fabulous. He has an ideal family of seven sons and three daughters. What is more, success has come early, for none of his children are yet married. No wonder he worships God. No wonder he tries to keep on the right side of God by making sacrifices, not just for himself but for his sons as well, in case they forget. He's got everything going for him. No wonder Job is good.' So might a cynic speak of Job.

The story tells us that the court of heaven was meeting, and naturally God was in the chair. An important member of the court was the public prosecutor whose God-given task was to test human beings to find out how good or bad they really were, not how good or bad they seemed to be, or claimed to be. This court prosecutor was called the Satan, and he is not to be confused with the Devil, the personification of evil. In the Book of Job, the Satan is a valued member of the court of heaven.

Satan is a little late for the meeting, and God asks him where he has been. 'Doing my job,' says the Satan, self-righteously. 'I've been going all over the earth, testing people.' It's clear that he enjoys his job, and likes to find that someone is not as good as they claim or people think. So, 'doing my job' he says with a certain smugness. And it's then that God says, 'Have you considered my servant Job?' There is no one like him on the earth, a blameless and upright man, who fear God and turns away from evil?' And that testimony from God is the beginning of all Job's troubles.

The cynical Satan says that Job is good because his life is good. He's rich, he wants for nothing. 'But touch his possessions,' Satan says to God, 'take away his riches and his comfort and his security and he will curse you and show that he is no different from anyone else.'

The story continues. One day, all Job's sons and daughters were together at the house of one of them, celebrating some family occasion, a birthday perhaps. Job was at his own home with his wife. A messenger arrived at Job's house to tell him that bandits had attacked one of the farms. They'd stolen cattle and the asses and killed the workers. He alone had escaped to tell the tale. Before he had finished speaking another messenger arrived. A sudden violent storm had struck the flocks and killed all the sheep and the shepherds. He alone had escaped to tell the tale. While he was still speaking a third messenger arrived. Three groups of raiders had stolen all the camels and killed the herders. He alone had escaped. And before he'd finished came the final blow. A fourth messenger reported that a freak wind had struck the house where Job's sons and daughters were celebrating. The house had collapsed and they were all dead.

And so, from being the richest man in all the East, with the future securely in the hands of his children, Job became not only a pauper but that saddest of all people, a bereaved parent. It is a terrible thing to lose a child; it seems so unnatural. And Job lost ten children. He went into mourning, tearing his clothes and shaving his head. But he did not react in the way that Satan had predicted. He did not curse God. Indeed he still blessed God. He said, 'Naked I came from my mother's womb, and naked I shall return; the Lord gave, and the Lord has taken away; blessed be the name of the Lord. (1:21)

The court of heaven met again and God could not resist pointing out to Satan that Job had fulfilled all God's expectations; he was 'blameless and upright'. But Satan hadn't finished yet. He accuses Job of a selfishness and hardness that is perhaps really his own. He claims that Job is untouched even by the death of his children. But, he says, if Job himself is harmed then he will curse God. This leaves God no choice but to let Satan pour more affliction on the patient Job.

It seems as if Satan arranged for Job to be struck with leprosy. He is covered with 'loathsome sores' from head to foot. And because of his condition he cannot stay at home with his wife; he has to go outside the city, and he sits in the rubbish on the town dump, scraping his erupting and itching skin with pieces of broken pottery.

By this time, Job's wife has had enough. After a life of comfort, surrounded by her family and servants, she has been dragged into poverty, and she has suffered, just as much as her husband, by the death of her children. And now, helplessly, she has to watch her husband suffer in the grip of a disease she can do nothing about. She cannot bear to see him suffer any longer. She wants it all to end, and in her misery she pleads with Job to curse God and die and be free of his suffering. But he won't. Job says, 'Shall we receive good at the hand of God, and shall we not receive evil?' Unwittingly, Job fulfils all God's hopes and confounds Satan's opinion of the selfishness of all human beings. Job proves that at least one man's faith in God does not depend on favours from God, real or imaginary. So he sits and scratches and suffers.

Job had three good friends who came to comfort him. If we have been used to thinking of the words 'a Job's comforter' as meaning someone who gives no comfort at all, then perhaps we ought to think again. The three men, Eliphaz, Bildad and Zophar, not only weep when they see the state of their friend, they join in his mourning. For seven days they sit with him in silence, sharing his misery. And that is true friendship.

At this point in the Book of Job there begins a series of poems – or perhaps it is one long poem – and in these poems Job, his three friends and a fourth who joins them later, argue vigorously about the problem of Job's suffering. The questions are: why should a good man suffer? Why does God let it happen? Does God send suffering? Does God care? These are still important questions and they are asked by someone every day.

As the book breaks into poetry, so Job breaks his silence. His legendary patience has gone, shattered by his bitter experiences. Job cries out and curses – not God, but the day of his own birth. He wishes he had never seen the light of day, because then he would have avoided the pain and misery that now fill his life. It is a bitter, pain-filled cry.

When at last Job falls silent, Eliphaz, the first of his friends, speaks. He reminds Job of the many times Job himself has comforted men in trouble, and he offers the advice which Job had often given to others. In essence, it is that justice will always be done in the end. 'Think now,' he says, 'who that was innocent ever perished? Or where were the upright cast off?' (4:7) Eliphaz tells of how, in a vision, he learnt that the misfortunes that come to men are the result of their sins. And all men sin. So he encourages Job to be patient. God punishes, but he also heals. 'Despise not the chastening of the Almighty,' he says, 'for he wounds, but he binds up; he smites, but his hand heals.' (5:17,18)

Each of the friends try to get Job to admit that for all this misfortune to come upon him, he must have done something wrong, even if he cannot remember it. They say, 'Admit it; God will punish you and then he will forgive you, and all will be well again.' What they were doing was putting forward as forcefully as they could the accepted wisdom of their day regarding suffering. People needed answers as to why they suffered, and especially why good people suffered. Bildad puts the traditional view very bluntly, apparently with very regard for Job's feelings. He says that Job's children must have sinned for them all to have been killed, and as for Job himself, 'if you are pure and upright, surely then he (God) will rouse himself for you and reward you'. (8:4,6) There was precious little that looked like a reward in Job's life at this time.

The friends' way of dealing with the problem of suffering is still very much alive. How often do we hear people say, 'What have I done to deserve this?' How often do we say it ourselves? And we have to be very careful of pouring scorn on this way of looking at things, because it is there, very clearly, in Scripture. Psalm 37 is full of it. 'Fret not yourself because of the wicked, be not envious of evil-doers! For they will soon fade like the grass, and wither like the green herb.' (Psalm. 37:1) It goes on, 'I have been young and now am old; yet I have not seen the righteous forsaken or his children begging bread.' (Psalm 37:25)

That wasn't Job's experience. Nor was it the experience of Jesus as he died on the cross saying, 'My God, my God, why have you forsaken me?' And it is not the experience of many people in the world whose suffering seems dreadfully out of proportion with any wrong they may have done.

The problem of suffering is more difficult and complicated than being a simple matter of merit rewarded and sin punished, and Job knew it. He did not claim that he was perfect, but he knew he had done nothing to deserve so terrible a fate. The friends' attempts at arguing sense into Job push him into revolt against the traditional belief that there is a just balance in life by which virtue is always rewarded and sin punished. Job knew that that was not true.

The third friend, Zophar, is the least understanding of the three. As he speaks, we get the suspicion that there is jealousy behind all he says. Perhaps he and Job had known each other a long time, and Zophar had seen Job grow rich and far more successful that he was. But whatever is behind it, there is a bitterness in Zophar's words. He says that God is treating Job lightly; 'less than your guilt deserves', are his words. (11:6) In the end he comes to the same point as the others; Job should admit his sin and repent.

Job has no doubt that God is powerful. He sees the evidence of that all around. He sees it too in the calamities which come upon people. 'He leads counsellors away stripped, and judges he makes fools ... He pours contempt on princes, and looses the belt of the strong.' (12:17,21) But while he doesn't doubt God's power, he does doubt his justice. He asks permission to argue his case in court. He says, 'Behold, I have prepared my case; I know that I shall be vindicated.' (13:18)

The arguments go on. The friends stand firm and repeat in as many ways as they can their conviction that whatever Job says, virtue will always be rewarded and sin punished. While they stick to the old familiar arguments, Job is ready to think new thoughts and to take risks in his exploration of God's ways. He feels as if God is attacking him on a battlefield, wounding him and trying to kill him. 'He set me up as his target,' he says, 'his archers surround me ... He runs upon me like a warrior.' (16:12,13,14)

Job is isolated. God is attacking him, his friends bring no comfort in their words, his relations and friends shun him, his servants no longer obey him, and in his misery he says, 'I am repulsive to my wife.' (19:17) Poor Job. But he argues on. He says that contrary to the views that his friends keep repeating, the opposite is the real truth; the wicked flourish. He asks, 'Why do the wicked live, reach old age, and grow mighty in power? Their houses are safe from fear, and no rod of God is upon them.' (21:7,8) But just when he seems to have reached rock bottom, his thoughts are lit up by rays of hope that shine through all the darkness. He is convinced that God is aware of his innocence: 'Even now, behold, my witness is in heaven, and he that vouches for me is on high.' (16:19) Then there is a great surge of faith when he declares that he knows that his Redeemer, the one who will speak of his innocence in the courts of heaven, lives and will avenge him. 'I know that my Redeemer lives, and at the last he will stand upon the earth.' (19:25)

Job is caught in an agonising conflict. One the one hand he feels hounded by God, and that God is the cause of his suffering. On the other hand he trusts God's justice and God's mercy, and expects God, the advocate, to plead for him before God the judge. A Jewish poet, a long time ago, wrote a beautiful poem about this conflict going on in Job's mind. And of course, Job's conflict is our conflict. This is the poem:

> Therefore though you slay me, I will trust You.
> For if you pursue my iniquity
> I will flee from You to Yourself,
> And I will shelter myself from Your wrath in Your
>   shadow,
> And to the skirts of Your mercies I will lay hold
> Until You have mercy on me,
> And I will not let You go till You bless me.
> – *Solomon ibn Gabriol*, eleventh century

As the arguments between Job and his friends rumble on a new figure appears. He is a young man called Elihu. He speaks with the confidence of youth and criticises both Job and his friends. Despite being over-sure of his own wisdom, Elihu does make two powerful points. The first is that suffering accepted as a discipline can be turned into something positive. The second is that the ways of God are not, and cannot be, open to the minds of mere human beings.

Job is silent. He neither responds to Elihu nor turns back to his other three friends. It is as if he has exhausted all his pleas, used all his arguments, and still he does not know the answer to the question, 'Why am I suffering like this?' Exhausted, he stops crying out to God for justice.

But if there are no words on Job's lips, there is turmoil, even a whirlwind, in his heart. And it is out of the turmoil that he receives his answer. 'Then the Lord answered Job out of the whirlwind.' (38:1) What God says is not a direct answer either to Job or to the friends. God does not bother to say that the friends have been accusing Job unjustly, nor does he take Job's points one by one and try to satisfy him. God's words are a revelation of the vast gulf that separates man from God and man's thoughts from God's.

He begins by reminding Job how little he knows, how little he understands of the universe in which he lives. 'Where were you when I laid the foundations of the earth?' (38:4). 'Have you entered into the springs of the sea, or walked in the recesses of the deep?' (38:16) 'Where is the way to the dwelling of light, and where is the place of darkness?' (38:19) With question after question, all unanswerable, God reveals to Job the limits of human understanding. He describes the stars and their mysterious movements. He reminds Job of the great creatures of the wild – the lion, the crocodile, the hippopotamus, the eagle. Man cannot tame or rule any of them and yet, like the stars, they are the works of God. What can man understand of this? If God cares for the lower creatures how much more must he care for man? And perhaps man isn't the lord of creation, despite what the stories in Genesis suggest. What can man know of the mind of God?

Job, for all his goodness – and God never changes what he said about Job being the most upright of men – can only see things from his own, or at best from a human, point of view. And that is a very limited point of view in God's mysterious universe. The universe is God-made and God-centred. It is not man-centred, and as long as Job asks questions only from man's point of view, he is asking the wrong questions.

God's words are for Job as if God had lifted him to a point high above the world and above worldly matters, and enabled him, for a moment, to glimpse things from God's side. He has been allowed to see things through the eyes of God.

At last Job breaks his awe-struck silence. No longer does he justify himself; no longer does he charge God with injustice; no longer does he look for answers. This time he speaks very briefly. He says that now he realises that earlier he had been speaking only at second-hand; he knew nothing from experience. But now all that has changed. 'I had heard of thee by the hearing of the ear, but now my eye sees thee; therefore I despise myself and repent in dust and ashes.' (42:6)

That is really the end of the story of Job. He is a humbler and wiser man. But his troubles have not miraculously disappeared. God has helped him to see them in perspective and so helped him to bear them. But the Book adds a final, short prose narrative in which Job becomes even richer than before. He has a second family – again, seven sons and three daughters – and he lives to see his great-grandchildren. We may not think that the story of Job with its profound exploration of human suffering needs such an artificial happy ending, and we may prefer to stop at the point where Job had learnt that a purely human point of view is a very limited one in God's marvellous and mysterious creation.

A Final Word

One of Job's questions was 'Does God care?' All the narratives we have looked at proclaim loudly that God does care. Long ago he formed a plan to bring blessing to all people. The plan was that he would choose a man, Abraham, to found a family which would become a nation, and through that nation all mankind would be blessed. God guided and cared for his chosen people, sending them prophets, priests and wise men, preparing them for their greatest work, the birth of the Messiah.

Christians believe that Jesus fulfils the hopes and longings of the Old Testament and that through his life, his teaching, his death and resurrection, blessing and salvation are offered to all.

Printed in the United Kingdom
by Lightning Source UK Ltd.
115188UKS00001BB/1